Ian Scott

To Make a
Difference

To Make a
Difference

a memoir

Ian Scott
with Neil McCormick

Stoddart

Published in 2001 by Stoddart Publishing Co. Limited
895 Don Mills Road, 400-2 Park Centre, Toronto, Canada M3C 1W3
180 Varick Street, 9th Floor, New York, New York 10014

Distributed by:
General Distribution Services Ltd.
325 Humber College Blvd., Toronto, Ontario M9W 7C3
Tel. (416) 213-1919   Fax (416) 213-1917
Email cservice@genpub.com

05 04 03 02 01 1 2 3 4 5

Canadian Cataloguing in Publication Data

Scott, Ian, 1934–
To make a difference : a memoir

Includes index.
ISBN 0-7737-3292-6

1. Scott, Ian, 1934–   .   2. Ontario. Legislative Assembly — Biography.
3. Legislators — Ontario — Biography.   4. Cerebrovascular disease — Patients —
Ontario — Biography. I. McCormick, Neil. II. Title.

FC3076.1.S36A3 2001   328.713'092   C00-932948-X
F1058.S36A3 2001

Jacket design: Angel Guerra
Text design and typesetting: Kinetics Design & Illustration

THE CANADA COUNCIL | LE CONSEIL DES ARTS
FOR THE ARTS | DU CANADA
SINCE 1957 | DEPUIS 1957

*We acknowledge for their financial support of our publishing program the Canada Council, the Ontario Arts Council,
and the Government of Canada through the Book Publishing Industry Development Program (BPIDP).*

Printed and bound in Canada

Contents

Prologue   *vii*

One   Out of Ottawa   1
Two   Learning the Law   19
Three   Cameron, Brewin & Scott   47
Four   Getting into Politics   75
Five   Once More into the Breach   91
Six   The Romance of Government   115
Seven   First-Term Challenges   141
Eight   Second-Term Blues   173
Nine   Over and Out   195
Ten   The Hardest Job   207
Eleven   Starting Over   219
Twelve   The Long Road Back   235

Index   245

Prologue

MOST PEOPLE DON'T BELIEVE most political advertising. I was as cynical about it as anyone until I tried politics myself. In 1981, I ran for a seat in the Ontario legislature for the downtown Toronto riding of St. David. I lost. Four years later, I ran once more in the same riding, again as the candidate for the Liberal party of Ontario. As part of that campaign, I produced this piece of political advertising:

IAN SCOTT — CAMPAIGN COMMERCIAL 1985

In the last four years since 1981 I have met thousands of you on your doorsteps or in your apartments. Since the election was called I have met thousands more in the course of our campaign. I have listened carefully to your concerns and have valued the chance to discuss the issues and the future of Ontario with you. It has been a rewarding and eye-opening experience.

I am a candidate in this election because I believe that if you care enough about people and issues that concern people you can make a difference. I care deeply about the people of this riding and the diverse communities that make it up. I am deeply troubled about the unwillingness of Queen's Park to listen to the concerns of our people. That is why I am running. If elected I believe I can make a difference.

Somewhat surprisingly, I was elected. Even more surprisingly, that election saw the defeat of the Ontario Conservatives after forty-two years of power.

After a short period of parliamentary jockeying for position, the Liberals and the New Democratic Party entered into an accord that brought my party to power and me to the office of attorney general.

In that office, I did try to make a difference.

Then, just as suddenly and unexpectedly as we had been brought to power, we were swept from office in the election of 1990, though I narrowly retained my own seat. This loss of power made me realize that if you want to make a difference, you had better do it quickly. You may not have a long time to try.

In August 1991, I got a call out of the blue from Neil McCormick, someone I had never met before. He had been interviewing David Peterson about the fall of the Liberal government, and David had suggested that he see me about a talk I had given the previous month. Neil and I had several interviews. In one of them, he asked me if I was interested in writing an autobiography, or in having a biography written about me. I replied that I had not the slightest interest in such an operation. I did tell him that I had kept a campaign diary about the 1985 campaign that Jack McClelland wanted to publish. But I won the election, and I didn't think I should publish it while I was in office.

I was much too busy leading my life to want to write about it.

In 1992, my partner, Kim Yakabuski, was seriously ill with AIDS. I resigned from the legislature, accepted a teaching position at York University's law school, and eased myself back into the practice of law.

In the fall of 1993, Kim died.

In the spring of 1994, I had a stroke. It was severe. My right arm became incapacitated. My right leg worked, but only just. My ability to read and write was compromised. I could speak, but with difficulty. I knew what words I wanted to say, but I had no assurance that those words would come out of my mouth. I was suffering from aphasia, a result of a break in the "hard wiring" of the brain. Only by finding new circuits around that break could I regain my speech. Until those new neural connections were forged, there was only a random chance I would come up with the right words.

It became clear that I would never be able to practice law again. Steve Goudge and my other partners at Gowling Strathy & Henderson took over my law practice for me. One of the cases I was working on prior to my stroke was before the Ontario Human Rights Commission. Rather improbably, given my long history of espousing rights for disadvantaged groups, I was acting for the landlords.

By chance, Neil McCormick was working for the Centre for Equality in Rental Accommodation, the organization representing the claimants in this case. He attended the hearings one day, introduced himself to Steve Goudge, who had taken over the case, and inquired about me. Steve suggested Neil visit me, and he did.

Our first post-stroke meeting took place on a sunny spring day on the steps of the Church of the Redeemer at the corner of Bloor Street and Avenue Road in downtown Toronto. Neil explained that we had met before. I could only say, "I remember, I remember," though my short-term memory at the time was in quite dreadful shape.

He asked about my campaign diary. I had forgotten about it. He asked me whether now I might be interested in having a biography written. If so, he would like to write it. I told him I would think about it.

As part of my recovery, my wonderful speech therapist Bonnie Bereskin had given me a range of exercises designed to recover my speech by using basic "building blocks." She had a series of flash cards, for example, with simple words like "red" or "cat" printed on them. When she showed them to me, I was supposed to read them. Little words gave me the most trouble. After a while, the exercises bored me. Then they frustrated me. My mind was still active beneath the rubble of my brain's hard wiring for speech. I needed something more. Working with Neil on a book seemed like that something more. I agreed to start the project.

The first time Neil came to my house, I had found the campaign diary. I could not, however, find the words to tell him this. The situation was a textbook example of the problems my aphasia caused me.

I knew enough to search for a copy of the manuscript, but I could not say something as simple as "I found it." Instead, I grabbed Neil by the arm and took him upstairs to show him the copy of the diary. I got him to read it to me over the course of his next few visits.

Eventually, I decided that I wanted Neil to write memoirs, rather than a biography. I also decided that I wanted him to write in the first person, as if he were me. I wanted to tell my story with an emphasis on humour. I had a good time doing what I did, and I wanted the world to share that sense of fun.

In the beginning, I couldn't remember very much. It was hard for me to think of things. When I *could* think of them, it was even harder for me to be able to say them. I couldn't read very well. In the course of working on this book, Neil spent many hours reading to me, listening to me read to him, asking me questions, and guessing the replies when I could not think of the right words. Even when he got it wrong, which was most of the time in the beginning, his efforts helped narrow down the possibilities. With his help, I improved, though it still seems to me that I'm stuck in low gear. Because of the stroke, I have had to rely on Neil to put the words down on paper for me. Fortunately, he still had transcripts of some of our original interviews from 1991. Those transcripts helped fill in some of the gaps in my memory. Neil has read every word of this book to me at each stage, and I have criticized and made suggestions, and sent him back to the computer until we arrived at this version.

We have no assurances in life, no guarantees that we will be healthy, enjoy a long life, or be able to control our destiny. What we can control is our attitude. We can still strive to make a difference, whether or not we achieve anything concrete.

I am writing these memoirs to show how important it is to try to make a difference.

This is my story. My hope is that it will inspire its readers, whatever their walks of life, to make a difference too.

ONE

Out of
Ottawa

◆

I WAS BORN ON JULY 13, 1934, at the Ottawa Civic Hospital.

My parents were Audrey and Cuthbert Scott. They had married the year before, my mother only eighteen and just out of Elmwood, a private girls' school, my father, ten years older, a practicing lawyer.

Their marriage brought together disparate elements of Ottawa society. My mother was a Gilmour, part of a clan that in the nineteenth century made its way from Scotland to Quebec City and then to Ottawa, clearing forests and selling lumber. More exciting, they also produced three brothers who played for Ottawa hockey teams that won Stanley Cups in the era before the NHL. My grandfather, Sutherland Gilmour, played rover, a position that was eliminated when hockey teams went from seven to six players. Unfortunately, Sutherland himself was also eliminated early. He died before my parents were married, of a stroke brought on by complications of diabetes. He was forty-nine.

My Granny Gilmour, left a widow at a relatively young age, never remarried. She was born in New Brunswick, where her father,

A.J. Blair, was attorney general and then premier. He subsequently moved to Ottawa to act as minister of railways and canals in Sir Wilfrid Laurier's government. There, he served with my paternal great-grandfather, Sir Richard Scott, who for many years was the government leader in the Senate.

The Gilmours and the Blairs were Protestants, the Scotts and the Sullivans, my paternal ancestors, Roman Catholics. In an era when "mixed" Catholic and Protestant marriages were frowned upon, the solution was for my mother to convert to Catholicism before her marriage. This she did, and as often seems to be the case became much more devout as a convert than my father, born into the church, ever was.

This must have pleased her father-in-law, who took a very active role in promoting the interests of the Catholic Church, and in conducting scholarly research into the liturgies of its various Middle Eastern offshoots. It is not surprising, perhaps, that my grandfather had such an interest, given that his father, Sir Richard Scott, had much success in sorting out Catholic-Protestant issues in Canadian politics. In 1863, he proposed that education in Upper and Lower Canada should be divided on religious, not linguistic lines, thus breaking a political logjam about the vexing questions of language and education. The principle of separate schools, later enshrined in the British North America Act of 1867, allowed Confederation to take place.

Before that, as mayor of Bytown in 1853, the forerunner of Ottawa, Sir Richard had learned that the Orangemen were going to take their July twelfth parade through the Irish Catholic shantytowns. Trying to avoid bloodshed, he agreed to ride at the head of the parade, thinking that the presence of a Catholic would forestall riots. In some versions of the story, he rode a white horse, but the more prosaic truth was that he had a bay horse draw his buggy in the procession. Whatever the colour of his horse, it was a tense occasion. While his actions were well intended, and widely credited with defusing a riot, they were not very politically astute. Sir Richard lost the next mayoral election, as people on both sides of the religious fence took umbrage at his action.

While he was mayor, my great-grandfather attended a musical

evening featuring the Heron family, a well-known travelling show. He fell in love instantly with Mary, one of the singing Heron sisters, and returned the next night with a huge bouquet of flowers for her. He followed her back to New York, persuaded her to marry him (thus breaking up the show), and brought her whole family to live in Ottawa. Perhaps it is from this great-grandmother that I inherited my love of music and the ability, on occasion, to act dramatically.

An abstainer from alcohol and a vegetarian, Sir Richard established a model farm on the Quebec side of the Ottawa River, where he planted fifty-three varieties of grapes, hoping to find some that would withstand the rigours of an Ottawa Valley winter. His interest in growing grapes was perhaps unusual, given that he was the author of the Canada Temperance Act, sometimes still called the Scott Act. But his abstinence and vegetarianism were not imposed on his guests, if his daughter Lilian Desbarats's account of Christmas dinner 1892 is to be believed:

> I have always kept a diary so I can tell you what we had for our Christmas dinner in 1892. This is the menu — meat soup, lamb rissoles, fricassee chicken, turkey, roast beef, spiced beef, peas, potatoes, plum pudding, brandy sauce, whipped cream, chocolate jelly, orange jelly, cheese and celery, pears, peaches both preserved [and] whole, grapes, apples, oranges, crystallized fruits, sucre a la creme, chocolates, stuffed dates, Christmas crackers, one dollar's worth of flowers.

Of the family home at 274 Daly Avenue, she wrote:

> On the west side was the cold pantry, where were kept perishable food like butter, eggs and milk, which was put in flat pans to set, then the cream was taken off with a skimmer. It was so sweet and much thicker than the whipping cream we get now — no table or cereal cream were heard of then. Next came the wine cellar. No window in it and always kept locked. There were cases of most kinds of wine and liquor. Though my father was the author

of the Scott Act, and he and my two brothers were absolute tee-totalers, father never tried to impose his views on his guests and they were given anything they wanted to drink.

For three years, when Sir Richard rented his Daly Street house and moved the whole clan to the model farm in Quebec, his children had to walk across the river ice to get to their schools in Ontario.

Oh, the cold and snow of the winters! My sister Mary and I walked the four or five miles from our house to the Rideau Street Convent twice a day. In winter we went on snowshoes nearly always breaking the track. We stood at our front door and made a beeline for the Parliament Buildings going across Bringham's Creek and the Ottawa River which of course were frozen over and covered deep with snow. We had to start at 7:30 to get to the convent at 9.

Sir Richard's son, my grandfather W.L. Scott, survived the rigours of this upbringing, followed his father to the bar, and supported some of his same enthusiasms. He was, for example, president of a Catholic Temperance League, part of the family history that I have done my best over the years to avoid. He also helped draft the Juvenile Delinquents Act of 1906, a forward-looking piece of legislation premised on the understanding, now sadly once more under attack, that children should be treated differently by the law than adults. And he was active in promoting the interests of the Catholic Church through a myriad of organizations.

He was on a bicycling tour of the Maritimes when he met my grandmother, May Sullivan, whose father was chief justice of Prince Edward Island, and before that, its attorney general and premier. My Scott grandparents had a long and happy marriage. They were a bit old-fashioned in some respects. They never owned a car. My grandfather usually walked home from his office for lunch every day. He was an amateur musician of some skill, playing the violin in the Ottawa Symphony for many years. He loved listening to opera, something

I did with him on one or two occasions, and something that I have done with much pleasure for all of my adult life.

My grandfather had a wonderful garden and was a keen observer of nature. He often wrote letters to the paper about sightings of birds that were early, or late, or well outside their normal range. He also wrote letters and articles about arcane matters of liturgies, trying to decide such questions as whether the Coptic Church belonged to the Catholic or the Eastern Orthodox Christian tradition.

In more contemporary matters, he was an active supporter of Mitch Hepburn, the leader of the Ontario Liberal party, thinking mistakenly that, if elected, Hepburn would extend full funding to Catholic schools. A report in the *Ottawa Journal* of a speech my grandfather made on June 18, 1934, the day before the election that brought Hepburn to power, shows him in full oratorical mode: "It is the duty of every Catholic to vote against the [George S.] Henry government in this election. Mr. Henry is an Orangeman and his government is absolutely dominated by the Orange Order. Unless we as Catholics enforce our views by our votes, we will never get anywhere."

My grandfather was greatly interested in family history, and wrote a number of articles exploring the various branches of the family. His grandfather, William Scott, had had a picaresque career as, variously, a surgeon with Wellington's troops in the Peninsular Wars, a factor for the North-West Company in Fort William, a suitor of one of the five granddaughters of a Macdonnell clansman who had fought for Bonnie Prince Charlie at Culloden and then resisted the republican forces of the American revolution, and as a doctor at Prescott.

My great-aunt, Lilian Desbarats, described the courtship of my great-great-grandparents Scott in these terms:

> My grandfather had been an Officer in the British Army. He had been stationed in Quebec but was sent to Fort Wellington near Prescott in the autumn of 1817 where he met his fate. He was recalled to England but refused to go preferring to give up the Army and his pension rather than part from his lady love.

Young people were just as foolish then as now. They were married when he had no job and no prospect of getting one.

A few months later however, he entered the service of the North West Company and was sent to Fort William. He took six weeks to get there by canoe. There he stayed three years. Then coming back to this same stone house where his bride had remained with her family and being met at the garden gate by a bevy of fair young girls, he was perplexed to know which was his wife. This was denied by my grandmother and even when she was over eighty she would get quite annoyed if it were mentioned.

The Macdonells were a warlike clan. One of them lost an arm in the battle of Ogdensburg. The legend was, as Lilian Desbarats put it: ". . . after the battle Captain John's daughter had advertised in the papers for her father's arm as he had worn a valuable bracelet. The arm was returned with the bracelet still on it."

Simon Fraser, the explorer of the British Columbia river system that bears his name, married one of my paternal great-great-grandmother's sisters. Something of my grandfather's quickness in defending the honour of his extended family can be seen in this letter to the *Canadian Bar Review*, denying that Simon Fraser fathered any children with native women:

I have been unable to find, in the Dominion Archives or elsewhere, any suggestion that Simon Fraser was otherwise than a most moral man. He was my father's uncle by marriage, and after his death, one of his daughters made her home with us and helped bring me up. I was, therefore, in a position to know something of how he was regarded among his relatives and connections and I can affirm that he was looked on as a very religious man, devoted to his wife, by whom he had a number of children. Indeed, his affection for her was such that he survived her by only a few hours, his death as it was said, having been caused, or at least hastened, by the shock due to her death.

My grandfather's research into family matters was exhaustive. He found ancestors who sold books to the famous English writer, Dr. Samuel Johnson. Perhaps optimistically, he traced one branch of the family back to Eleanor of Aquitaine. He named my father "Cuthbert" after the first native-born English saint.

So the political and legal genes run deep in the paternal half of my family. On the maternal side, there were the Blairs, who were active and successful in politics for several generations, if one includes grandchildren like Andrew Brewin, and great-grandchildren like John Brewin and me. Lilian Desbarats had this to say of my maternal great-grandfather's ability to obfuscate:

> Everyone bicycled in those days often going one way by train and checking their bicycles, which the railways carried free. However, they [the railways] eventually protested and wanted to charge. The matter came up in the House of Commons. The Hon. George Blair being Minister of Railways spoke for an hour and a half on the subject. He said to us afterwards: "I am sure no one knows which side I was on."

Even the Gilmours, lumbermen in Canada, could find legal and political potentates as ancestors in Scotland, and one distant Gilmour aunt married into the Birmingham political dynasty of the Chamberlains.

My mother, despite her somewhat limited education, was the intellectual in our family. She loved books and reading, interests she passed on to me at an early age. She was a slim, lovely woman whose life centred on her family. She was only nineteen when I was born. My brother David was born fifteen months after I was, and then my sister Nancy in 1940. We were the "pre-war family." As my father was away for much of the war, engaged in training troops, most of my early memories and experiences involve my mother and not both my parents.

We had idyllic times together. In the summers, we went to our cottage at McGregor Lake in the Gatineau Hills in Quebec, about thirty miles from Ottawa. There, we fished and swam and boated with

Mother and Granny Gilmour. My mother's best friend was Cairine Wilson, the daughter and namesake of Senator Cairine Wilson, the first female senator in Canada. The Wilsons had a home at St. Andrews in New Brunswick that was quite grand in scope. Each summer, we would pile into the car and drive to her house for a couple of weeks of vacation. It was a wonderful place. We got to swim, eat seafood, play golf, and enjoy a life that could have been featured on *The Lifestyles of the Rich and the Famous*. We weren't rich, but Cairine Wilson definitely was.

The rest of the year, we lived on Besserer Street in Sandy Hill, close to downtown Ottawa and our Scott grandparents, who had a house with a marvellous garden a few blocks away on Stewart Street. On Sundays, when I got older, I would help my grandfather deliver copies of the *Catholic Register* after mass. I went to a Catholic primary school, where the teachers were nuns in full regalia — black habits, wimples and all. They were, in my recollection, a stern and fairly demanding lot.

They would not have approved of my decision, when I was eight, to skip out from home in the midst of a polio epidemic scare to go to a movie playing downtown on Bank Street. My mother, not surprisingly, was frantic. Our housekeeper, Minnie, tracked me down and hauled me out of the theatre before the movie was over. How did she know where to find me? For years, I wondered how the movie ended. I did know that my decision to go to the movie was not very popular at home.

In later years, when I appeared at the Court of Appeal for Ontario, one of the most fearsome judges was Mr. Justice Schroeder. Rather uncharacteristically, he always treated me with respect, verging on kindness. He had grown up with Minnie in a district of Ottawa called Germantown, so at some point she must have put in a good word for me, movie escapade or no movie escapade.

After the war, my father came back to Ottawa. He rebuilt his practice in patent law, which had been put on hold during his army service. And, with my mother's help, he produced a second set of children:

Brian, Martha, and Christopher. There was such a gap in age between the "pre-war" and "second" families that Martha and Christopher were not born before I would decamp from Ottawa for St. Michael's College in Toronto.

My father was very gregarious and a great joiner of organizations and clubs. He was president of the Rideau Club, a Master of the Hunt at the Ottawa Valley Hunt, and active in many service organizations. He was also old-fashioned in some ways. While he was happy to send David and me to university, he thought that Nancy might be better off not going. She went anyway, to the University of Western Ontario, and took sociology, of which he also probably disapproved.

After my father's return to Ottawa, we moved from Sandy Hill to Rockcliffe, then as now reckoned one of the best areas in the city. We needed a bigger house to accommodate our growing household. The move also meant that David and I would be closer to our new school, Ashbury College.

Ashbury was, at the time, run by people who believed firmly that the battle of Waterloo had been won on the playing fields of Eton. It had the trimmings and trappings of a British public school. Many of the teaching masters were British, or at least anglophiles, and many of them had served in the war. Most of its pupils were boarders, but David and I were day students. We wore uniforms, studied a traditional curriculum featuring Latin, and were expected to participate in games every day. *Mens sana in corpore sana.* The day started with chapel, from which, as a Catholic, I was excused. A group of Catholics, Jews, and other odd souls, gathered every morning under the ministrations of the gym teacher while formal Anglican services were conducted in the school chapel.

A small contingent of Spanish-speaking students from Mexico and Cuba studied at Ashbury. One of them, a Cuban named Hiram Morales, used to tease me that I would be the prime minister of Canada. I used to tease him that he would become the chief of the Cuban army. His life did turn out to be very adventurous. He and another old Ashberian, Juan de Sousa, took part in the Bay of Pigs

9

invasion. They were captured by the Cubans, and Juan lost 110 pounds during his imprisonment. Eventually, Hiram was traded in a prisoner exchange to Puerto Rico, where he now lives and prospers.

As in the British public schools of the time, my school emphasized corporal punishment as the way to ensure that standards of decorum and behaviour were met. I don't remember getting caned, but I do remember being threatened with it for my achievement of getting 10 percent on a surprise English test. An English master once hit me on the head for something he took exception to, an incident that taught me a valuable lesson: to be wary of that particular master.

My brother David tells a story of his hockey team swarming a variety store on the way back to Ashbury from a practice. The team swooped into the store, and ran out with pilfered chocolate bars or gum. The school was notified, the miscreants were all summoned for an interview, and punishment was duly meted out.

The first of the punishments was "gating." If you were gated, you could not leave the school grounds for the duration of the penalty. If, like David, you were a day boy, then you had to come in on weekends for the duration. You had to do assorted physical activities, like running laps in the gym and doing push-ups till you dropped. In addition, you were caned by the headmaster, Ogden Glass. As he administered the stinging blows, he would say, "I take no pleasure from this. You must think of your family, and the shame you have brought upon them."

David recalls that I skipped seventh grade, to go into a form called "Transitus." When he started classes there, however, after a few weeks of also being skipped, he was demoted to Grade 7, being less of a brain than I was. He also remembers trying hard to keep up with me as we rode to school on our bicycles during the first week of classes, and flying "ass over teakettle," as the expression goes, as a car door opened in his path. He remembers me circling back impatiently on my bike, and my pained expression as I had to put up with an incompetent younger brother who had ripped his new pants.

The best account that I know of what it was like to go to Ashbury is Robert MacNeil's memoir, *Wordstruck*. MacNeil went on to fame in journalism as part of the *MacNeil-Lehrer NewsHour* on PBS in the United States and the author of the best-selling book *The Story of English*. There were other illustrious, or soon-to-be-illustrious, people there as well, including John Turner. Brenda, his sister, used to play with us when we were kids.

I have fond memories of some of my teaching masters at Ashbury. In particular, I remember my music teacher, Irene Woodburn, with great affection. Somewhat surprisingly, given the quest for respectability that Ashbury pursued, she was kept on staff after her husband was one of those implicated in the Gouzenko affair. Igor Gouzenko was a cipher clerk in the Soviet Embassy in Ottawa. His defection to the West, and his revelations about the Communist infiltration of assorted institutions, helped fuel a witch hunt in Canada and the United States. To the best of my knowledge, her husband's involvement in the affair did not have any great impact on Miss Woodburn's teaching, nor on her encouragement of musical gifts, wherever these might be found. She certainly encouraged me in my appreciation of listening to music, a lifelong passion.

I helped start, and was the first chairman of, the Music Club. *The Ashburnian* gives the following account of one of its meetings:

On December 1st, 1950, the Music Club assembled at the home of Mrs. Barwick. The purpose of this gathering was to hear Mrs. Barwick play the harpsichord. She began by telling us how the harpsichord had been derived from the psaltery, virginal and spinnet. To illustrate the virginal music, she played a piece composed by William Byrd in 1612. When this wonderful recital was finished, we left Mrs. Barwick's home feeling that we knew much more about the harpsichord than we had done previously; and we left very grateful to have had the opportunity of such an educational and inspiring evening.

Some of the other teaching masters were less inspiring, but the great thing about Ashbury was that the school was small, and participation was expected. Hence, it was possible to learn a great deal through the clubs and societies that proliferated like mushrooms around the place. My first published writings were done for the school magazine; prophetically, my first piece was about my admiration for the North American Indian.

> Among the tribes of Western Canada there is a religious rite known as the Sun Dance in which the whole tribe took part. During this dance one of the braves will become a warrior. This is done by piercing the muscles of the chest, tying thongs through the opening and lifting the brave above the crowd. If he can survive this painful test he is considered a warrior . . . So the Indians have lived in Canada. I believe they are the most interesting people on earth.

Whether this explains my later career path as commission counsel for the Berger Commission in 1974, I leave to others to decide.

The great bugbear of my youth was my stutter. I had difficulty with words that started with or contained S sounds. I had two options. I could shut up, which was difficult for me given my disputatious nature, or I could attempt to conquer it. My classmates' assessment of me in the 1948 yearbook shows that silence was not part of my strategy: "Scott: Though the general opinion is that he talks too much, he has proved that there is more than chatter under his skull."

In addition to talking a lot, I tried to overcome my stutter through participating in debates and drama. Debates were a regular part of the English classes, and the school also held formal competitive debates. My great friend and friendly rival in the debates was John Fraser, son of Blair Fraser, the noted Canadian journalist. John went on to have a distinguished career in External Affairs, serving in China and Portugal, among other places. At Ashbury, John and I shared many activities and competed for assorted academic prizes. He almost always won, though in my last year there we tied in the speech competition. *The Ashburnian* reported: "The quality of the speeches and of their enunciation was high however — remarkably so in the Senior Division. In this class the adjudicator found it impossible to arbitrate between Ian Scott and John Fraser. An additional prize has therefore been awarded by the school."

John and I had a subversive view of the power structure of the school, though he rose through the ranks to be head student, staying on at the school for one more year after I left to go to St. Michael's College.

Although his father maintained an independent stance as a journalist, John and I were then, in his words, "rabid little Liberals." The Scotts had been Liberals since that day in the 1830s when my fourteen-year-old great-grandfather Richard played hooky from school in Prescott, went across the river to Ogdensburg, New York, and heard the exiled rebel leader William Lyon Mackenzie speak. Blair Fraser took John and me, aged about fourteen, to witness a debate in a federal by-election. The Conservative candidate was George Drew, the former Ontario premier. The CCF candidate was Eugene Forsey, and the Liberal candidate had the unlikely name of John A. MacDonald. During the debate, we heckled Drew as much as we could.

Blair Fraser, wisely choosing to sit a respectable and professional distance away, happened to choose a seat in front of Drew's wife, the formidable Fiorenza Drew. He told us afterward that, each time we heckled, she kicked the seat of his chair quite firmly. He was not pleased by our behaviour. When I did get into politics, however, I loved both heckling and responding to heckling, so my early training served me well.

I was a page at the Liberal party convention in 1948 that selected Louis St. Laurent to replace Mackenzie King as leader and prime minister. My early political involvement, however, went beyond that of fulfilling the duties of a page. With my friend Dick Wright, I wrote some speeches that were delivered by Brooke Claxton, the minister of defence in the St. Laurent government. Mr. Claxton was quite unaware that the speeches had been written by a schoolboy. That I was able to write a credible speech for a politician at a relatively young age is a tribute to the school I attended. Ashbury gave me many opportunities to stretch my wings in speaking and writing, good preparation for my subsequent career in law and politics.

That I would have a career in law was predicted in the final year-book article about me in 1951. The italicized line beside my name, meant to suggest my most characteristic remark, was, *"May I ask you a personal question, sir?"* The entry said:

Ian is another of the form's intrepid debaters, and many of his most bitter disputes can be heard in History Class, where he is either trying to argue an extra mark, or hotly disputing one of B.J. Genesove's more fantastic statements. Ian is going in for law, and with his nimble brain he should be a good man to get hold of when you run afoul of the laws of the land. If any of you are interested, he can be found in about five years or so at Cell 23580, North Block, Kingston Penitentiary.

The prophecy was out only by about fifteen years; in 1970, I was indeed in Kingston Pen, but as commission counsel for my friend Bill Swackhamer's inquiry into the causes of the riots there.

I still have mixed feelings about Ashbury. It was a bit like the curate's egg: parts of it were very good indeed. It did prepare me well for university, but I could have done without the cuff on the head. According to a clipping in the family scrapbook, on Monday, August 13, 1951, I.G. Scott received the following Grade 13 grades: Eng. Comp. 1st; Eng. Lit. 2nd; Hist. 1st.; Bot. 3rd; Zoo 2nd; Lat. Auth. 1st; Lat. Comp. C; Fr. Auth. 3rd; Fr. Comp. C. The pattern was established early. If I was interested, I did well. If I was not, I did enough to get by. Ashbury did its job in getting me through high school and into university, and for that I should be grateful.

Ashbury also made me participate in a number of activities that I would not otherwise have taken up voluntarily. There is a picture of me in *The Ashburnian* with the cricket team, for example. Everyone else is in full cricketing whites. I am wearing a tweed jacket. I managed to escape from actually having to play cricket by becoming the scorekeeper, solemnly recording things like "Out — LBW" ("leg before wicket," to those not familiar with the arcane language of cricket), or "Out — caught silly mid-on."

This insistence on playing games reflected the Victorian values of Thomas Arnold and Rudyard Kipling. It was thought, of course, that participating in sport was a great preparation for life. I took a slightly more cynical approach to it myself. In any event, I have not watched or scored cricket since I left Ashbury.

My general skepticism about received opinions and values started early. Perhaps it is just in my character, or perhaps it has something to do with my sexual orientation. From quite early on, when I was as young as five or six, I had realized that there was something different about me, something not quite "cricket." I knew I was different from the general run of boys. By the time I was eight, I was pretty sure. By my early teenage years, I knew for certain that I was homosexual.

I had sexual encounters with other boys and men before I left Ottawa to go to university in Toronto. I remember being invited to fill out the table at dinner parties given by Senator Cairine Wilson. She entertained in great style, but was superstitious about having thirteen at the table. So sometimes I attended to ensure that the dreaded number thirteen would be avoided. I can remember that I would catch the eye of one of her servants; we would exchange phone numbers, and arrange to meet later, sometimes leading to a sexual encounter. Given the prohibitions attached to such acts at the time, it was imperative to keep quiet about them, which I did.

This lesson of silence was made abundantly clear during my first relationship, with Dick Wright. He was twenty-eight, and a friend of my parents. He and his friend Paul Pare, later head of Imperial Tobacco, had rented a cottage on McGregor Lake one summer while I was a teenager. I spent a great deal of time at that cottage. My relationship with Dick Wright merely confirmed what I knew about myself before I became sexually active. He and I remained friends long after we ceased to be lovers. If people had known we were lovers, though, all hell would have broken loose. We both knew this. My relationship with him altered my life permanently. It confirmed my long-standing feelings about who I was, but it also called for exceptional vigilance in keeping my private life private.

I never discussed my homosexuality with either of my parents.

From the time I was eight, I was sure that my mother knew that I was different, and accepted me for who and what I was. I always had a special bond with her. But both of us preferred to keep private matters private.

My father was less approachable. And as he got older, he grew less in tune with the times. He was not prepared, for example, for the world of the sixties in which his younger children grew up. As adolescents, David and I had had our share of escapades involving drinking and driving. Our father would lecture us about it, but he was mostly concerned about our safety, in not doing anything foolish when drinking. But when Christopher, the baby of the family, was at Ashbury, he got into some trouble, allegedly for selling dope to his classmates. The "dope" turned out to be tea leaves. The family crisis revolved around Christopher's wish to be charged; he did not want his classmates to know that he had not been selling them real dope. He left Ashbury under a cloud of smoke, as it were. My parents were horrified. Drugs were just completely beyond their ken.

David and Nancy and I remembered our parents, our mother particularly, as young people with lots of energy. My mother skated with us, swam with us, went out in boats with us, played tennis with us. When Brian, Martha, and Christopher reminisce about our parents, however, they tell very different stories about very different parents from the ones I remember. Maybe we older kids wore them out.

I knew from the time I was fourteen or fifteen that it would be difficult to remain in the relatively small world of Ottawa and conceal my sexual orientation. So when I had just turned seventeen, I headed out to St. Michael's College at the University of Toronto. After that, the amount of time I spent in Ottawa was minimal. I did not wish to inflict any pain on my family by forcing them to confront my homosexuality, something that would have been difficult for them, given the role that the Catholic Church played in their lives. My family respected my privacy. I kept my personal life quiet. That was the implicit deal we kept for many years.

For me, it was better to keep my life in Toronto quite separate from my family in Ottawa. My father, for example, once came to my farm when my friend Jimmy Smith was there. He noticed that Jimmy was wearing a signet ring that had been passed down through the Scott family. He questioned me about it, but let the matter rest without inquiring into any of the details of my arrangement with Jimmy. By that point in my life, my father had given up on his oft-repeated advice to me that I should get married and settle down. Without saying anything to each other, we had decided simply to enjoy the times we had together, without delving into too many details of my personal life. My parents continued to be devoted to each other, though their health, particularly that of my mother, was not good in their later years.

One story about my parents is instructive about how much they cared for each other until the end. They were both aged and quite infirm, living in the apartment they moved into after selling their big house in Rockcliffe, when my mother got a call from Roland Ritchie, who lived in the same building. He was then retired from the Supreme Court of Canada, but he and his brother Charles, one of the most distinguished diplomats that Canada ever produced, both had well-deserved reputations as ladies' men, as any reader of his brother's four-volume memoirs could attest. He called my mother to see if she could come over to help him tie a bow tie. My father grumped, "Let him tie his own damn tie. You're not going over there."

In 1983, we had a wonderful party for my parents' golden wedding anniversary. We dressed in period costume, the men with striped jackets and straw boaters, the women in white dresses with parasols. There were many toasts proposed and drunk, and many stories told. Some of them were even true. The party was a fitting tribute to our parents, and to the energy that they had unleashed in the world. We were lucky to have had such a wonderful party. Within a few years of it, both of my parents died.

My brother David, who had gone into partnership with our father, had his four children there that day. My sister Nancy, her two sons, and her husband, who was then very ill with cancer, came back from England for the party. My younger siblings had not then had any children, but my brother Brian would later be a father of four; my sister

Martha a mother of three; and Christopher, the baby of the family, a father of two.

As he and I worked on this memoir, my sister Martha once told Neil McCormick, "Make sure that you write that Ian was always Mother's favourite. That will really turn David's crank." My own suspicion was, to the extent that Mother had favourites, it was Brian who topped the charts. This is what he, speaking for all of us, said at her funeral mass:

> For in fact she was full of life and full of fun — and the mortar that held us together. At McGregor Lake where she swam every summer of her life, at Acacia Road where Christmas was a major cultural, social and religious festival, the preparations for which began as soon as she came back from the country in September. And thus we thought it no accident that on her last day she said that she was looking forward, on her first day on the other side, to playing bridge with her friends who had gone before: Aunt Cairine, Mary Price, and Peggy Heeney.

My father's death followed my mother's by a year. My parents had given me all the support and encouragement over the years that anyone could want.

Learning
the Law

WHEN I ARRIVED AT ST. MICHAEL'S IN 1951, I had two possible careers in mind. The first was teaching history, the second, practicing law. Despite the prophecy in the Ashbury yearbook, I was leaning toward the former. I had a bursary for one thousand dollars, a lot of money at that time, which was designed to bring me into the teaching fold. As I stayed longer in the system, however, the idea of law began to appeal to me more and more.

St. Michael's College is the Catholic college of the University of Toronto. In my time, there were some famous scholars associated with it, including Jacques Maritain and Etienne Gilson. When I went there, the college was in something of a transition. At one point, most of the professors were priests, but as they retired a new generation of lay professors replaced them. About half my classes there were taught by priests, and half by laymen, of whom the most notable was Marshall McLuhan, my instructor in English. I took many of my modern-history classes in the university's other colleges, but St. Mike's was the place where I took most of my courses.

St. Michael's had a debating club, the Senators, which had a distinguished list of alumni, like Morley Callaghan and Paul Martin. I wanted to join, but Jim Jerome, the head of the club, later to be a Speaker of the House of Commons and associate chief justice of the Federal Court of Appeal, thought my stutter was too much of a handicap to overcome. So he kept me out of the club for a year. When I got in the next year, the act of debating helped me get rid of the stutter.

I had fun at St. Mike's. I lived in residence for two years. There, I met my future roommates. Four of us were offered a chance to live rent-free in a nice apartment. The rent was free because the apartment was over a funeral home and we had to field the nighttime telephone calls requesting hearses to collect the bodies. Frederick Rosar, who owned the funeral home, did not want his three daughters' rest disturbed by phone calls in the middle of the night. So I lived there for two years, getting used to the occasional late-night call about the location of a corpse. Good training for politics, I suppose.

In my last year at St. Michael's, I had my first taste of electoral success: I became the president of the student council. I was also active in the university's student parliament. I had the honour of meeting Senator John F. Kennedy at one Hart House function. I enjoyed debating, and the camaraderie of the mock party system.

Of the professors I studied with, Frank Underhill made the biggest impression on me. There was a kind of divide in the history department, between people who took classes from Donald Creighton and those who took them with Underhill. Creighton was a famous conservative historian who wrote a definitive biography of Sir John A. Macdonald. Underhill was either a left liberal or a socialist, depending on your point of view. Either way, he was interesting and provocative.

While I was an undergraduate, I developed some study habits that stood me in good stead throughout my legal career. First, I didn't study too far in advance of the deadline. Second, I tried to read all the relevant material, organize that material in my head, and then write my papers based on what I retained. If a typical undergraduate essay consisted of a string of quotations linked by passages of the student's own writing, mine consisted of my own words, based on my absorption of the material. This gave me early practice in marshalling my thoughts and organizing them into a coherent argument, something required of every courtroom lawyer. Peter Russell, now a distinguished constitutional scholar, says that I used to infuriate all the other history students by arriving late to all my exams, dressed in a blazer and tie. He says I would pick up the exam books, write a page-and-a-half answer to each of the required four questions, and then be the first one to leave the exam room. What made it particularly infuriating, he says, is that I would get just as good a mark as people who sweated a lot more before the exams.

Although I enjoyed my classes, and even enjoyed writing history essays, my best memories of my undergraduate days revolve around the friends I made, and the fun I had there.

In second year, I joined the University Naval Training Division, or UNTD, a program designed to train naval officers. University Reserve Training Plan, or URTP, was the Air Force plan, and the Canadian Officers Training Corps, or COTC, the equivalent Canadian Army plan. Serving in UNTD entailed going to one training session a week during term, and spending one summer in Halifax and one at Royal Roads in British Columbia, learning how to command ships. Although graduates of these programs received the Queen's Commission, and were duly certified to be officers and gentlemen, we were not obligated to join the regular forces.

My late grandfather might have hoped that my enlistment in the Navy was in keeping with my great-great-grandfather's career as a ship's surgeon in the Peninsular Wars. Probably however, as my friend Jimmy Smith would later say, it had more to do with the way I looked in the navy-blue uniforms we were issued. They were much more dashing than the drab khaki that my brother David wore when he was in the Armoured Corps in COTC. For years, I used to wear my Navy greatcoat skiing, wearing it up on the T-bar or chairlift, and sending it back down on the lift, where it would be waiting for me on my arrival after I skied down the hill.

The other great thing about UNTD was that, with people like Bill

"Max" Saunderson (later a minister of industry and trade in the Mike Harris government) and the aforementioned Peter Russell, I got paid for spending my summers in ships. On occasion, in keeping with the great tradition of the Royal Navy, alcoholic beverages were consumed — sometimes in excess. Following one after-training stint at the Colonial Tavern, I was briefly detained by one of Toronto's finest for attempting to stop a trolley in the middle of Yonge Street. Max Saunderson, to this day, claims credit for persuading the officer not to press drunk and disorderly charges against a future attorney general.

Perhaps the high-water mark of my naval service occurred when I was plucked by helicopter from the deck of the ship on which I had completed my summer's training, so I could return to Ottawa in time for some function at which Brooke Claxton, the minister of defence, thought my attendance desirable. And the low-water mark was undoubtedly the occasion when I snapped off my oar in some demonstration of lifeboat skills, and the supervising bosuns all shouted at me, "Cadet Scott, Cadet Scott, ship your oar, ship your oar!"

The summer of my fourth year, I worked in Quebec City for a company that was a precursor to Hydro-Québec. Roy McMurtry and I were the only Anglos in a work crew of twenty-five or so. We lived with French-Canadian families, one of the objects of the exercise being to learn French. On the work crews, we learned a lot of not-very-polite French. My landlady was very refined and charming, but for the first few days, when I unpacked my lunch, I discovered that she had made me cucumber sandwiches with the crusts delicately cut off. I had to beg her to provide more robust fare that would not provoke quite so much mirth among the Hydro workers.

One day, Roy and I missed the last company truck back across the river from Lévis to Quebec City. Neither of us had a cent on him, and the fare for the ferry across the river was twenty-five cents each. Roy had recently broken up with a French-Canadian girl whose family lived in Lévis. It took several hours of argument from me before he would agree to go to the girl's home to see if we could borrow the necessary fifty cents to get across the river. We were in our work clothes, dusty and tired after our day of construction work.

When we rang the doorbell at his ex-girlfriend's home, her father answered the door. He spoke only French. It fell to me to explain who we were and why we needed to borrow fifty cents. After some hesitation on the father's part, he reluctantly gave us the money, and we made it home. Roy heard later from a friend of the girl that her father had grounded her for a month for lying to him about what kind of boyfriend she had. She had told him that Roy was a law student. Her father thought it obvious from Roy's appearance that he was a bum without money or any apparent prospects.

At some point in my fourth year, I had decided that I would apply for admission to law school. If I didn't get in, I reasoned, then I would be a teacher. But I was accepted at Osgoode Hall Law School, so I decided to go — the fourth generation of Scotts to embark on a legal career. I picked Osgoode, then still at its original site in downtown Toronto, for the eminently practical reason that it took a year less to complete than did the law school at the University of Toronto, at the time the only competing school of law in the province. Osgoode would not be affiliated with York University until some years after my graduation.

When I was a student, there was a rather sharp division between the two schools concerning the teaching of law. Osgoode Hall represented the old, practice-driven kind of legal instruction. The U of T, on the other hand, took a much more academic approach. People like Bora Laskin, the noted constitutional scholar and future Canadian chief justice, taught there. The separation between the two institutions was quite pronounced. As I explained many years later, when I was honoured with an invitation to deliver the Goodman Lecture to the U of T law school:

The other memory that suffuses me in this company tonight is of the twelve years that I taught Civil Procedure in the law school in succession to my friends David Kilgour and Horace Krever. I was not a graduate of the law school and for that defect I was frequently called to account. The truth was that in the fifties Osgoode Hall was one year shorter. Nonetheless at the urging of my undergraduate classmates, Marty Friedland and Harry Arthurs, I undertook to attend a number of first year lectures including those given by Dean Wright in Torts, J.B. Milner in contracts and Edson Haines in civil procedure. Not many classes had gone by when Dean Wright detected my presence, summoned me following a class to his office, and with little formal ceremony, threw me out. He made plain that the intellectual deficiencies I had elected to bear by enrolling at Osgoode were not to be offset by surreptitious attendance at his university. I was not to be permitted to end run the benchers; the end did not justify the means.

I got to know the Dean better when he participated in a Hart House debate on divorce in which I played a small speaking part. In the discussion in the Warden's quarters following the debate as I sought to question the Dean, I was quietly coached by a member of the law staff who thought it would be amusing to watch the Dean's face when the Faculty member's own ripostes came from a new and juvenile quarter. My coach later became chief justice of Canada.

I was one of the youngest students at Osgoode, but I must confess that I was not one of the most diligent. I lived in my fraternity house, Alpha Delta Phi, and occasions for social get-togethers were numerous. My attendance at classes, as opposed to attendance at parties, was spotty. I did enough work to finish in the middle of the pack, and I learned that I wanted to do litigation, but I was not fully engaged as a student.

In my final year at Osgoode, a representative from Harcourts came to display the gowns, striped pants, vests, and jackets that lawyers must wear in court. Alan Leal, the dean, had just been made a Queen's Counsel and had decided to attend this presentation wearing his new silk robes. When the man from Harcourts had finished his sales pitch, he asked if there were any questions. I stuck my hand up and asked him how I could get a shiny robe like the one the dean was wearing. The dean, like Queen Victoria, was not amused.

In a speech honouring Coulter Osborne on his elevation to the Court of Appeal of Ontario in 1990, I made the following remarks about him, and about the intellectual atmosphere of Osgoode Hall in those dim, distant days of 1955:

I first met Coulter Osborne, our guest of honour, when we entered the first-year class at Osgoode Hall Law School in 1955. We were by and large an undistinguished lot and not much was expected of us. Caesar Wright's Law School at the University of Toronto had recently been accredited and it was well understood that any student showing ability or aptitude for the profession or perhaps even ambition had sought enrollment there. Our old school itself was at a particularly low ebb: very large classes, very small permanent faculty, an imported dean of uncertain distinction, black letter law, printed notes, few questions asked, fewer answered. On all sides it was expected that we would be the drones of the profession. I still smart when I recall the intellectual condescension of my old friends in the U of T elite corps.

In such an environment, lifelong connections and good friends are easily made. Coulter appeared then much as he does now: a tall figure in the class, open faced, good natured and dryly amused by his circumstances. In a classroom of young men who had barely ceased being school boys, he gave off an air of maturity and distinction solely on account of his distinguished athletic career. For he, alone among the lumpenproletariat of our class, exhibited the physical grace of an athlete. This was more than enough, in our circle to mark him, albeit cautiously, as a person with a future.

Whatever the vicissitudes of Osgoode Hall, it prepared me for articling with William Howland at McMillan Binch. It was a large firm for the times, as it had about twenty lawyers. Mr. Howland had a large mortgage and real estate practice. I had met him when he taught me mortgage remedies, then a compulsory course. So I spent a lot of time searching titles in the Registry Office and attending at the Sheriff's

Office to see if there were any liens on property. I liked the work and was good at it, though it was not very intellectually challenging.

One day, when I was supposed to be at the Registry Office, I decided to take in a matinee instead. When I emerged from the movie theatre, blinking in the brightness of the afternoon sun, I encountered the rather large frame of Mr. Howland at the theatre entrance. Although our brief conversation then was entirely cordial, I was not asked back to work for him at the conclusion of my articles.

In later years, when I was attorney general and Howland was the chief justice, it is hard to say which of us was more surprised by our respective career paths. He was always most charming and helpful to me, though I couldn't help feeling that he harboured some reservations about me.

My father wanted me to come back to Ottawa to join his practice. I did not want to do that, so I was relieved when my brother David went to law school and joined our father in Scott and Aylen. David's firm, however, like so many others, has recently merged with several other firms, and is now part of Borden, Ladner, Gervais.

Instead of going back to Ottawa, I sent out fifty or sixty letters of application to law firms in Toronto. The only offer I received in response to all those letters came from Andrew Brewin. I joined his firm, Cameron, Brewin, Weldon, McCallum and Skells, and began my real legal education.

Andrew Brewin was my mother's first cousin through her Blair relatives, which made him a second cousin of mine, or a first cousin once removed, if one is being pedantic. At any rate, he was a first-rate courtroom advocate. His mentor and former partner was J.C. McRuer, the father of the Ontario Human Rights Code and later the chief justice of Ontario. Many years later, in 1984, I was the host at the University Club for a remarkable dinner in honour of the seventieth anniversary of J.C. McRuer's call to the Ontario bar. At the dinner, he was alert and in remarkable shape for someone in his mid-nineties.

McRuer taught Andrew Brewin well. Before politics consumed most of his energies, he was one of the top lawyers of his generation, which included people like John Robinette, Arthur Martin, and my old articling supervisor, William Howland. Mr. Brewin (and I always called him that throughout our years of practice together) had somewhat chaotic work habits. He took on any case that interested him, so that his practice ranged widely from criminal cases to civil litigation. If he believed in the cause, or in the principle raised by a particular case, he did not even notice if he got paid for his work. In those days, there was no formal system of legal aid, but people like Andrew Brewin ensured that cases were heard regardless of finances. Though I had been an indifferent law student, my time with Brewin inspired me. I found that I loved practicing law, and I worked hard learning how to be an effective advocate.

Brewin practiced law from an office at Bay and Richmond streets in downtown Toronto. His firm operated on a loose kind of partnership arrangement, but the lawyers operated essentially as individuals, with quite distinct practices. When I started as Brewin's junior, he paid me a salary for the first couple of years. I occasionally worked for the other lawyers in the office, but the bulk of my work flowed through him, at least initially. The first thing he taught me was how to deal with clients. As I did not have an office, or even a desk of my own, for the first year I worked with him, I hung about in his office and got to see directly how he listened to clients and gave them advice. Sometimes, if the matter was sensitive, or the client wary about having a junior listening in on the conversation, Mr. Brewin would kick me out of the room for the duration of the interview, depriving me of the only desk I had in the office.

A steady stream of people needing help came into his office: people charged with minor criminal matters, people in need of free legal services, and lots of people who wanted to appeal rulings, referred to us by other, mostly out-of-town law firms.

From Mr. Brewin, I learned two major lessons. First, everyone is entitled to legal representation, and the job of the legal counsel is to give the best legal advice possible in the circumstances. Second, if an important legal principle is involved, it does not matter if the client is solvent: the principle should be defended.

Hence, Brewin often took on more cases than he could comfortably handle, which meant that I got to do interesting cases from the beginning of my career. Circumstances would sometimes catch up with him. Cases that he thought would be settled would be set down for trial, and documents would have to be prepared at the last moment to meet court deadlines. At times, the whole office mobilized to get the papers in on time. Mr. Brewin would have dictated something to the secretary, who would transcribe it as quickly as she could. As soon as she finished a page, someone would run it over to the courtroom where Mr. Brewin would have it added to the factum, even as he addressed the court.

Later, in my own career I sometimes had to resort to similar tactics. My friend and former articling student Ian McGilp recalls a story that one of my articling students was sent to file some documents, produced rather tardily, that did not quite comply with the formal court requirements of the day. The clerk would have been within his rights to refuse to accept the documents. If he had done so, however, it would have meant that a big trial that was about to begin would have to be rescheduled, with all the attendant grief rescheduling would entail. The court clerk looked at the student, looked at the documents, pensively contemplated the consequences of refusing to accept them, and then, slowly, began to stamp them to make them part of the official record, all while saying, "That Mr. Scott has more gall than a poacher's dog."

All I can say is that I learned at the feet of a master.

Andrew Brewin sometimes got so bound up in his work and quest for social justice that he neglected more mundane matters. He was good-hearted, but sometimes lacking in concern for the prosaic details of ordinary life, a crime I was guilty of myself on more than one occasion. Occasionally, I fielded calls from Mrs. Brewin, asking me to intervene in some domestic crisis involving plumbing or electricity. On one occasion, she called me from a pay phone, asking me to get Mr. Brewin to pay the phone bill, as the service at home had been disconnected.

Brewin had great confidence in my ability to appear in court for him on short notice, to make arguments on motions and to represent his clients on minor matters in criminal courts. And I discovered that I loved being in court.

As I gained more experience, he let me take on bigger and bigger cases. My breakthrough case with him concerned a Fort Erie motor court, situated across the road from a gas station. The station started to operate twenty-four hours a day to provide fuel for transport trucks. The noise the trucks made pulling in and out of this truck stop made it difficult for the patrons of the motor court to sleep. Business dropped off. We brought a motion in nuisance to force the truck stop to abate the noise by restricting its hours of operation.

Mr. Brewin and I went down to St. Catharines, Ontario, for the trial. He presented the opening arguments. Then he went out for lunch. He did not come back after lunch, but I was there, and had done the research on the case, so I simply carried on. The judge hearing the case was Wishart Spence, who later sat on the Supreme Court of Canada. He decided for our side: my first major victory. On appeal, Walter Williston, one of the great figures of the Ontario bar, represented the other side. I won at the Court of Appeal as well.

In later years, when I felt that my junior counsel were ready to handle cases, I sometimes left them to it in the same way that Mr. Brewin did me that long-ago afternoon in St. Catharines. Linda Rothstein, a partner of mine at Gowling's, remembers one day at the Court of Appeal when I did not come back after lunch to make a reply. When the judges asked her if there would be a reply, she said yes, got up, and did it — and was well launched on her successful career as a litigator.

Whether this teaching technique is a good one probably depends on having fairly apt pupils. In any event, Andrew Brewin and I made a good team in the few years we worked together before his work as the NDP member of Parliament for Greenwood made him only an intermittent visitor to the office. He was elected in 1962 after some six or seven unsuccessful previous attempts. His son John, later an NDP member of Parliament himself, and I assisted him on his last appearance in the Supreme Court of Canada, some years after his election to Parliament.

The case was an important one for freedom of political expression. Moses MacKay was a union official who had bought a house in an upscale neighbourhood in Etobicoke. He had put up a sign for the NDP candidate in a federal election. Etobicoke, however, had a strict by-law regulating signs on private property. It might have been that Moses' upscale neighbours objected to the NDP nature of his sign, or they might have thought that the whole tawdry election process was not in keeping with the dignity of the neighbourhood. In any event, Moses' election sign was deemed to be illegal, according to the Etobicoke by-law. The Supreme Court, however, held that the Etobicoke by-law was *ultra vires*, beyond the legal authority of the city. Moses MacKay was entitled to put up his sign.

Andrew Brewin took on small cases as well as large ones, right up to the end of his professional career. In 1967, for example, he attended a meeting of the Metropolitan Toronto Parks Commission to argue for an extension on the leases of the houses on Toronto Island. He managed to persuade one commissioner to change his vote. The extension was granted, a first step in preserving the island community.

In those days, I would show up in criminal court at least once a week, ready to assist anyone who needed representation. People in need of lawyers were a captive audience there. There was usually no pay for representing these clients, but that was how one learned how to practice law. The late Supreme Court of Canada judge, John Sopinka, told a story of the first time he remembered meeting me. He was sitting in the court, waiting for his case to be called, when I burst into the room shouting, "I have a case respecting the liberty of the subject, liberty of the subject!" It was an application for *habeas corpus*, one of the oldest writs in the canon of the English common law, and one of the foundations of the political and civil liberties that flowed from it. The practice was for cases involving the "liberty of the subject" to go to the head of the docket. According to Sopinka, the judge was not impressed, and threatened to have me incarcerated unless I shut up.

The number of lawyers practicing then was very much smaller than it is today. Lawyers got to know one another's strengths and

weaknesses very quickly. It imposed a kind of discipline, as one's reputation depended on keeping one's word. People who were regarded
as "benders," in Sopinka's terminology, had a hard time obtaining the
little accommodations that all busy lawyers need from time to time.

It was possible, then, to meet the leaders of the bar in any number
of informal settings. As I put it in my introduction to the Goodman
Lectures:

When I began to practice with the late Andrew Brewin in 1959
we were a six- or seven-man law firm, which in those days was
regarded in Toronto as a firm of very significant size. Down the
block from us on Richmond Street was David Goodman's firm,
which had entered into some incestuous relationship with the
Charles Dubin firm, which we did not precisely understand, a
conglomeration in total of probably six or seven.

It was Mr. Goodman's custom to take coffee most mornings
at Muirhead's Restaurant, a ramshackle enterprise representing
the cross-pollination of the Honeydew and a low-grade Arcadian
Court. He often brought with him Ed Eberle, all pop-eyes and
enthusiasm, and Horace Krever, then as now a walking symbol
of malnutrition. Eddie [Goodman] and Charlie [Dubin] were
too busy building their careers and rescuing the Progressive
Conservative party from one political difficulty after another,
to attend. Most mornings it was thus in the company of never
more than a half dozen young lawyers that David Goodman held
a kind of court. He listened, gently prodded the odd provocative question into our circle, and was always both intelligent and
wise. Like others of these lucky few, I will not quickly forget
those mornings, the lessons taught us, and the experience given
to us by this gentle, thoroughly civilized man.

A less civilized place to learn the law was in the Ontario Court of
Appeal. When I began practicing law, the courts were in the last
throes of their adherence to the system of common law built up
through precedent. English cases and decisions were the ultimate

controlling authorities. To win a case, one had to show how the facts fit into one of the prevailing canons of interpretation.

In my first reported case from the Court of Appeal, *The Queen* v. *Yule*, I faced two problems, one practical, the other legal. The practical problem was that my client had been denied permission to open a restaurant, quaintly called a "victualling establishment," without having been given a hearing by the town official in charge of such matters. The legal problem was that I had to find a legal principle to invoke, as the courts customarily treated such matters as purely administrative and outside the purview of the courts. The only principle I could use was that of an improper delegation of authority to a subordinate. To make this argument, I cited an 1895 case, *Merritt* v. *City of Toronto*, and a 1916 case from Alberta, in an attempt to persuade the court that the principles enunciated in those cases should take precedence over an Ontario Court of Appeal case decided in 1948, *Re McGillivray and Hamilton*. My argument was based on the principle that the council could not delegate its powers to a subordinate official without clear words to that effect in the enabling legislation. I was trying to show that a provision regarding auctioneers in an Edmonton by-law, which was struck down by the courts, was similar to the Eastview, Ontario, by-law, and hence that the Eastview by-law should be struck down as well. I was not successful.

The court held: "While the argument based on the special provision relating to auctioneers is persuasive, nevertheless, in view of the statement in the McGillivray case based upon the legislative history of s. 247(4) the plain meaning of the words of that section ought not to be limited by an implication based upon a special provision relating to auctioneers."

The legal principle of *stare decisis*, the principle that courts are bound by previous decisions, was then the controlling judicial notion. For the judges to call my arguments "persuasive" meant that they approved of my style and my gallant attempt to get around the rather large obstacle of the 1948 Ontario Court of Appeal case. They just weren't buying my argument. In some ways, arguing from precedents made practicing easier, as there were a limited range of principles and cases on hand. In other ways, it put you squarely in the power of the judges to decide if your precedents were persuasive or not.

Judges on the Ontario Court of Appeal, like Justices Shroeder, MacKay, and Aylesworth, had a well-deserved reputation for eating junior counsel alive. Some members of the bar disliked appearing before them, afraid that past errors would be forcefully recalled to them, and applied to the facts of the present case. Sometimes I got work from lawyers who simply did not want to appear before certain judges on the Court of Appeal.

Andrew Brewin, however, was a skilled advocate at the Court of Appeal. He had as much appeal work as he could handle. And after a short time of working with him, so did I. Dick Trainor, now a distinguished judge, reminded me recently of our first professional meeting. He had come down from Sudbury to retain Mr. Brewin to do an appeal for him. When Dick finished outlining to him the importance of the case, Mr. Brewin said that it "sounded like a good appeal for Ian to do." Dick had been a couple of years ahead of me in law school, and thought that I was far too young to do such a big appeal. But I did it — and I won. Dick and his partner Jimmy Hinds retained me to do any number of appeals for them after that.

Several factors helped me become a successful appellate advocate.

First, I had learned to write factums that had persuasive power. A factum is the statement of how the facts of the case fit into the existing legal framework. In order to write a good factum, I had to learn how to anticipate and defuse the arguments that my opponents would likely use, while setting out the facts in a framework that would give the judges a way to find for my side in the appeal. In the case of legal arguments, this practice almost always entailed going back to the basic legal principles that applied to the case, and then showing how an interpretation of those principles could lead to the results I wanted.

Once I had the lines of the argument worked out in my head, I could craft a factum quickly. Malcolm Ruby, one of my partners at Gowling's, remembers being on a routine case as my junior. As the other side was making its arguments, I was writing away furiously on a pad of legal paper. He glanced over to see what it was that I found so interesting about the other side's presentation. But I was writing the factum for a completely unrelated case, and finished it before the other side had finished talking. This, it must be stressed, was not my usual way of writing factums, but it shows that all the early appeal work I did helped to hone my ability to make legal arguments concisely and effectively.

Second, I thrived in the Court of Appeal because early in my career I developed a thick-enough skin not to let comments from one case carry over to subsequent ones. I regarded myself as an advocate. Someone had to win and someone had to lose each case. The important thing was to make the best possible argument in the case at hand, and then move on. There was absolutely no point in wallowing in introspection about lost cases, or in gloating about victories either. There would always be another case coming down the road, and it was important to be clear-headed going into each one.

Third, I learned fairly quickly how to tailor my oral argument to suit the panel of judges assembled to hear it. Some judges were more bound by convention than others. While some were receptive to creative attempts to find ways within the existing framework of the law to reach a just conclusion, others were solely concerned with finding previously decided cases that seemed to be on point. I learned to assess on the spot which argument had the best chance of success before which judge.

On one of the first cases in which Steve Goudge accompanied me to the Court of Appeal, I attempted an innovative argument. While I was speaking, Mr. Justice Aylesworth, the most senior of the panel hearing the case, sent a note down to the most junior judge, sitting on his left. Twenty minutes later, I was still in full rhetorical flight. The note came back. Mr. Justice Aylesworth read it, looked at his colleagues, who nodded at him, and then said to me, "I think we've heard enough, Mr. Scott." Then they retired to consider their verdict. As they did so, Mr. Justice Aylesworth threw the note in the wastebasket.

Steve, consumed with curiosity, waited until they had left the courtroom, and then retrieved the note from the wastebasket. On it,

Mr. Justice Aylesworth had written, "Let me know when you have heard enough of this argument." The junior judge had scrawled, "Enough," and sent it back to Aylesworth. Another innovative argument squelched in its infancy.

Despite such setbacks, I loved being in the Court of Appeal. Appeal work involved the basic principles of law. The findings of fact had been made at the court below, so my major concern with the facts was to show how they justified applying one set of legal principles over another. After a relatively brief period of practice, I always felt that I could argue how basic legal principles should apply. Therefore, I could go into court on quite short notice and make arguments that had at least a chance of persuading the two judges I needed to convince to win the appeal.

The practice of law is nothing if not an exercise in realism. You take your lumps and you get on to the next thing. Andrew Brewin gave me the space to find that out for myself and I am still grateful, after all these years, to have been given the chance to learn from him. Nepotism works. At least it did in my case.

If Andrew Brewin was my mentor in taking on cases that needed to be argued, and opening the door to whomever needed representation, John Robinette was my model in how to conduct cases. When I started, I had the privilege of learning from a number of distinguished advocates, like Brewin, Charles Dubin, and Arthur Martin. As skilled as these lawyers were, however, the one who impressed me most was Robinette. He did his own research and his own writing. He operated within the confines of his law firm as if he were a sole practitioner. He was thorough, capable, and tough-minded. Like everyone else at the bar, I admired him for his principled approach to the law. He provided a wonderful example of what a skilful advocate could do. I was not alone in seeking to emulate him.

During my first few years with Andrew Brewin, most of my time was spent with run-of-the-mill criminal cases. They provided a good grounding in learning how to think on my feet and how to shape arguments. But as time went by, I found myself doing less criminal work, and more and more labour cases, a development that helped me develop an expertise in administrative law. As a result, I was well prepared to take part in the great explosion of administrative law cases in the late 1960s and 1970s.

By the mid-sixties, the outlines of my later professional life were taking shape. I was an advocate. I was active in professional organizations. I was interested in reforming the legal system. I founded a Toronto chapter of the John Howard Society. I was expanding my contacts in the profession, which gave me a steady stream of appellate work. I worked hard, but made lots of room for fun in both my work and my private life.

Then I added another string to my bow. In 1968, I started teaching civil procedure at the University of Toronto Law School. I recently had lunch with a student from that first class. He told me that the thing he remembered best about my class was that I enlivened it with "war stories" based on my own experiences in the courtroom. My examples, he said, were pithy and helpful. Of course, I was buying him lunch when he told me this, but as he is now a judge we must give him some credit for probity.

More than anything else about teaching, I enjoyed meeting the students. Over the years, I taught many people who went on to have distinguished careers, though I do not claim to have had much to do with their later accomplishments. Rob Prichard, later president of the University of Toronto, was one of my students. Bob Rae was also a student of mine, and the first time he ran federally for the NDP, in 1978, I did some canvassing for him. Later, when he was leader of the Opposition at Queen's Park, he was an effective and occasionally harsh critic of our policies. When he became premier, and I spent two years in opposition, I tried to return the favour.

Students over the years found me approachable when they had problems. Steve Grant, later one of my partners at Cameron, Brewin & Scott, first saw me when I was in court defending a student charged with assault and creating a disturbance during one of the many demonstrations that enlivened campus life during the late sixties and early seventies.

Later, students at a bar admission course retained me to sue the

Law Society of Upper Canada to stop it from changing the rules of the bar admission course partway through their exam year. I agreed to represent any student who was willing to retain my services for a dollar. So they set up a table to sign up students and collect the dollars. Having been retained, I went to a meeting of Convocation, the rule-making body of the law society, to discuss the case. We went behind closed doors. I made a simple opening statement: "Do you know how much fun I am going to have taking you [the Law Society] to court on this case?" The Law Society immediately backed down.

I was also retained by students at Rochdale College to represent them in a tax assessment case with the City of Toronto. Rochdale had gained a national reputation as a haven for drug-dealing and loose living. Accordingly, the city had concluded that Rochdale was no longer entitled to an education discount on the tax rate. The city's position was that not much education of the traditional type was taking place at the college. Through intense negotiations, we managed to get the city to acknowledge that 35 percent of the space at Rochdale was being used for educational purposes, and the city agreed to lower the tax bill by that amount.

The settlement was endorsed by Mr. Justice Richard Holland. The students of Rochdale were so impressed by his impartial handling of the case that they decided to present him with a plaque commemorating the trial. We met in his chambers, and I presented him with the plaque, which depicted three leaves of *cannabis sativa*, along with an inscription of gratitude for his role in finding a solution to the case.

Through teaching, I met interesting students who helped keep me abreast of the world outside the rather narrow cloisters of the courtroom. So I kept teaching, right up until the time I became attorney general of Ontario in 1985.

A couple of years into practice, I met the first of my three long-term life-partners. I was on vacation at the time, at Ogonquit in Maine, when I noticed a young waiter named Paul Cohen. He was a student, from Florida, working in the summer to earn his tuition. He would later become a prominent stockbroker. I eventually persuaded him to come to Toronto to be with me. When I met him, he was young, energetic, and lots of fun. We started living together in a downtown apartment, but we shortly thereafter bought a place in the country as well. It was an old stone farmhouse, on fifty acres of land, near Erin, about an hour from Toronto. A stream ran through the woods at the front of the property, the water making its way to the nearby Forks of the Credit River.

The farmhouse needed a lot of work. Among other things, I put in a massive stone fireplace in a kitchen I designed myself. We also transformed the landscape around the house. I put in a large vegetable garden and worked hard at landscaping. I planted thousands of trees by the stream. I loved seeing the plantings mature. I planted thousands of bulbs for a spring show of flowers, and each season was marked by a procession of blooms. For a couple of years, I boarded a horse called Copper at a neighbouring farm, and rode him when I got the chance on weekends.

That I had a country property before I owned any place in the city was telling. I needed a place where I could unwind, do physically strenuous work, and prepare — physically and mentally — for the upcoming week in court. The farm was my place of refuge. It was a lot of hard work, but the work was so different from what I did during the week that it recharged my batteries. It was a place where I could entertain friends and be myself.

On weekends, Paul and I would load our cat, Louise (originally found in the barn at the farm), into my car and head off for the country place. The country air must have been healthy, as Louise lived to the ripe old age of twenty-one.

Having a place of my own meant that I spent relatively little time in Ottawa. A routine developed whereby I would fly in to Ottawa on Christmas Eve, or even Christmas morning, to participate in the family Christmas that my mother had been planning since September. She loved organizing and wrapping presents and having the family all around her. My younger brother Brian describes me sweeping into town on Christmas Eve, laden with presents from places like Holt Renfrew, having an uproarious time, and then departing for Toronto on Boxing Day. Then I would go to the farm with Paul for our New Year's celebrations with our chosen family of friends.

When I first went to Toronto as a student, there were relatively few places where one could meet other homosexuals. One such place was Letros, across from the King Edward Hotel on King Street. It was open long into the night and famous, or notorious, depending on your point of view, for its parties in The Nile Room. There were other places where one could meet, like the Murray's Restaurant on Bloor near the Park Plaza. One needed to be circumspect about whom one met and where, as consequences were attached to being mistaken about someone's sexual orientation.

Over the years, I built up a network of homosexual friends who became, in some ways, my extended family. Among them were people like Darrell Kent. Darrell was one of the first to see the real estate potential in Cabbagetown. He ran a real estate company that specialized in two types of property: upscale Rosedale homes and Cabbagetown fixer-uppers. Such was his influence that I bought a house in Cabbagetown, on Carlton Street across from the Riverdale Zoo, as it then was. For the first few years, I rented it out, and continued to live in apartments near Church and Carlton, not then the gay quarter of Toronto it would become. Darrell and his partner Peter Brown lived very well, and I always had fun with them in activities that ranged from dinner parties to trips to exotic places like Brazil.

Darrell and Peter bought a house an hour east of Toronto in Port Hope, close to Lake Ontario. From the outside, the house looks like something out of *The Great Gatsby*. It was built in the days before air conditioning, by a rich American family from the South who wanted to come to Ontario and catch the cool lake breezes in the summer. The house sits on a couple of acres high above the lake; a portico runs across its entire front, and the rooms inside are built on a grand scale.

Peter and Darrell entertained lavishly and often. In later years, however, their happiness was marred by Darrell's illness; he developed a brain tumour that eventually ruptured while he was on a trip to Brazil with Peter in 1989. He died almost instantly.

As I said at the memorial service held to honour him:

Darrell Kent's last two years were terrible — the ghastly inevitability of a tumour — . . . but throughout it as before Darrell enjoyed life richly, lived it every hour and very much wanted to go on living . . . He never shut himself away or cut himself off, gave in to despair or forsook determination. Throughout, he presented himself to the world and equally to his friends as he liked to believe he was: and, thus happily, he became for us what he believed he was: A man who relished life with all its pleasures and even with all its misfortunes; a man who challenged himself as well as the fates that surround; a man who found savour in the human carnival of which for a moment a living part.

I miss him. Peter has carried on being a gracious host, and his dinner parties are still noted for their camaraderie and good cheer. Like so many of my friends, Peter has had to cope with the untimely death of a lover. He still travels a lot, but it is not the same without Darrell at his side.

Another of my friends from that period is John Manuel. He is an interior decorator with a flourishing business that caters to people with both good taste and money. There are records of one of my Gilmour great uncles fishing in New Brunswick with a "John Manuel," described as the nephew of my Gilmour relative. John likes to say that we are related. I don't think we are, but over the years we have had a lot of fun together. Sometimes he brings clients to my house to show them the colour scheme he says he selected for it. Of course, I maintain that I was the one who thought of it.

Another friend from the sixties on is Robin Glasgow, an unrepentant conservative verging on the Attila-the-Hun school of social welfare. He has done real estate and interior design and has been a wonderful friend over the years, despite his antediluvian social opinions.

One of my best friends was Jim Inch. He was the Canadian representative for one of the big American movie companies. I could always talk to Jim about anything that was on my mind, and he helped me through all the major disruptions in my romantic life.

Unfortunately, he died a number of years ago. It is a sad truth in my community that too many people have died too young.

Another who falls into that category was Bill Swackhamer. He was a lawyer with an incisive mind and an elegant lifestyle. In many ways, he was my mentor in how to lead one's life. He had a country property five concessions away from mine, and there were many occasions for weekend get-togethers at one place or the other. Bill was a good bridge player, and we spent many enjoyable hours playing bridge together. Another friend, Bob Pouper, had a country place a few miles away; on many evenings, we made a progression from one place to another for drinks or bridge or conversation. This pleasant routine ended abruptly after Bill's drowning death in the pond on his farm. It was a great loss.

The country properties gave us the privacy we needed to lead our lives free from the scrutiny of neighbours. Another way to achieve privacy was to travel. For several years in a row, I spent the American Thanksgiving weekend at a big house in Acapulco, staffed with three servants, that was owned by the Mexican film star Cantinflas. He lived in an even grander house on the same street. We would all hang out on the beach in the day and have dinner in at night. It was possible to be much more uninhibited there than in staid old Toronto.

There are those who think that the repression of homosexuals is responsible for the flamboyant side of gay life — turning social disapproval of "fairies" into the extravagance of drag queens, for example. I think that the truth is far more complex. There are homosexuals who spend their lives denying their sexual desires. There are homosexuals who haunt bathhouses and have hundreds of sexual partners. I have known gays who committed suicide over the break-up of a relationship. There are tormented gays and happy gays. There are interesting homosexuals and boring homosexuals. I had a friend who liked rough trade. All kinds of marginal people had keys to his apartment. One day he arrived home to discover that all his furniture had been looted from his flat. He went over to the cocktail lounge at the Ford Hotel, a none-too-salubrious haven for the types of people he was interested in, posted a note offering a reward for the return of his furniture, no questions asked, and got it all back the next day. His tastes were like those of Christopher Isherwood in his days in Berlin, now famously preserved, in a sanitized way, in *Cabaret*.

All of the above observations could be made about heterosexuals as well. As I always defined myself through my work, other people's sexual practices were not at the core of my concerns. I saw no reason why mine should be anyone else's business either.

If the people mentioned above are, or were, at the core of my social life, it also included a shifting kaleidoscope of other people who shared my interests in music, art, and lively conversation. If there is a common thread in my friendships, it is that the people are lively and don't mind engaging in polemical arguments, whether those arguments are about politics, paintings, or bad haircuts.

No account of my friendships would be complete without mention of Mary Kiervin. When we first met is lost in the mists of time. We shared a love of good music and fine dining, not to mention the occasional exchange of information that lesser minds might call gossip. Mary is one of the kindest people I know. When I went into politics, she organized innumerable coffee parties for me.

Marilyn "Pete" Milner, my secretary for practically the whole time that Mary and I have known each other, once described us as being like an old married couple: always squabbling about something inconsequential, and then making up and going on to the next thing together.

Mary was one of the few people who moved back and forth with me between the "straight" and "gay" worlds. She was there for me when I had tough times. I was there for her when one of her relationships, usually with a man unable or unwilling to commit to her, would break down. However others may classify the relationship that Mary and I have enjoyed over the years, we have, at the least, made things interesting for each other.

People were especially discreet about relationships in the years before the 1968 change to the Criminal Code decriminalizing homosexuality, because some people moved back and forth between, or inhabited both, the straight and gay worlds. I have a male friend, for example, who has had an affair with a married man that has lasted for something like thirty years. Such a relationship depends on secrecy, as do clandestine affairs in the heterosexual world. Generalizations about human sexuality are always risky.

In fact, Paul Cohen left me to get married, an occasion for much wry comment from my homosexual friends. After a series of brief encounters, I found myself chatting in a bar with the man who became my next partner. He was Jimmy Smith, a Scot some twelve years my junior. We experienced much joy and much grief in our years together. He was charming and full of fun, but like me he had his opinions and stuck to them. We had some titanic battles over the years, but we had a lot of fun as well.

When Jimmy and I started living together, my renters' lease was expiring. I asked Darrell Kent what an appropriate rent for the house should be. Darrell, always in favour of pumping up real estate values in Cabbagetown, named a figure that was much greater than the rent I had been charging. I thought, well, he's the expert in real estate, so I'll just slip a notice of the rent increase through the mail slot. After I hadn't heard from the tenants for a couple of months, I walked over one evening to discover that they had decamped, unwilling or unable to pay the new rent that Darrell thought I should get.

I decided then to renovate the place and move in. It took several months to do everything, so that Darrell's advice resulted in my losing several months' rent. Years later, when I ran for office the first time, and lost, I used a three-storey townhouse belonging to Darrell as my headquarters. At the end of the losing campaign, I announced that his contribution to the campaign was the rent for his building, and considered myself even.

Jimmy and I lived in that house together for eight or nine years. We acquired a black standard poodle, Boo. After a period of tense stand-offs between Louise, my cat, and Boo, they worked out an agreement to tolerate each other's presence. This meant that on the weekends, both Boo and Louise would be put in the car for the trip to the farm.

Jimmy was originally from Edinburgh, and had immigrated to Canada with his family as a young man. His first thought was to join the police. He spent a year as a cadet before he and the police reached the mutual conclusion that he was not cut out to be a policeman. It was the last gasp of his hoping and pretending to be straight. Jimmy sold advertising for CFRB Radio, a career that obviously suited him more than being a police officer; he made as much money from that as I earned at the time from law.

Jimmy and I used to throw big parties at the farm every few months or so, parties notable for their hilarity and the prodigious amounts of alcohol consumed. Jimmy and I both loved to cook and entertain, though he enjoyed having lots of people around more than I did. Quite often, I would retreat to a quiet spot with my book and my drink while others engaged in more boisterous pursuits.

He always claimed that I was born "lucky," though he might have used a somewhat more earthy expression involving horseshoes and anatomy. His favourite example was the story of how I rolled and totalled my car going to the farm from Toronto one night. I went off the road, and the car flipped as it went into the ditch. There was just enough room for me to roll down the window and squeeze out. As I sat by the roadside, pondering what to do next, an OPP car with two policemen stopped. There was no doubt that prior to this incident, I had had a few drinks. The policemen asked if I was hurt. I said no, but I would like a cup of coffee. So they took me to a coffee shop on the way to Guelph, where they were going to take me to the police station. I bought them a coffee, too, though I don't recall any doughnuts figuring in the transaction. I said to them, "Look, I know what drunk is, and I wasn't drunk." They accepted my submission, called in the station, and said that this incident did not warrant charges. And, as Jimmy put it, "Not only did they not give you a Breathalyzer test, they drove you out to the farm!"

A Breathalyzer test might have detected more than trace amounts of alcohol in my breath on that and many other occasions. Alcohol played a central part in my social life, and had done so since I was quite young. Legal culture was suffused with alcohol. John Sopinka used to say that his first job each morning when he was articling for Walter Williston was to find out at which of his favourite drinking spots Mr. Williston had left his car the previous night. Having found where the car was, Mr. Sopinka then had to go and get it, so that the whole process could start all over again. Walter Williston was one of the most respected experts on civil procedure that Ontario ever produced, so his drinking cannot have incapacitated him.

The pattern, then, was set relatively early. I worked hard at becoming a good lawyer. I was active in many community organizations. I was also good at keeping my life in quite separate compartments: private and public, social and professional. My friends knew who I was. Steve Goudge, my closest professional colleague over the years, was only at my farm once in the twenty-five years we practiced law together. He only met most of my gay friends when I went into politics, and then mostly for the purposes of the campaigns.

When the pattern started, it was necessary to conceal my homosexuality if I wanted to practice law. After Pierre Trudeau took the state out of the bedrooms of consenting adults, prejudices still lingered that might have hampered my career had I been open about my sexuality.

I was too busy and having too much fun in my life and my profession to want to rock that particular boat, so I didn't.

THREE

Cameron, Brewin
& Scott

IN THE 1960S, MY LAW FIRM changed dramatically. Jim McCallum joined a corporate law firm, taking John Brewin, Andrew's son, with him. The firm was renamed Cameron, Brewin & Scott. Andrew Brewin and Pat Cameron were both busy with federal politics. Andrew Brewin was the NDP member for Greenwood and Pat Cameron was the Liberal member for High Park, though he usually showed up in the office on the weekends to tend to his real estate practice.

The firm had an infusion of new members. One of the first of these was Alick Ryder, who articled at the firm and then joined it. Alick's family had a cottage on Stoney Lake, north of Peterborough. The Brewins also had a cottage there, and that is how Alick initially came into the ambit of the firm. His family ran a large heavy-equipment business, J.H. Ryder and Sons, that was, and continues to be, extremely successful. On the basis of background and family interests, one would have assumed that Alick would practice corporate law, or real estate, or, perhaps, construction law. Instead, he followed me into my labour-law practice, representing unions in various arbitrations and negotiations.

Being a union-side labour lawyer in the late sixties was not the most lucrative way to make a living in law. The work itself was interesting, although the same issues tended to recur. The problem was getting a steady flow of work. The big unions tended to have their own in-house counsel who did the bulk of the routine work, and those lawyers had links to favourite outside firms for any work they could not absorb themselves. If you represented the Steelworkers union, for example, you would have a steady stream of work because of the sheer size of the union. We did not have a formal retainer from any large union, but took whatever work we could get from any of them.

One union that consistently gave us business was the Bartenders' Union, which though it was relatively small still generated a lot of grievances. Bartenders were always being dismissed for one reason or another, and there were always good cases involving hotels and bars. Alick came to master the sometimes arcane and convoluted fact situations involving personnel clashes at assorted bars. His knowledge of the minutiae of each case was extremely useful for me, as I tended to concentrate on the broad principles of law involved, and was delighted when he provided factual underpinnings for my arguments. Alick and I had a lot of fun together in the bargain, an essential requirement for anyone who worked for us.

Steve Goudge also possessed a great sense of humour. Unlike some of the other members of the firm, however, he was not blessed with keen instincts for a good party. He articled with us, and then joined the firm. Over the years, he became the colleague closest to me. I could always bounce ideas off Steve, and get a frank response from him about possible strategies or arguments to employ.

Steve's father, Thomas Goudge, was for many years the head of the philosophy department at the University of Toronto. Steve must have inherited something of his father's rigorous mind, as he has a razor-like ability to cut through the persiflage and get to the heart of the matter. Steve is also a good administrator, so he always managed to keep things on an even keel in the office. Almost from the beginning of our association, I could trust Steve to go into any court to make an argument for me, often on short notice.

My colleagues often joked that the firm expanded only when its most junior member had been beaten up by judges one too many times while begging for an adjournment or a rescheduling for me. I always believed that 90 percent of my cases would settle without going to trial. As a result, I often had to work out double-bookings, and, in some cases, triple-bookings. I could not have done it without my associates, who were all capable of filling in for me at a moment's notice. On one such occasion, I was in another court and had sent Steve to face a particularly formidable judge. Steve had strict instructions from me to get the case rescheduled. The judge was all for hearing it that day, whether Steve was prepared to argue it or not. Eventually, Steve got the postponement, but it was obtained at such a cost to his psyche that we were forced to hire another junior lawyer to serve as judicial cannon fodder for a while.

Ian McGilp, another articling student who later joined the firm, remembers getting a call from me one morning, requesting that he show up in the Court of Appeal that same morning to explain to the judges that I was unable to attend. I told him to tell them I had an important discovery to do. This request, not unnaturally, filled him with apprehension, as judges on the Court of Appeal are not used to being passed over, and certainly not for such a preliminary matter as a discovery. They were probably aware that I had not done a discovery myself in many years. He rushed over to the court to beg the opposing counsel to explain to the judges why I couldn't be there. The counsel wisely declined. McGilp, not yet called to the bar, was technically unable to appear in the Court of Appeal. So he rushed back to the office to get Ian Roland to gown and explain to the judges that Mr. Scott had been unavoidably detained, and that if they would grant him the courtesy of adjourning until one in the afternoon, he would definitely attend then.

Stories still conflict as to where I was that day. I was a believer in Benjamin Jowett's maxim "Never apologize, never explain," and I probably did not enlighten my colleagues on why I did not show up in court that morning. The prevailing suspicion was that I was in New York, where I had gone to see the opera and had enjoyed myself a little too much, deciding to stay over an extra day. Frantic phone calls were made. I was located and duly appeared in the Court in the afternoon.

The next person to join the firm was Chris Paliare. He had been a student in a labour-law class taught by my friend Harry Arthurs. Harry had invited me to come to his class to take part in a discussion. I was representing the union side and John Saunderson, a well-known corporate lawyer, the management side. I extolled the virtues of unions and the evils of the powers inherent in the capitalist class. Chris, favouring management at that point in his life, thought it was the most radical thing he had ever heard.

After that class, however, he underwent something of a meta-morphosis. He got a summer job at the Steelworkers union and began working on arbitrations with in-house counsel. That summer, all the outside counsel normally used by the Steelworkers were on vacation or otherwise unavailable for a hearing coming up in Thunder Bay. Chris, remembering my classroom performance, suggested that the union hire me. They didn't want to use me, however; I had appeared across from them on some other matter, and their policy was not to use people who had ever opposed them. When they couldn't find anyone else, they did hire me, and Chris and I went up to Thunder Bay for the arbitration. We had a fine time together.

In the fall, I invited Chris out to lunch at an expensive steakhouse and offered him a job. He was startled, because he was still in law school. He asked me instead for an articling job for the next year. We had already hired two students, for what was then a five-man firm, and I didn't think that I could offer him a position on the spot. By the time I called to offer him an articling job, however, he had decided to go to the University of Texas for a master of laws degree. We agreed that he would article with us upon his return. Chris has been with Cameron, Brewin & Scott and its successor firms ever since.

The next acquisition for the firm also came out of a university contact. In one of the first classes I taught at the University of Toronto, in 1968, a student, Ian Roland, approached me with a survey, inspired by the LeDain Commission on Drug Use in Canada, that he had prepared on drug use among the faculty and students of the school. Apparently, I was one of only four faculty members who agreed to respond to the survey. When he returned from a European trip the summer of his last year at law school, Ian did not yet have an articling position. His roommate, John Campion, had already accepted one at Cameron, Brewin & Scott. Then Campion got an offer from Faskens, a much bigger law firm with a corporate department. Ian persuaded John to accept the offer from Faskens, and then called Steve Goudge and asked for an articling job. When Steve said that the position was filled, Ian broke the news about Campion's defection, was interviewed, and accepted on the spot.

He told me he wanted to work for a year as my junior. He did. He remembers two cases during that year that illustrated sharply the pleasures and pains of winning and losing at the bar. The first involved a group of mostly middle-aged women who had been charged with obstructing the police who were trying to escort scabs across a picket line. The prospect of going to jail filled the women with dread. Ian noticed that the Crown had failed to provide one of the links in the chain of evidence needed to convict. I was able to point this out to the court and the women were acquitted. They were so excited they mobbed me. I pointed out that Ian Roland was the one they should be mobbing, so they thanked him enthusiastically. As he was driving me back to Toronto, the car ran out of gas. I told him, "Welcome back to the real world."

In the other case, he had discovered an Alberta case that supported the position we were arguing. As I was on my feet, making arguments about how this case helped our cause, the opposing counsel slipped a note to Ian that the Alberta case had been overturned on appeal. Ian passed me the note. I read it, informed the court of its contents, then proceeded to add, "As I was saying, the Alberta case does not stand for the proposition . . ." After my argument was over, I told Ian if he could remember for the rest of his career always to update cases, then that little incident would have been worth it.

People who joined the firm were expected to be competent and flexible. Stephen Grant, for example, was recently cited by his colleagues as being the best family-law lawyer in Ontario. At the time he joined our firm, however, we effectively had no family-law practice. Stephen mostly practiced labour law at the beginning of his career, then segued into family law, partly because no one else in the firm wanted to do it. It was becoming a trend to move from being an all-rounder, to use a cricketing term, to being a specialist.

Obviously, we had no great business plan for Cameron, Brewin & Scott. It grew through accretion. Its strength was that all of the people who worked for it worked hard and worked effectively. Of course tensions and pressures arose, resulting from missed deadlines or similar catastrophes, but the tensions were usually dispelled by a flash of humour, or, perhaps, by a quick burst of temper. I did blow my stack on occasion, but it was almost always quickly forgotten, and we would continue on as before until the next crisis.

Excitements and alarums were part of my style. People who couldn't deal with it went elsewhere. One person who stayed for twenty years was my secretary, Marilyn "Pete" Milner.

The life of a legal secretary is never easy, but this was especially true in the days when documents had to be produced on a typewriter. Not only did Pete juggle all my often double-booked court appearances and hearings, handle my appointments, and make excuses for why I was not someplace that I was expected to be, but she also typed my factums, sometimes transcribing from the Dictaphone page by page while I was in court making opening arguments. Articling students were kept in shape running the pages to the courtroom to be inserted in the factum as soon as they were produced. This technique had served Andrew Brewin well, and it worked for me on the few occasions I had to use it.

Pete was tough enough to withstand my occasional outbursts of impatience brought on by the realization that documents were needed instantly. I trusted her judgement and her competence. She ran all my personal finances for years. Her system was to retrieve some money from my bank account and split it into three portions.

One she put in an envelope in the centre drawer of my desk, one in a locked filing cabinet by her desk, and the third in the office safe. When I needed the money in the safe, she knew it was time to go to the bank and start the cycle all over again. When I cleared out my office prior to moving to Queen's Park to be attorney general, I found dozens of these unopened envelopes of cash. I opened them all and spent the windfall.

When Pete left in 1990 to have her child, after two decades of working for me, I had no clue whatsoever about my banking arrangements, except that my bank was at the corner of Bay and King. So I dispatched John Moffat, my new executive assistant, to get me some money. Unfortunately for him, there were banks at each corner of the intersection. He had to go to all four before he found the one with my account. When I eventually found my chequing account, I discovered that Pete had deposited a cheque representing my share of my mother's estate, where it had remained for a number of years. I took out the money and bought some art.

Our firm managed, over the years, to attract some of the best and brightest articling students to work for us. I think they knew that with us they would get to work on interesting cases and accrue a varied litigation experience. In one year, for example, 1979, the three students were Ed Waitzer, later head of the Ontario Securities Commission; Beth Symes, first head of the tribunal system in the Pay Equity Office; and Rob Herman, later deputy head of the Ontario Labour Relations Board. Early in our firm's existence, Ted Matlow, now a judge, asked to switch his articles to us from another firm. He said he would work for nothing if we would give him a better grounding in the practice of law than the firm he was then working for. We said yes, but did not accept his offer to work for nothing.

Dick Trainor, for whose Sudbury firm we did a lot of appellate work, always said one of the reasons he sent us so much work was that he knew we always would have the brightest students working for us, and that all the basic legal research would be impeccably done.

One former articling student of whom I am especially proud is David Baker. He left our firm to work with Ralph Nader in

Washington. When he came back to Toronto, he founded and for many years was the head of ARCH, a legal clinic for people with disabilities. He remembers that during his first week as an articling student, he was assigned to write a legal memorandum on a complicated issue in tax law. As no one in the firm did tax law, his impression was that the senior lawyers all looked at the research and writing skills displayed on a student's first assignment and then decided what kinds of files could be safely entrusted to him. Once a student was assigned the file, it became his responsibility.

Our firm might have been small, but it was lively and ready to take on challenging assignments. I jumped at an opportunity to work as commission counsel on the inquiry into the causes of disturbances at Kingston Penitentiary. In 1970, there had been a bloody and prolonged riot at Kingston Pen. The prisoners had taken control of several cellblocks, where they held some guards hostage. The inmates then meted out prison justice in horrible ways. Some prisoners were forced to run the gauntlet, taking fearsome blows from the other prisoners as they did so. Others, who had offended prison codes of conduct in some way or another, were tried in kangaroo courts and then beaten severely.

My friend, Bill Swackhamer, an extremely competent lawyer at Faskens, was one of the commissioners. I had dealt with prisons and prisoners through my work with the John Howard Society, but nothing could have prepared me for the devastation caused by the riots. I enlisted Steve Goudge, newly called to the bar, as my assistant, and we set out on our investigation.

Canada was not alone in the phenomenon of prison riots. They were erupting all over the world. In one sense, then, the prisoners at Kingston had just been part of the *Zeitgeist*. In another sense, though, the riot seemed un-Canadian: this sort of thing was supposed to happen in the United States, not north of the border.

In many respects, Kingston Penitentiary symbolized the debate that still rages about the purposes of the detention system. Physically, the place had not changed much since it was built in the nineteenth century. It was dark, dank, and foreboding. Its high walls and stone construction spoke volumes about its main purpose: to contain and punish wrongdoers. This ambiance was not much improved by the riot, either. The first time Steve and I toured the prison after the riot, we were almost overwhelmed by the sight of the burnt-out cellblocks and other signs of damage.

Our job was to get at the root causes of the riot and recommend changes to the system to ensure that such an event would not happen again. We interviewed people like Donald Oag, one of the principal instigators of the riot, a man with a long history of violence both inside and outside correctional facilities. We also interviewed guards and prison administrators, and heard expert testimony.

The inquiry into the riot was the first public commission I had worked on, but it would not be the last. I next worked for the Law Society of Upper Canada with Mr. Justice John Osler on an investigation into the funding of legal clinics. At that time, there were only a few legal clinics in Ontario. Many members of the profession regarded them with some suspicion. Clinic lawyers were paid a salary, and their clients were not charged for the legal services they received. I saw clinics as one way to make the law more accessible to people who ordinarily would not have been able to afford legal services. One of the few then in existence, Parkdale Legal Clinic, served the diverse community that lived in one of the poorest areas of Toronto. Most of its clients would have had no easy access to lawyers without it.

We produced a report that recommended that the government finance legal clinics throughout the province and that they fund them indirectly, through the agency of the Law Society. The clinics would be able to build up expertise in relevant areas of law; landlord-tenant law, for example, was an area where landlords had far better access to legal representation than their tenants. I had always believed that one of the chief functions of lawyers was to even up the sides, and I hoped that a system of legal clinics across the province would help even things up for people who would otherwise have a hard time getting legal help.

I discovered that I had a taste for the making of public policy through commissions of inquiry. In 1974, I was fortunate enough to be invited to work for one of the most influential commissions of inquiry in Canadian history, the Berger Commission. The commission was one of the most satisfying and interesting things I have ever done.

John Diefenbaker might have hoped that his 1962 Canadian Bill of Rights would usher in a new era of Canadian law. The problem, however, was that the Bill of Rights was not entrenched in the Constitution. Its effectiveness, rather, depended on the willingness of judges to use it to override other statute law. After the Supreme Court of Canada did just this in *Drybones*, a case that used the Bill of Rights to overturn sections of the Indian Act, the courts retreated. In *Lavelle* and *Bedard*, two cases involving the rights of women denied status under the Indian Act, for example, the Supreme Court withdrew from its activism in *Drybones*, dashing expectations that the courts would make significant changes in the way that aboriginal people were treated. The courts seemed mired still in traditional and narrow interpretations of the law, especially in comparison with the judicial activism in the United States. There, courts were staking out bold new territory in the wake of *Brown* v. *The Topeka Board of Education*, and the Civil Rights Movement was making important headway. The differences in the legal environments between the two countries were striking.

The issue of native rights in Canada arose in an acute form in the late 1960s and early 1970s, when oil and gas discoveries were made in Alaska and the Northwest Territories of Canada. It was clear that any pipeline built to transport the oil and gas would have a substantial impact on the traditional hunting grounds of the indigenous peoples of the North. After the 1972 election, the federal government, then a minority Liberal government dependent on NDP support, determined that full public hearings should be held before approval of assorted proposals to build an oil and gas pipeline through the Mackenzie Valley.

They appointed Mr. Justice Thomas Berger to head the inquiry. Before his appointment to the bench, Berger had been the lawyer for the Nisga'a people in their efforts to negotiate a land-claims settlement with the federal and BC governments. He had also, briefly, headed the NDP in British Columbia, so he was a good choice to secure the support of the federal NDP for the inquiry. Echoes of the 1957 pipeline debate, with its disastrous consequences for the federal Liberal party, might have been behind his selection. Whatever the deeper political motivations behind the appointment, there could not have been a better man to conduct such an inquiry.

Berger had hired Ian Waddell to be his assistant on the inquiry. Waddell called up Steve Goudge, a close friend from their days in university, to see if I would be interested in being commission counsel. Steve contacted me in Ottawa, where I was arguing a case before the Supreme Court of Canada. Berger and Waddell flew in from British Columbia, and Steve came up from Toronto for a dinner meeting to discuss it. By the end of the evening, I had agreed to take the job, which turned out to be the most interesting one I'd had, at least until I became attorney general some years later.

Part of my job was to keep the oil and gas and pipeline companies from filing and winning procedural motions against the way Berger proposed to run the commission. To help me do this, I made arrangements for my colleagues Steve Goudge, Alick Ryder, and Ian Roland to join me at the commission. Chris Paliare, fresh out of law school, was conscripted to cover any lectures I might miss at the University of Toronto.

Almost as soon as I had agreed to do the job, Berger took me on a tour of the North. Ian Waddell describes such a tour in Carolyn Swayze's book, *Hard Choices: A Life of Tom Berger*:

> We flew to Inuvik on a beautiful June day. There a helicopter pilot met us and took us up the Arctic Coast, up the Mackenzie Delta to Demarcation Point on the border of the Yukon and Northwest Territories. Then we went right across the ice to Herschel Island, up the Firth River, over the British Mountains and down the Pelly River, right down the Alaska border parallel to the coast. When we got over the mountains we saw migrating caribou, three grizzlies, several wolves and dozens of seals on the sea ice.
>
> As tired as Tom was when we got to Old Crow, he accepted

the chief's invitation to go to his home for caribou. And there was no darkness, remember. It was hard to sleep.

The next day he said to me, "Do you realize the magnificence of what we've seen? It's the last of North America, the eighth wonder of the world."

By the time we had finished the preliminary tour, Berger had worked out his strategy for the whole commission. We started by summoning all the groups who had an interest in the pipeline to meet in Ottawa for procedural hearings to determine how the inquiry would be run. Then, the twenty-five-member-commission research team got to work preparing for the substantive phase of the hearings, while similar work was undertaken by people hired by the pipeline companies.

One of Berger's great insights was that the commission could be used as a giant exercise in democracy, to explore the needs of indigenous peoples and to explain those needs to the great mass of the Canadian people who had little direct experience of the North. It was his idea to hold the bulk of the hearings away from Ottawa and in the North, a major change in the way in which public inquiries were usually run. This brought the media to the North, resulting in a whole spate of stories published by people like Martin O'Malley, who was covering the hearings for the *Globe and Mail*. Berger went into small towns and listened to what the elders had to say about their traditional ways of life and the importance of not interfering with traditional migration routes of the caribou herds on which the communities depended for their major food source. The companies had major reservations about the process. How, they asked, could you rely on testimony that had not been subjected to cross-examination and discovery and all the other procedural safeguards of the judicial system? It was my job to ensure that what the aboriginal elders said in these informal sessions was treated as seriously as the testimony of the oil-company executives in more formal hearings, where the usual rules of evidence applied. We also commissioned anthropologists, zoologists, and botanists to give expert testimony about expected impacts on native ways of life.

The commission put environmental concerns squarely on the public agenda. Oil and gas and pipeline companies had to explain how they could construct a pipeline and its attendant infrastructure without damaging the fragile ecosystem of the Arctic. For almost the first time in the history of Canada, whose economy had historically been based on the exploitation of natural resources, including cod, fur, lumber, mines, oil, and gas, companies had to justify economic development against the competing claims of a traditional way of life.

Just as the formal hearings were beginning in Yellowknife, however, I had to leave for two weeks, for one of the strangest cases in my legal career. Steve Goudge took over for me in Yellowknife. I left the world of oil and gas pipelines and entered into a trial featuring underworld characters with Runyonesque names, a murder, a missing gun, cigarette butts, and forensic evidence that hinged on whether or not the victim's kidney had been completely frozen. The contrast between the two worlds could not have been more complete, except, I guess, for questions about freezing tundra and frozen kidneys.

Muggsy Dean, a man with a long record of charges, was a client of my partner Chris Paliare, whose practice in those days was about 50-percent criminal law. One day, Chris picked up the newspaper and read that Muggsy had been charged with the murder of a local thug, nicknamed "the Chinaman."

The facts of the case were thus: sometime before the murder, Muggsy and the Chinaman had met in a restaurant on Queen Street, in Toronto. Muggsy had a reputation for being a hitman, and the police had staked out the restaurant. After the meeting, the Chinaman got into Muggsy's car and they headed north, trailed by the police. Somehow, Muggsy managed to give the police the slip. Ten days later, they discovered the Chinaman's body, with five bullet holes in it, in a barn north of Toronto, around Major Mackenzie Drive.

Muggsy was charged with the murder and retained Chris to represent him. Chris had just been called to the bar a couple of years earlier, and did not want to do a murder trial by himself. I agreed to do the trial with him and a bright articling student named Paula Knopf on two conditions: that I did not have to speak to Muggsy directly, and that I would not call him to take the stand, where his lengthy criminal record might be opened up on cross-examination.

The circumstantial evidence strongly suggested that Muggsy was guilty as charged. He was the last person known to have seen the Chinaman alive. When last seen by the police, the two of them had been in a car heading in the general direction of where the body was found. The bullets that killed the Chinaman were of a calibre that fitted a six-shooter like the one witnesses had seen in Muggsy's possession. There were some du Maurier cigarette butts by the body, and witnesses would testify that they were Muggsy's brand.

The weak point in the Crown's case was that the Chinaman's body, when discovered, was consistent with a stage of rigor mortis of thirty-six hours after death, as opposed to ten days. If he had been killed only a day and half before his body was discovered, then anyone could have done it, as the murder would have occurred well after the time when Muggsy and the Chinaman were seen together.

The Crown's pathologist was Hillsden Smith, the chief pathologist for Ontario. He would testify that this degree of rigor mortis was consistent with the earlier time of death if it could be shown that the body was entirely frozen for that period. The last organ in the body to freeze is the kidney, as it is enveloped in its own wrapping of fat. Smith was prepared to testify that a slide of the tissue from the Chinaman's kidney would show that a certain process of putrefaction had begun, consistent with the kidney's having been completely frozen.

Chris and I knew we had to find a pathologist who disagreed with Smith's interpretation of the kidney slide, to cast doubt on the body's being completely frozen. We also had to find out if any other kind of gun could have taken the calibre of bullets used to kill the Chinaman.

Chris called about twenty pathologists, asking them about Hillsden Smith's analysis of the kidney slice. None of them would testify for us, either because they agreed with him, or because they did not want to show up Smith; as chief pathologist, he ladled out work to them all. Then we heard about a retired professor of pathology at the University of Western Ontario. He had an impeccable reputation, and had testified for both the Crown and the defence in many previous cases. Paula Knopf and Chris went down to London to interview him in his home. In a scene that mixed the worlds of Agatha Christie's Miss Marple and the hard-boiled world of Elmore Leonard, Chris and Paula were entertained with tea and home-made cookies by the professor's white-haired wife, while he cheerfully provided a grisly interpretation of differing rates of putrefaction of kidney tissues. The upshot was that the professor said that while Hillsden Smith was an excellent pathologist, he was wrong in this instance. In his view, the kidney had not been completely frozen. It was a lifeline for Muggsy.

Chris and Paula also learned from the owner of a gun shop on Yonge Street that several other guns besides the six-shooter allegedly belonging to Muggsy used the same calibre of bullets that did the Chinaman in. We informed the owner that we might call him to testify. He called the police and told them what we had been up to. In a conference with the Crown, about another matter, we were told that the gun-shop owner wanted to keep his good relationship with the police, and that we shouldn't call him, as he would not be helpful to Muggsy.

At the same conference, however, the Crown told us he was going to call a policeman who had driven in the squad car with Muggsy when he was arrested. He would testify that Muggsy had offered to show them where the gun was if they would drop the charge from first- to second-degree murder.

We were shocked. Before the trial started, we had agreed with the Crown not to hold *voir dires*, on condition that what the Crown had disclosed to us of Muggsy's statements was complete. A *voir dire* is a hearing done in the absence of the jury, where technical arguments about the admissibility of evidence or other legal doctrines can be made. So we had a *voir dire* with the judge, Mr. Justice O'Driscoll, not exactly a pro-defence judge, and complained that the policeman's promised testimony was a violation of the undertaking that the Crown had given us. The judge said that notwithstanding any discussions we might have had with the Crown, he could not exclude the policeman's statement as evidence. Fortunately for us, the Crown respected our previous bargain that full disclosure had been given, and never tendered the statement as evidence. The police were furious with him.

About ten days into the trial, Muggsy called Chris down to the cells and asked him when he was going to be called, as he wanted to present his alibi evidence. Chris told him that his alibi evidence was full of holes that the Crown could exploit, that he was not going to be called, and that the main defence witness was going to be a doctor.

Muggsy's comment was that it wasn't looking too good.

I called the retired professor of pathology from Western to testify. He was elderly, impressive, and, I think, reassuring for the jury. He discussed the intricacies of rigor mortis in terms the jury could understand. He also clearly explained his theory about the state of the kidney, and why, in his considered opinion, Hillsden Smith's interpretation of the evidence was incorrect.

I used his testimony to raise the concept of "reasonable doubt" in my address to the jury at the conclusion of the trial. I took some risks in the way I addressed them. I admitted that my client was not exactly a sterling character and might well be found guilty of any number of offences. But I reminded them forcefully that they were there not to pass judgement on the general character of Muggsy Dean, but rather to assess whether the Crown had discharged its burden of proving beyond a reasonable doubt that Muggsy had murdered the Chinaman. Chris Paliare claims that my address was electrifying. He remembers that I took a package of cigarettes out of my pocket and said, "Look, I smoke du Mauriers. Just because there were du Mauriers found at the scene of the crime doesn't mean that I was there. Lots of people smoke du Mauriers."

The jury retired, and they weren't out for very long, considering that it had been a two-week trial. They came back with a "not guilty" verdict. Muggsy also faced a lesser charge of conspiracy to murder the Chinaman. As soon as the verdict came down, we made an immediate application for bail on the conspiracy count. It was successful. I took Chris, Paula, and Muggsy out for dinner, the only time in the whole proceedings that I had any direct contact with our client.

Two days later, Muggsy fired us as his counsel for the conspiracy trial. Thirty days later, he tried to rehire us, but we all refused.

Going back to Yellowknife for the continuation of the Berger Commission was a relief. I quickly left arcane forensic evidence of differential freezing rates of human tissue far behind me and re-entered commission-counsel mode.

After the hearings in Yellowknife, we flew to many different communities across the North. We met people who had grown up in traditional societies, with values and skills that enabled them to survive in one of the harshest, yet most vulnerable, environments on earth. I learned so much from Tom Berger. He had a great gift for listening. He also had a gift for eliciting information from people unaccustomed to talking in formal settings. The concept at the heart of the Anglo-Saxon judicial process, that truth will emerge from an adversarial process, was completely foreign to the northern people's way of thinking.

Having extracted testimony from village elders and community spokespeople, Berger was then intent on explaining that testimony to the urban south. We used the commission as a teaching tool. We had hearings in Vancouver, and took the commission to places like Winnipeg. And we produced a report that changed forever the way in which aboriginal and indigenous peoples are treated in Canada.

The report helped ensure that economic development in the North would not be at the expense of the interests of aboriginal people; it provided training and jobs for many of them; and it ushered in a new era in taking the constitutional rights of aboriginal people seriously. It put the concerns of aboriginal peoples ahead of the interests of oil companies. This did not exactly please the government of the day, but it had never been our intent to please them, nor to arrive at recommendations that they would find easy to endorse. We wanted to do right by the aboriginal peoples. Whether any outsiders can do this, of course, is a question of more than moot significance.

At the same time that the Berger Commission was reshaping the way Canada treated its native peoples, wide-ranging changes in administrative law were affecting individual rights. Important changes in the law occurred in the 1970s. In Britain, a whole series of decisions in administrative-law cases started to break down barriers to remedies for aggrieved individuals.

When I was in law school, judges distinguished between judicial, quasi-judicial, and administrative hearings, and applied different standards based on that distinction. Matters classified as judicial were entitled to the highest standards of procedural fairness: the right to know the nature of the allegations made against one, the right to cross-examine adverse witnesses, and the right to a fair hearing, for example. Hearings classed as quasi-judicial offered a smaller range of protections. Administrative matters were usually held to be beyond the purview of the courts.

By the 1970s, however, boards and commissions were increasingly occupying fields once filled by legislatures, and there was growing pressure to extend more procedural safeguards to the ways in which boards conducted business. Courts began to recognize that boards often had the power to determine matters that profoundly affected the lives of the people who appeared before them. Boards could determine property rights, the ability to earn a living, or admission to certain professions. I spent much of my career appearing before tribunals, and I welcomed the extension of procedural safeguards. Indeed, I was retained by the College of Physicians and Surgeons to come up with new procedures for discipline hearings that ensured a separation between the investigative and trial branches of the College.

The most important expansion in administrative law, however, was in the recognition that people affected by administrative decisions also had rights that had to be respected by their employers. This was the toughest fight to win, as there was an extensive history of the courts washing their hands of any overseeing responsibility for administrative decisions. A case that I eventually took to the Supreme Court of Canada had a large role in changing the law in this area.

Mr. Nicholson was a police officer with the town of Caledonia. With the creation of new tiers of municipal governments in Ontario, his employer changed to the Regional Municipality of Haldimand

Norfolk. Shortly thereafter, the police board terminated his employment and alleged misconduct. The problem was that Mr. Nicholson was not allowed to see the allegations brought against him, nor was he allowed to cross-examine the people making them. The police board made its decision, and Mr. Nicholson was not allowed to be present or to present his side of the case. It was all rather Kafka-esque.

The divisional court unanimously found that there was a duty on the part of the police board to give Mr. Nicholson a hearing. The Court of Appeal for Ontario reversed this decision, holding that the action was administrative, and that there was no obligation on the part of the police board to provide a hearing for Mr. Nicholson.

Then the case went to the Supreme Court. As I put it in the appellant's factum, "The point in issue in this case is whether the Board of Commissioners of Police has the power to dispense with the services of a police constable without notice or hearing or reasons, or even any minimal duty to act fairly in the circumstances."

I made six submissions. First, that the Court of Appeal was wrong to hold that the police board possessed the common-law authority of the Crown to dismiss its servants "at pleasure." The police board was a creature of statute, not an emanation of the Crown, and hence was not entitled to claim Crown privilege.

Second, that "even if a police constable serves 'at [the] pleasure' of the Police Board and the Board is empowered to exercise that wide discretion, there still exists the duty to act fairly and to provide an opportunity to be heard." I was able to find some English cases that supported the principle that fairness required Mr. Nicholson to have the right to a hearing. As Lord Reid put it in *Malloch* v. *Aberdeen Corporation*, "Acting at pleasure means that there is no obligation to formulate reasons. Formal reasons might lead to legal difficulties. But it seems to me perfectly sensible for Parliament to say to a public body: you need not give formal reasons but you must hear the man before you dismiss him."

Third, that there was an increasing recognition in the jurisprudence of the Commonwealth of the "duty to act fairly" in a wide variety of areas of law previously deemed to be administrative only.

The fourth, fifth, and sixth submissions were more technical in nature, but their thrust was that the Court of Appeal for Ontario had erred in not allowing a hearing for Mr. Nicholson.

The court found for my client, by a five-four vote. It was, as the Duke of Wellington once remarked, a close-run thing. The significance of the case was that the principles of procedural fairness were now available in matters previously deemed administrative only.

Nicholson was an example of the most important kind of case that I did. Principles were at stake; new law had to be made for us to be successful; and wider social consequences would flow if the case could be won.

I also acted for unions in the *Reference on the Anti-Inflation Board* case. The federal government had instituted a wage and price freeze for civil servants. Some provincial governments adopted the program and froze the wages of their public servants. I acted for the Ontario Public Service Employees Union. In the end, we were successful in having the courts throw out the program's applicability to Ontario's public servants.

For every case like *Nicholson* or the *Anti-Inflation Reference*, there were dozens of more ordinary cases to be argued, hearings to attend, negotiations to take part in. I loved the variety of work that my practice engendered. I represented people from all walks of life with all sorts of legal problems. The more experience I got, the more interesting the cases became. Like Andrew Brewin, my policy was to accept each case that walked through the door. Like Brewin, if the case interested me, or raised an important issue, I would do it without getting paid, if that was what it took to get the matter before the courts.

For example, two young homosexual men had been assaulted at a restaurant close to their home. They had eaten at this restaurant for many years without incident. The police had been reluctant to press charges, so the men had launched a civil action for assault, but were having trouble getting the courts to take it seriously. Mutual friends gave them my name. I took the case. According to one of them, when I walked into court with them as their lawyer, the demeanour of the judge changed instantly. They were able to get vindication for the gay-bashing they had endured. I never did send them a bill, a decision I am sure Andrew Brewin would have endorsed.

An example of a more lucrative case involved Tom Ryder, the brother of my colleague, Alick Ryder. I knew Tom well from trips to the Ryder cottage on Stoney Lake, as well as our travels together in 1972 to the former USSR to watch the final games between Canada and the Soviet Union in the Summit series, when Paul Henderson scored the famous goal that won the series for Canada.

Tom retained me to act for him after he had been stopped for speeding while going to his cottage. He had been delayed leaving Toronto, and he was late. He was travelling along Highway 135, at great speed, when he was pulled over by a policeman whose car had been parked behind a billboard. Tom asked how the officer knew that he had been speeding, and the constable replied that a plane had been attempting to track him, and because of the headwinds had had a hard time keeping up. They reckoned that Tom was travelling around ninety-five miles per hour.

If Tom was convicted, he would lose so many points that he would lose his licence, a major handicap for someone who travelled routinely around the province, selling and inspecting heavy equipment. I managed to get the Crown to postpone the case to a later date. Somewhat later, the Crown and I discovered that the agreed-upon date happened to be a date on which the court could not meet. Not surprisingly, the Crown wanted a new date set, and convened a second hearing for that purpose. I was able to convince the court that the bargain about court appearances had been entered into in good faith, and if it turned out to be a bad bargain for the Crown, then that was too bad for them. The case disappeared into legal limbo.

I then sent Tom Ryder a bill for my legal services. He claims that the bill was four times the amount of the substantial fine that he would have had to pay if convicted. At first, he refused to pay it. I sent him a note saying that it was a cheap lesson for him to learn about the dangers of speeding, that he had not lost any points, and that he should just pay up. He did.

Toward the latter part of the 1970s, I began to be retained in a

whole series of cases in which I acted for individuals who had grievances with rather arbitrary decisions or actions of the Ontario
government. For example, I acted for officers in a correction facility
who had been suspended without hearings for alleged abuses within
the facility. I also acted for a Pickering, Ontario, woman whose land
had been bought by the province as part of an Ontario government
program. This case was a watershed for me.

Two land assemblies were in process at the same time at Pickering.
The federal government took land for a proposed airport, and the
province was assembling land for a "planned community" that it was
going to build around the airport. The province sent around a negotiator, offering people a low-ball price for their land and telling them
that if they did not accept it, the land would be expropriated and they
might not get as much. On this basis, many people entered into an
agreement for the purchase of their land and then regretted it. They
thought their property was worth more, and that they had been
misled by the government's land agents. In fact, the federal government did pay more per acre for the land it acquired.

Twenty-nine people wrote to Arthur Maloney, the province's
ombudsman, complaining about the process. He launched an investigation and produced a report saying that the provincial government's
agents, knowing that the land was worth more, had improperly
induced the landowners to sign. His call for a royal commission into
the matter caused something of an uproar, as one provincial agency
had accused another of having acted in bad faith. Roy McMurtry, the
attorney general, appointed Mr. Justice Frank Donnelly to head
the commission. Maloney and Donnelly disliked each other intensely,
for some reason known only to them. Maloney had ceased to appear
before Donnelly in any matter when he was practicing law, sending
juniors or colleagues if he had a case that Donnelly was going to hear.

Mr. Justice Donnelly appointed Bob Armstrong to be the commission counsel. John Sopinka was on for the provincial government's
land agents. Armstrong and Sopinka's position was that we were
alleging fraud, and that we had to go on first to prove our case. Our
position was that it was a public inquiry: Armstrong as commission

counsel had an obligation to call all the evidence, and we had the right to cross-examine. Donnelly ruled that Sopinka and Armstrong were right, and that we would have to go on first.

I appealed this ruling to the divisional court, and won. John Sopinka was astonished. In a conversation with Neil McCormick in 1996, he still remembered vividly the facts of the case. He attributed my success at the divisional court to my eloquence in presenting what he called "an astounding" view of the law. Sopinka then took the matter to the Ontario Court of Appeal. He recalled that as I was impressing the judges there with my argument, he stepped in to warn them that they were in danger of losing sight of the law by listening to my "eloquence," as he called it. Unfortunately, he won. This presented us with a real challenge.

All we had was the evidence of the complainants. I was representing Heather Dinsmore, one of the people whose property had been taken, and she of course had no direct knowledge of whatever conversations took place in the ministry. It was a severe evidentiary hurdle to overcome, to put it mildly.

So I walked out of the hearings, on the ground that they were being improperly conducted. One of the commissioners, David Humphrey, also walked out at the same time. He had been the only commissioner who agreed with my submission on how the evidence should be tendered. This created something of a sensation, as it was not every day that a commissioner resigned from a public inquiry on a point of principle.

I then went to the legislative committee set up to oversee the office of the ombudsman, which was headed by Jim Renwick, an NDP member of the legislature. He agreed to hold hearings. We had other witnesses called to testify before the legislative committee. They then set up a separate committee under the auspices of the ombudsman, and that committee awarded substantially more money to the landowners. As a result, we got more money for Heather Dinsmore.

The whole process was frustrating. The government had gone through the motions of providing for an inquiry, without empowering the inquiry with the means to get to the bottom of the accusations of a serious abuse of public trust on the part of public servants. The government tried to cast the matter in terms of bargaining: if some people made a bad bargain, they maintained, they had only themselves to blame.

In this and other cases, when I believed that a simple injustice was being done through an arbitrary action of the government, I fought it in as many forums as I could muster. I had students come up with novel arguments. I was determined not to lose, or at least to go down with all guns blazing. In the end, although we did get more compensation for our client, I was becoming disillusioned with the provincial government.

This period in my legal career coincided with a period of some turbulence in my domestic life as well. Jimmy Smith and I had lived together for eight or nine years. In 1977, he decided to leave me to go to New York City to make his fortune. This was a shock. Jimmy and I did have our moments of strife, but we also shared many happy times together.

One of the continuing sources of strife was that Jimmy liked to go to bathhouses, something I didn't like. Once, I came home late from work and found him at home, with hair made frizzy and curly from what I could only assume was the humidity of the bathhouse. This was usually all the proof I needed that he had been there. He denied it; I didn't believe him. Eventually, he convinced me that his hair had curled for some more innocent reason. After the *Sturm und Drang*, I needed a cigarette. I pulled one out and he offered to light it for me. He produced a book of matches with the bathhouse name emblazoned on it. I rested my case.

I don't think that this was why he left. Jimmy just decided that Toronto wasn't a big enough theatre for him to operate in. I wasn't happy about it, but there wasn't much I could do, as I had no intention of giving up my law practice to go with him to New York City.

I had been working "like a madman," as one of my law partners once described it. I decided I needed a change of pace. At the law firm, we had put in a system for a sabbatical leave, but no one ever left the firm to take it. I thought that we should either get rid of the policy, or I take up the opportunity. Accordingly, I made arrangements to go to Queen's University in Kingston for the academic year 1978–1979. I was to teach two classes, and more surprisingly for a visiting professor I would enroll as a student in two classes.

I arranged to rent a delightful stone house on Wellington Street, which I shared for a while with my friend Peter Brown, and I set off for the great adventure. I did not entirely give up my practice, but I was serious about the need for change and to recharge my batteries.

At a cocktail party at the start of term, I met three law students who would later play major roles in my political life: John Ronson, Chuck Birchall, and Peter Lukasiewicz, collectively known later in my political career as "The Queen's Mafia." They all took classes from me, but more important, they all suggested that I should get into politics.

At the time, the Ontario Conservative party had been in power for thirty-five years. I thought that I might spend my entire adult life being governed by the only party that rivalled communist regimes in its longevity. My young Queen's friends helped convince me I should do something to change the situation. When I got back from my sabbatical, I began to explore the possibility of entering provincial politics. Tom Ryder, still a friend despite the size of the legal bill I sent him, asked me why I was considering running provincially when the chances of being elected federally seemed so much better.

"Because that's where all the action is," I told him.

In some ways, it was an odd thing for me to consider. I had one of the most interesting legal practices in the country. Going into politics would mean a big drop in income and a major disruption to my personal life. And there had already been two big changes in my personal life since I finished my sabbatical at Queen's.

The first change was romantic. A short time after I returned from Queen's, I met a young man, Kim Yakabuski, in a bar in Toronto. Shortly thereafter, we decided to live together. Kim's father, Paul, owned a hardware store in Barry's Bay, in northeastern Ontario. From 1963 to 1987, he was also a member of the Ontario legislature, one of the Tory rural MPPs who helped keep the Robarts and Davis governments in power. There were fourteen Yakabuski children. Kim's mother, Doreen, was a cousin of Sean Conway, first elected to the legislature for the Liberals at the tender age of twenty-three. Assorted ancestors on both sides of Kim's family had been members of the legislature.

Kim's mother died when he was a child. His father remarried, and his second wife did a marvellous job of coping with all the children and running the hardware store when Mr. Yakabuski was in Toronto while the legislature was sitting.

When I first met him, Kim was a physical education student at the University of Waterloo. He was in Toronto for a sports meet the weekend I met him. He was lively, a good athlete, and like all of his many brothers and sisters bright and determined. Shortly after we started living together, he went off to Queen's to do a law degree. He would come back to Toronto for weekends and holidays. Though he was much younger than I was, we shared a similar outlook. We enjoyed travelling together and had some wonderful trips to exotic locales.

He loved to play tennis, so I had a court built at the farm, and we played many uproarious games. He was much better than I was, but I had no compunctions about giving myself the benefit of line calls, so things tended to even out. Each summer he organized a good-natured tennis competition, usually held at Hanlan's Point on the Toronto Islands.

Kim was my junior by some twenty years. Through him, I met a whole new circle of friends, including Ron Beck, Wayne Briede, Bob Watkin, and Scott DeWare, who somewhat later became Jimmy Smith's partner when Jimmy moved back to Toronto from New York.

The second change in my personal life was geographic. In 1980, I bought a house on a cul-de-sac south of Bloor, bounded on one side by the Rosedale Valley ravine, and on the other by the Don Valley. It was a leafy and quiet enclave close to downtown. I had first seen the house some years earlier, when Kay Graham, an artist who had lived there for many years, put it on the market. I tried to buy it from her, but she sold it to a young couple from South America. A few years later, they were transferred, and the house came on the market again.

I bought it as quickly as I could. Shortly after my offer had been accepted, Bob Macaulay, a friend of mine, long a power in the Conservative party of Ontario, offered to buy it from me for fifty thousand dollars more than I had paid for it. But I wanted the house more than I wanted his money, and so I set about transforming it.

The house was large, with five or six bedrooms. I converted it into a two-and-a-half-bedroom place, with a large master bedroom with a vaulted ceiling and lots of light. I also had the gardens redesigned, planting cedar hedges for privacy and installing formal gardens at both the front and back of the house. A deck was built off the kitchen and dining room, and a canopy installed. This became the summer living room, as it was possible to sit out and have a drink or dinner on the patio table in complete privacy.

I now had the best of both worlds. My place in the city had enough trees and hedges to ensure that it felt like the country, even though traffic streamed across the nearby Bloor Street Viaduct in huge volumes. My place in the country had lots of urban refinements, with even more property around it to ensure privacy.

I had achieved a high degree of privacy, and I had found someone to share my life. My ambition to run for public office, I knew, would put my privacy and my need for solitude at risk. I did not want my private life splashed over the tabloids. My decision to run was a measure of my disquiet at the long series of Tory governments that continued to do things the way things had always been done, and in the process excluded many citizens, perhaps the majority, who did not share their views.

At a time when my personal and professional lives were better than ever, I entered into the ring to make my mark politically. Given the tenor of the times, it meant that Kim would be forced into the background, as, in my estimation, the public was not then ready to deal openly and honestly with homosexuality. In the best of all possible worlds, such discrimination would not exist. But Ontario in 1981 was not ready to deal with the issue, and I saw no reason to make what would have been a futile attempt to change it.

Getting into
Politics

◆

AS A PRACTICING LAWYER, who dealt with the government and its agencies on a regular basis, I felt strongly that the Tory dominance in Ontario was absolutely unhealthy. I didn't have any personal grudge against the Tories — I counted some of them, as the saying goes, among my best friends. But when one government dominated the public law process for as long as the Conservatives had, the system became distorted, enhancing the bureaucratic exercise at the expense of the political. I thought: "This has to end. I will be very troubled if my whole adult life is spent under one government."

Now, at that stage I had worked for various NDP candidates. Andrew Brewin, my law partner, was a sitting NDP member in the House of Commons. I had done a little work for Bob Rae when he ran federally. I didn't really have a provincial party. Had I concluded that the NDP were the best shot at getting rid of the Tories, I might have gone to them. But I found Stuart Smith, the provincial Liberal leader, a more sympathetic figure than the NDP leader, Michael Cassidy. I thought that the Liberal party of Ontario had the best shot at getting rid of the Tories.

I set up a meeting with Smith. I was very naive; I didn't know anything about that kind of politics. I simply asked if I could run. He laughed and said, "You certainly can if you can get a nomination. Nominations for the Ontario Liberal party aren't hard to get."

There was some talk of what riding I might run in. Smith offered to set aside for me what passed for a relatively safe Liberal seat, like Downsview in northwestern Toronto. But, again naively, I wanted to run in my own district, St. David. That was regarded as a fatal error because I was running against a cabinet minister, Margaret Scrivener. She was widely thought to be unbeatable. Her patrician manner seemed perfectly suited to the Rosedale types who dominated the northern third of the riding. The NDP was strong in the south end of the riding and the section across the Don Valley, south of Danforth and Broadview. There were a lot of apartment buildings around Davisville Avenue whose inhabitants, mostly young people concerned about things like rent control, were the easiest for me to reach with the Liberal message.

Once I got the nomination for St. David, I decided to run on my own name, rather than relying on the Liberal party's material. I had campaign buttons designed. In black and white, rather than Liberal red, they said, simply, "Ian Scott — a man you should know." Because the party had never done anything much in the riding, I relied on rallying people who did not normally think of themselves as provincial Liberals.

Steve Goudge was the chairman of the campaign. His main functions were to give wise advice and take over my law practice to free me for the rigours of campaigning. Organization of the campaign fell to the Queen's Mafia: Chuck Birchall, Pete Lukasiewicz, and John Ronson, supplemented by Bob Hawkins, a University of Toronto graduate. All of them were doing their bar admission course at the time, so they had lots of time to devote to politics. One of my law partners, David Rubin, handled the money side of the campaign; he would do so in all my subsequent campaigns.

As a measure of the idealism animating that first campaign, the entire top floor of our Cabbagetown headquarters was devoted to policy, an organizational feature notably lacking from my future, more successful, campaigns.

I found the whole exercise exhilarating. A group of us always hit subway stops, bus stops, or apartment lobbies first thing every morning to catch people on their way to work. The idea was to get me to meet as many people as possible. The problem with this approach was that at big subway stops like Broadview, most of the people passing through did not live in the riding. A better idea was to arrange for me to meet as many potential voters as possible.

This we did in the time-honoured way of Canadian political campaigns. We divided the riding into zones, and the zones into polls. We designated zone captains and poll captains. Each captain was responsible for canvassing his or her territory: knocking on doors to find out how many people lived there, how many were eligible voters, and what the voting intentions of the voters were. If they found anyone who intended to vote for me, then another series of questions followed: Would they put up a sign for me? Volunteer to work for me? Make a donation to the campaign?

The second set of questions was designed in part to put a check on over-enthusiastic campaign workers. There are very few paid campaign workers in Canadian politics. The NDP tends to have the biggest pool of them, as many labour unions release organizers to volunteer to work for NDP candidates. At least, they did so at the time of my first campaign. We, however, had no pool of experienced campaign workers. We had to find out first which volunteers would show up when they said they would before we could get to the next level of discovering which volunteers were reliable in estimating the voting intentions of the people they canvassed.

Many years earlier, in the *MacKay* case we did together, I had helped Andrew Brewin establish the constitutional right of Canadians to put up election signs. In many ways, it was easier to deal with theoretical sign questions than the practical problems of getting signs up in all the right places. First, the party objected to my black-and-white signs. We replaced them with signs that were supposed to be Liberal red. Then the printer made a mistake, and the second set of signs came back more orange than red. The NDP used orange. I didn't mind the ambiguity myself, but Senator Keith Davey called up and told me to get proper Liberal red signs.

We had a sign crew that went around erecting signs. We thought it especially important to get signs on major thoroughfares like Mount Pleasant Road. Each time we put them up, however, someone (we darkly suspected the Tories) would tear them down. Getting the signs up proved to be surprisingly tricky. In the riding, the Tories had an inherent advantage in sign locations in Rosedale and Moore Park, where the residents lived in houses. Many of our supporters lived in apartment buildings where it was difficult for them to display signs that many people could see. It's difficult to tell if signs actually work in converting undecided voters to your cause, but there is no doubt that an array of signs is useful for convincing campaign volunteers of the value of their efforts.

As the candidate, I had to appear to be cheerful and enjoying myself to keep my troops motivated. This wasn't hard during that first campaign, because we were all coming to it fresh. There were lively debates about the content of the campaign literature. People vied to get endorsements for me from celebrities or local notables. I even got one from George Armstrong, the captain of the Toronto Maple Leafs, who did not know me from Adam.

I also was expected to be enthusiastically "up" on our candidate canvasses. The goal was to do three of these a day. In theory, I was supposed to go into areas identified by poll captains as having a strong Liberal vote. In practice, we did a lot of the basic voter-identification work on these canvasses. I loved going door to door. The riding was one of the most diverse in the province, with pockets of affluence almost cheek by jowl with public housing projects. I tended to have more fun campaigning in the latter areas. My weakness as a campaigner, however, was that I tended to get involved in what Chuck Birchall called Hegelian dialectical conversations with individual householders, when I should have been running down the street to knock on more doors. I took it as a challenge to debate issues with electors who were not predisposed to vote for me, a habit I never entirely broke throughout my political career.

After the first all-candidates' debate, Margaret Scrivener realized that debating me was not her best option and stopped going to them. Eventually, her decision helped me: the papers started calling her the "ghost of St. David's," the nickname of an apartment building in the riding that sat empty at a time when housing was in short supply. The link between this visible symbol of bad Tory planning and my absent Tory opponent was most helpful.

As the campaign progressed, it seemed that there was an outside chance that I could win. We felt we had put together a better campaign team than Scrivener had. We got our signs up. Our canvasses produced excellent results. We had a critical mass of enthusiastic campaign workers who were able to attract a large number of volunteers.

In an effort to keep up our momentum and make an impression on the southern part of the riding, we hired a band and piled on to a Queen Street streetcar. We should have checked the streetcar's route. Once we were on it, we were trapped, with the band playing rousing songs, all the way to the Victoria Park turnaround, miles out of the riding. The band, which would be a feature of all my subsequent campaigns, played in all kinds of bad weather, and sometimes in the face of an apathy that would have deterred people of lesser enthusiasm.

What we lacked in professionalism, we made up for with enthusiasm. Enthusiasm, however, was not enough to carry the day. Early in the campaign, we had canvassed in Regent Park, the largest public-housing complex in Toronto. We seemed to have made real headway there. In the last week of the campaign, however, the Tories pulled out all the stops. Limousines filled with Tories like David Crombie and Susan Fish would pull up to the project, and the Tory notables distributed flowers and posters to the residents. One of Scrivener's particularly effective strategies was to throw a picnic and barbecue for the residents of Regent Park opposite the site of the advance poll. Her workers handed out free hot dogs, gave the children balloons, and then persuaded the parents to go vote.

All our calculations of who was winning went out the window.

Margaret Scrivener carried Regent Park by a large margin. This made no sense from a class-based political analysis, but her strategy worked. She used her lead in Regent Park, as well as the traditional Tory ground of Rosedale and Moore Park, to beat me by roughly a thousand votes.

There is truth in Tip O'Neill's famous maxim that "All politics is local." But we thought we had done almost everything it was possible to do locally, and we still lost. It was small consolation that losing by this margin represented a definite upsurge in Liberal support in the riding. But Bill Davis and the Tories were rolling to a majority government, and we would have had to run strongly against that trend to win. I liked Stuart Smith. I found him an able and sophisticated man. But Davis, playing on Smith's profession as a psychiatrist, called him "Dr. No," after the James Bond villain, and managed to make the label stick.

The disconnection between local efforts and the province-wide campaign was discouraging. A number of other urban Liberal candidates did much better in 1981 than Liberals had done in previous elections. But the sad fact was that in the 1981 election, not many urban Liberals were elected to the legislature. Smith had made a valiant effort at recruiting new candidates. Some people he recruited, like Elinor Caplan and me, ran again in 1985 and won.

After the election, I made a proposal to Smith, suggesting that some defeated candidates should join the Liberals' elected caucus. The purpose of such an exercise was to help "urbanize" the largely rural caucus, and help it develop responses to urban issues like rent control, health care, and housing. Our objective was not to decide strategy day by day, as caucus has to do, nor to control question period.

The caucus was, in my view, simply out of touch with urban issues. For example, Margaret Campbell had represented St. George, the neighbouring riding to St. David, for a number of years. She beat Roy McMurtry in a by-election the first time he ran for the Tories, a not inconsiderable achievement. She'd been very effective in the legislature in calling for rent control, but she was an outsider in the caucus, which regarded her as an extreme figure.

Even though Smith supported my proposal, the caucus didn't. I was very disappointed when the caucus rejected it; I saw it as a sign that there weren't going to be significant changes in the way the party was run.

Some months later, Smith resigned and David Peterson subsequently beat Sheila Copps for the leadership of the party. I thought of him as much more to the right than Smith had been. I had no idea then how successful he would be in taking the party away from its rural roots and opening it up to the new communities that made up such a large percentage of St. David.

So back I went to Cameron, Brewin & Scott, feeling I had done my civic duty. My wonderful campaign team disbanded, and started working in various law offices.

In 1982, 115 years after Confederation, the provinces and the federal government finally managed the patriation of the Constitution. My old friend Roy McMurtry had his famous kitchen meeting with Jean Chrétien and Roy Romanow, and the deal was done. Quebec launched its angry rhetoric about being stabbed in the back and excluded from the Constitution. Thus, the stage was set for all subsequent attempts to deal with Quebec's grievances within a flexible Canadian Constitution, including the 1990 Meech Lake Accord, with which I was to be deeply involved.

Along with patriation, for the first time in Canadian history we had an entrenched Charter of Rights and Freedoms. With the charter came a greatly expanded role for the judiciary. For someone like me, who loved to argue constitutional cases, it was like being given a whole new box of legal toys to play with.

I became engaged in one of the first important charter cases in a rather unusual way. Each week, a panel of Supreme Court of Canada judges heard applications from refugees for leave to appeal negative rulings from the Immigration Board. This was a matter of routine, because there was then a right to apply for leave to appeal from decisions of the board that had been upheld by the Federal Court of

Appeal. Just as routinely, most of these applications were turned down. One afternoon, however, Mr. Justice Willard Estey was part of the panel examining the applications. By coincidence, most of the applicants that day had the surname Singh. Willard Estey, struck by the coincidence, thought the full court should hear the appeals in order to find out what was going on at the board. He convinced his fellow panel members to grant the leave applications. Rather unusually, the court made the applicants an offer of legal representation on the house, or on the court, as the case might be. They decided to nominate me to represent the applicants.

An official of the Supreme Court of Canada wrote to each applicant to say that the court had decided to appoint me to represent them and would pay for my legal services out of court funds. They were free to choose another counsel, the letter informed them, but in the event that they did, no court funds would be made available to them. In the end, all the applicants but one accepted the offer. David Coveney, a lawyer from London, Ontario, already represented one of them and appeared on his behalf.

The key legal issue here was how the charter applied to people who were trying to get into Canada. Underlying this issue was an important question of policy: did the government apply the same standards for determining refugee status to claimants from all parts of the world? There was some evidence that refugee claims from certain Commonwealth countries were automatically denied because the government did not want to offend its Commonwealth partners by allowing questions of political repression to be raised in Canadian hearings. Such claimants were sent back to their countries of origin, unless — and this was unlikely — they could find some other place that would accept them. Then they would have to pursue their appeal from the countries they alleged had mistreated them. In effect, this process meant that most of the claimants would never be able to appeal, and that some of them would be put in acute jeopardy by the governments they were fleeing.

Ian McGilp did a superb job of researching case law in other jurisdictions with entrenched bills of rights. We produced the factums under a tight deadline, and were soon in the Supreme Court of Canada, making our oral submissions. Unfortunately, I had forgotten my reading glasses that day and had to borrow McGilp's when I made my presentation. One of the judges asked me which section of the Immigration Act applied to the submission I was making, and I had to confess that I couldn't remember. So I looked frantically through the voluminous record for the right section of the Immigration Act. Meanwhile, McGilp rooted blindly through his copy of the material; he knew the section, but couldn't see it because I had his glasses. Finally, Mr. Justice Willard Estey suggested that I give McGilp his glasses back. McGilp duly read the correct section to the court.

It was a big case. Most of the provincial attorneys general were represented, as the costs of looking after refugee claimants would fall on their governments if we established the right of refugee claimants to remain in the country while they waited for hearings on the merits of their cases.

Eight months after we made our submissions, we received a letter from the Supreme Court of Canada asking us to produce, practically instantly, a factum on how the Canadian Bill of Rights, John Diefenbaker's contribution to Canadian constitutional law, applied to the case. This was unexpected. The Canadian Bill of Rights had been mentioned once in our factum, without any explication of how it might apply. There seemed to be no other mention of it in the other factums, and there were no oral arguments about it at the court. We produced a factum on the Bill of Rights and immigration law, and, shortly thereafter, the Supreme Court brought down its decision in our favour. Rather oddly, three of the judges who upheld the appeal used the charter to justify it, and three used the Bill of Rights. It was the most sweeping decision ever based on the Bill of Rights. Odder still, the Supreme Court, to my knowledge, did not build upon this interpretation of the Bill of Rights in subsequent cases.

The case rather dramatically illustrates the sea change in Canadian law brought about by the charter. Its results have some parallels with the busing decisions made by the US Supreme Court in the wake of the desegregation cases there. Thousands of people who had refugee claims became entitled to remain in Canada while their appeals worked their way through the system. They had to apply for permission to work, and often had to wait years for that permission to be granted. In the meantime, they had to be housed and fed by local governments while they waited for their appeals to be heard. It was perhaps one of the costliest Supreme Court of Canada decisions ever made. Hundreds of millions of dollars have undoubtedly been spent as a result of it.

I also argued a case, *Bhinder* v. *CNR*, involving the right of Sikhs to wear their traditional clothing at work. The issue was whether Mr. Bhinder had to wear a hard hat at work, as required by his employer, the CN Railway, or whether he could wear the turban stipulated by the tenets of his religion. I thought I had a stronger case, and made better arguments in *Bhinder* than I had in *Singh*, but I lost. It just goes to show that one is not always the best judge of the strength of one's legal arguments.

Another sea change in Canadian law occurred when Mr. Justice Samuel Grange presided over the inquiry into the deaths of babies at the Hospital for Sick Children in Toronto. The inquiry grew out of the dismissal of charges of murder against Susan Nelles, one of the nurses working on the ward in question. She had been charged when police became suspicious after she refused to talk to them without her lawyer present. The charges, after much anguish for her and her family, were thrown out at her preliminary hearing.

I represented the hospital at the inquiry; John Sopinka represented Susan Nelles. The inquiry was televised, and the public was galvanized by it. It raised basic questions about the conflict between the public's right to know what had happened at the hospital, and the rights of those whose conduct fell under some suspicion.

The evidence was complicated. All of the babies who died were in the hospital in the first place because they had serious health problems. The expert witnesses disagreed on toxicological issues concerning how to account for the digoxin levels found in the babies' tissues. There were two competing explanations. The first was that the babies had died from overdoses of digoxin. The second was that bad sampling techniques in the toxicology labs gave a false impression of how the babies died. The commission concluded that babies had been murdered. No further charges were ever laid, however, in part because of the difficulty of producing a fair trial, given the extensive publicity that surrounded the proceedings.

In a whole series of subsequent inquiries, including the Houlden Inquiry into the 1989 Patti Starr affair, in which I would be involved, counsel were able to use the charter to halt inquiries that had the potential to turn into criminal investigations. The 1974 Berger Commission had helped set a high standard for encouraging public participation in the making of public policy. The problem in extending its style to commissions that were investigating criminal, or potentially criminal, actions, however, was that public expectations would be raised without any real opportunity for closure.

Commissions of inquiry should be called and should be given proper funding so that different relevant points of view are represented. But it is difficult to avoid putting the people caught up in such commissions into double jeopardy. I have no doubt that the Berger Commission reached the right conclusions and used the right methods. I am, in retrospect, not so sanguine about the inquiry into the babies' deaths at the Sick Kids Hospital.

While these cases were going on, I began to think that Cameron, Brewin & Scott might have difficulty staying the same size. With our nine partners, we had carved out a niche in appellate work, labour law, and public inquiries. But a wave of consolidation was rolling over the legal profession. I began discussions with Gordon Henderson, one of the most respected people in the profession, about a possible merger with his Ottawa-based firm, Gowling and Henderson.

Gordon was remarkable because he had mastered three different areas of law: patent law, litigation, and corporate law. On top of that, he was prepared to take on cases he believed in, regardless of whether he would be paid. For example, he represented Leo Landreville, who had been forced from the bench because of his activities connected with the Northern Ontario Gas Pipeline while he was mayor of Sudbury. Mr. Landreville was a difficult client, who did not make things easy for Gordon, but he stuck with him to the bitter end.

Gowling and Henderson had a strong base in intellectual property law and did a lot of appellate work in Ottawa at the Supreme Court of Canada and the Federal Court of Appeal. The firm was interested in getting a larger presence in Toronto, where they had a small office. After some weeks of talks, I agreed to put a merger proposal before my partners.

There were now nine of us at Cameron, Brewin & Scott. Ross Wells, David Rubin, and Raj Anand had joined the six members mentioned previously. We met at La Scala, a charming and now defunct restaurant on Bay Street, to discuss the matter. Many bottles of wine accompanied the discussion. Speeches were made. A vote was taken. It was so close that another one had to be taken later that week when heads were somewhat clearer. The final vote was five to four in favour of merger.

As a result of the vote, Raj Anand left the firm, as he did not favour the merger. The rest of us joined Gowling and Henderson. In the new firm, the Cameron, Brewin & Scott team dominated the Toronto office, so it was not all that noticeable that a major change had occurred. There was a lot of work to do, especially as action on the charter front intensified.

The Ontario political scene of 1984 looked as if the Tories were going to go on forever. This made it extremely difficult for David Peterson, the new leader of the Ontario Liberal party, to make much of an impact. When George Orwell wrote his dystopian novel, *Nineteen Eighty-Four*, he envisioned a society where an all-knowing and all-pervasive authority watched the actions of ordinary citizens. In 1984, in the Ontario Liberal party, it seemed that Big Brother was not only watching, but also conspiring against, Peterson's rather fragile leadership.

In February of that year, Pierre Trudeau took his famous walk in the snow and vacated the leadership of the federal Liberal party. John Turner emerged from political exile and won the prize that his

Sir Richard Scott's clan, 1903. My grandfather, W.L., is in the back row, second from the left; my grandmother is seated, extreme right, holding my father, Cuthbert, seven months old.
— PUBLIC ARCHIVES CANADA PA 42457

ABOVE: My mother with David (right) and me.

BOTTOM: David and me at McGregor Lake.

TOP: A novel way to bathe, outside our Besserer Street residence.

LEFT: Nancy, David, and me, circa 1944.

RIGHT: Officially a schoolboy, 1946.

TOP: With fellow naval cadets at Royal Roads, B.C.: David Mitchell (left), "Max" Saunderson, me, Burke Smith, and Bill Patterson.

BOTTOM: With my parents and David in New York City, 1951.

TOP: I'm on the left, with Dick Wright and Chris Noel.

TOP RIGHT: Paul Cohen.

BOTTOM: Paul Cohen, second from left, David Ross, and Ted Braithwaite.

TOP LEFT: Jimmy Smith.

TOP RIGHT:
The farm, derelict.

MIDDLE: The farm,
in Spring.

RIGHT: The farm,
after renovations.

TOP: Tom Berger, inspecting pipelines.

BOTTOM: Ian Roland, Arctic fish, and me.

Christopher (left), Brian, David, and me, with Martha and Nancy, 1983, at our parents' fiftieth wedding anniversary party.

mother had always wanted for him: to be prime minister of Canada. His selection as leader boosted the poll ratings of the federal Liberals. They appeared to have managed the perennial challenge of transferring leadership while retaining power.

In the summer of 1984, with the prospect of a federal election looming, the Ontario Liberal caucus at Queen's Park started to leave for what appeared to be greener pastures. James Breithaupt resigned to become head of the Ontario Law Reform Commission. Sheila Copps and Don Boudria, among others, decamped to federal politics. Meanwhile, David Peterson was trapped at a Lake Huron cottage, being a househusband while his wife, Shelley, was on stage at the Red Barn Theatre outside Grand Bend.

I decided not to run again. My law firm was in its merger process. I had a lot of big cases coming up. I was not exactly enchanted with the direction the Liberal party had taken since Stuart Smith's resignation. I thought that my losing run in the 1981 election might be enough of a futile gesture for one lifetime.

But Steve Goudge told me I at least owed Peterson the courtesy of a face-to-face explanation if I was going to bail out on my promise to run. So I set out on Highway 401 to deliver the bad news in person. As I drove along, I began to think what a difficult interview it was going to be. There he was, up to his fanny in dirty diapers, doing laundry and cooking meals for the three small kids, with half his caucus departing. I thought to myself, "He's too nice a guy. I just can't do this to him. I'll take six or seven weeks off work, run in the election, lose, and that will be the end of my political career." So I turned off the 401 at Guelph, went up Highway 24 to my farm, and spent the weekend gardening.

Turner called a summer election, and the Liberals lost. Both Don Boudria and Sheila Copps found themselves in opposition again, albeit at the federal level. Peterson always maintained that he knew that when Brian Mulroney won federally, he would have a good chance of winning provincially. He might have been the only person in the province, however, who truly believed it.

Later that summer, the signs seemed to be pointing to a fall election.

The speculation continued into the fall. Davis, always capable of sphinx-like silences followed by vague pronouncements capable of multiple interpretations, spent the Thanksgiving weekend at his cottage retreat in Georgian Bay. Most pundits and politicians thought that he would call the election on his return. Instead, he stunned his cabinet by making two announcements to them an hour before the legislature was to resume sitting. Both decisions had major impacts. The first was that he was going to retire, even though the public opinion polls showed that he was far in the lead should an election be called. The second was that he committed the government to full funding of Catholic secondary education.

There was intense speculation about why he had chosen that moment for these two moves. Bob Nixon, the former leader of the Ontario Liberal party, thought Davis's motive on the full-funding issue arose from guilt from the 1971 election. Nixon's story was that he, Bill Davis, and Stephen Lewis had agreed to keep the issue of full financing for Catholic schools out of the 1971 campaign, but that Davis had broken the agreement, raised the issue of full funding only to oppose it, and won the election. Davis, on the other hand, maintains that Nixon first raised the question of full funding in the 1971 election, and he was just responding. His responses were highly effective, in any event.

My own suspicion is that Bill Davis supported full funding because he thought that its time had come, given the demographic changes in Ontario. Whatever the reasons, there is no doubt that his conversion on the issue produced major repercussions.

There would be no fall election. Instead, the Conservatives held their leadership convention. Larry Grossman and Dennis Timbrell split the Red Tory vote. Frank Miller was rumoured to have cast his own ballot for Grossman on the second-to-last ballot, to try to ensure that Timbrell would not be on the final ballot with him. If so, the strategy worked. Somewhat surprisingly, Miller won.

Miller was far to the right of most Tories, and unlike other successful Tory leaders before Mike Harris he did not move to the centre once elected leader. His selection gave his party a boost in the polls.

A couple of months later, he was at 52 percent, with the Liberals and the NDP trailing badly. Peterson's name was recognized by only about 13 percent of the voters polled. If an election was called, it was expected the Liberals would lose and perhaps even be relegated to third-party status.

Miller called a spring election in 1985. I was committed to running again, mainly because I did not think I could back out on Peterson and retain my integrity. However, I was not very happy about running. My expectations were low.

FIVE

Once More into
the Breach

IN THE 1981 ELECTION, I had been surrounded by a group of happy young political warriors with much time on their hands and energy to spare. We all had fun, even if it was in a losing cause.

In 1985, most of those young warriors were now working for law firms that expected them to devote their energy to the practice of law. Politics was now something they would have to do in their spare time — and law firms have always been good at limiting the amount of junior lawyers' spare time. At my own firm, we were still working out the kinks of the merger with Gowling and Henderson, and I had a particularly heavy caseload. Steve Goudge once again took over most of this work for me as the campaign got underway, but I still had some cases to argue.

Senator Keith Davey made it clear to me that I needed a full-time organizer. On his recommendation, I brought in Robin Russell, an experienced back-room person, to run the campaign. Robin was not used to working with lawyers, who once again provided the backbone of the organization. This led to difficulties and revolts, especially at the beginning of the campaign, when we had trouble finding people to canvass with me during the day.

This time around, the office was more prosaic — and more realistic — than the charming townhouse we had borrowed from Darrell Kent in 1981. There would be no top floor devoted to policy issues. Our new headquarters was on Danforth Avenue, on the south side of the street just east of Broadview.

Margaret Scrivener, my main opponent from the 1981 campaign, had decided to retire. There were rumours that Julian Porter, the son of former Ontario attorney general Dana Porter, was going to try for the Conservative nomination. Porter was running against Margaret Scrivener's son, Paul. I thought I had a fair chance of beating the younger Scrivener, but little chance of beating the younger Porter. For one thing, he was well known as a libel lawyer. For another, he was married to the well-known publisher, Anna Porter. He also was a member of the Toronto Transit Commission and got his name in the papers whenever some transit issue came up.

The NDP had nominated a young lawyer named Barbara Hall as their candidate. She eventually went on to become the mayor of the City of Toronto, losing her job in 1997 when the city was swept into the megacity, and the voters opted for former North York Mayor Mel Lastman's flamboyance over her quiet competence.

As in 1981, my early campaign literature focused on local issues, and on how I could be a more effective representative for the riding. The word "Liberal" only appeared once on the first pamphlet I produced, the name David Peterson not at all. The slogan had changed from 1981's "A man you should know" to "Count on him working."

The main headings of this pamphlet were "Ian Scott is no stranger"; "Ian Scott — advocate, teacher and community leader"; and "Ian Scott — a strong voice in St. David." The concluding argument went like this:

Now, more than ever, a positive, productive difference in St. David will come from our election of Ian Scott.

A difference that captures the communities of St. David, that recognizes the diversity and value of our citizens, that is committed to their active representation.

A vote for alternatives is wasted.

St. David needs new commitment, and the new ideas that can only come from a new elected representative.

The people of St. David seek fresh thinking and a political concern — a political commitment — that remains constant, honest and caring.

Count on Ian Scott working for you without fail and without distraction. Working for St. David and for you.

Count on his commitment, his experience and his understanding of the needs of St. David.

It is striking that there is no mention in this pamphlet of the official Ontario Liberal party policy on any issue. I was convinced that running on my own would give me the best chance of winning.

I decided to keep a diary of my campaign effort. I expected that it would be a minor contribution to the literature of what a losing campaign looked like from the inside. Jack McClelland, publisher of McClelland & Stewart, said that he would publish it and get Julian Porter, widely expected to be the next attorney general of Ontario, to write the foreword from the perspective of a graceful winner.

The tone of the first few days' entries is not too optimistic. In an excerpt from Thursday, March 28, 1985 — the third day of campaigning — I am musing on how to get unenthusiastic Tories to switch their votes:

For example, tonight in Playter Estates one man said he'd always voted Tory, but did not really like what they are doing. How do we provide a motivation for him to vote anything but Conservative?

In the last analysis, I think the whole point of this exercise is that I am an old-fashioned small-L liberal unhappily living in an unsympathetic decade. I do have a nagging suspicion, though, that there are people out there — I suspect mostly women, mostly lower middle class — who are sympathetic to this view. Can they be reached?

As I hobbled from door to door tonight, I found myself thinking that I was really not a suitable person for this exercise. Not that I lack ambition, but I am simply not aggressive enough. I do not insist that people vote for me. I do not press them to take signs. It is almost as if I back off at the critical moment. Maybe I don't really want them to vote for me, and want simply to return to my practice.

Driving home, I think about election night, when I lose and lose badly, and all the people who have worked for me are in the hall, and I come in and I want to say something to thank them for what they have done and to give all their work some meaning, some significance. I am hard-pressed for ideas at the moment, but I think this is not the least of the tasks ahead.

Entry for Monday, April 1, 1985 (April Fools' Day):

I am dictating this a day later and can barely remember what I did. I do know that we started out at the Queen and Broadview station with [Ian] Roland and Robin Nunn. It is a bus stop we should not have done. There are very few people; most of them are bored to tears and the rest live out of the riding. It is again bitterly cold. Hawkins turns up, but we quit at 8:30 because of the cold and lack of interest, and repair for a coffee.

Later in the morning, I canvass alone. In the afternoon I do Dearborne and Fairview. Again, very few people home. The whitepainters have arrived; many new householders, little interest in politics, no knowledge of me. How is it going to be possible to win these people to our side? I seem to have nothing in common with any of them.

In the evening, I quit early, partly because I have to write the speech for our "floppy disc" recording. I have already done two drafts and the third gets, under the influence of the odd martini, quite dramatic. I know Lukasiewicz will tear it to pieces.

Excerpts from Thursday, April 4, 1985:

This was, without any doubt, the worst day so far, and it provoked our first major crisis.

The subway stop is Summerhill, with Liz Yorke, Peter Gilchrist, and Alick Ryder. It is uneventful, though there is some difficulty in persuading Alick to force the pamphlets on people who do not grab them out of his hand. The crowd is not quite as sympathetic or supportive as I would have liked, bearing in mind that I have already canvassed part of this area.

I feel a heavy burden to persuade the others that we are having fun.

After a bowl of cereal at home I begin a canvass in the Tullis Crescent area. I am alone again, which means that I cannot accomplish a full poll.

I meet a number of people who vigorously assert they are already committed to Porter or who eye me with bleak suspicion.

At lunch I rush through the traffic to the law office, where pictures are to be taken for pamphlet #2. All is disorder. The photographer has not shown up, and the whole matter is postponed. The only redeeming note is the win in the Singh case. Perhaps I can get some publicity out of that.

Back to the office at 4:00 p.m. The place is in a shambles. No arrangements have been made for someone to canvass with me, which means I will canvass alone again this evening. I do not mind, but it is inefficient. I can barely canvass a full poll on my own, let alone the one and a half polls I would like to do in each outing. Robin is away again. Elsie is absent at her job, and poor Kathleen is sick.

By this point, I have lost my sense of humour, and I visit my unhappiness on poor Hawkins, who in turn calls Goudge, Ronson, and Birchall. Further news: no arrangements appear to have been made for the weekend blitz. I am despondent. Again, I ask myself, why am I doing this?

Wednesday, April 10, 1985:

The canvass system has fallen through this afternoon and I am
therefore alone on Broadview Ave., north of Queen and Hamilton
St. behind. A fair number of whitepainters here. Someone tells
me that Julian and a gang of fifteen people were on the street
yesterday. His little white cards are to be seen in a few of the
windows.

One young woman tells me in considerable excitement that
Mr. Porter actually came to her door and shook her hand. I have
grave doubt that she will make the same glowing report about
me to the next canvasser who happens by. Nonetheless, she
agrees to be fair and puts my sign in her window.

It is rather lonely, and I retire to the car for a cigarette. It is
all a question of getting one's stamina up, which is difficult when
you are alone. When you are in a group of even two or three
there is a heavy obligation to play your role, which I can then do.

Thursday, April 11, 1985:

Back to the committee room for a quiet lunch, only to be told
that I am supposed to be addressing a meeting of old-age pen-
sioners at the Salvation Army Retirement Shelter.

Mary and I rush up there to arrive on time and to confront
about fifty or sixty retired army officers, both male and female,
whose ages vary from probably sixty-five to eighty-five. They
are sitting almost motionless in chairs facing me in a large
assembly room furnished in particularly plain furniture, no
doubt Salvation Army furniture. I fear that because they have
just had lunch there is a likelihood they will doze. There is no
one to introduce me so I shake hands as they come in to their
chairs and Mary discreetly hands them pamphlets. I then begin,
hardly an idea of what I will say. And yet it turns out — to my
mind — to be the most successful event of the campaign to date.

I talk about my knowledge of the Salvation Army and their

commitment to social reform, and I emphasize that I want to speak to them about the problems of the young unemployed in Ontario, rather than the preferred topic of pensions, etc., which has been recommended to me. I speak for probably twenty minutes and there is good attention. I stop and ask if there are any comments.

There follows a dreadful moment of silence when no one says anything, and I fear they have all gone to sleep.

But then the fun begins. Five or six of them have quite pointed, sophisticated questions based on considerable knowledge. It is a discussion that is by far more intelligent than the average Rosedale coffee party.

One pensioner who must have been eighty refers me to the recent series of articles in the *Toronto Star* on the Swedish experiment. When I make comments on them, he is in a position to compare the economic history of Sweden and Canada.

I make a comment about the Conservative government's regime having lasted over forty-three years, the longest in the Western world except Albania. One elderly gentleman comments that the Albanian comparison ceased yesterday. I don't know what he means, so I let the comment pass and go away thinking he is quite dotty until later I hear on the news that the dictator of Albania died yesterday.

Friday, April 12, 1985:

On to the committee room, where the second kits are being handed out and all is enthusiasm and excitement. Most people seem to think the canvass has been either neutral or very good, and I am cheered by this atmosphere.

Hawkins tells me confidentially that there is a poll indicating that we are within three points (the margin of error) and this adds to my enthusiasm and elation. I return home with Mary for something to eat, about 8:00 p.m., after about three unnecessary glasses of white wine, which are about to knock me off.

At my door, I have received Julian's second pamphlet, which is absolutely superb. It is mostly testimonials under the heading "People for Porter" and contains the usual ones you might expect . . . David Crombie, Paul Godfrey, Margaret Laurence, etc. I am selfishly upset to note that a testimonial is given by June Callwood in which among other things she indicates that she "would trust him with my life." I am very disappointed because this obviously neutralizes the endorsement that June has given me.

The piece introduces a note of gloom because it is so obviously superior to anything that we are or can be doing. It is glossy. The photographs are relaxed and comfortable and it is, in short, a highly professional piece of work. I imagine it will be terribly effective, and I begin to think that the whole thing is now all over but the counting.

The tiring but exhilarating feature of an election is the constant succession of highs and lows that are unpredictable as to duration and occurrence. This day has been high. It has ended with a very, very low moment. But I am certain that there will be more highs in the future, and undoubtedly more lows. One simply has to adjust to them.

Saturday, April 13, 1985:

I have permission to sleep in until about 7:00 a.m. today, but in fact I wake up about 5:45 a.m. The *Globe and Mail*, arriving late, has good news. "Miller Loses Ground to Liberals, Tories Find Support Slipping." The stories point out a drop in Tory support from 55 to 47 percent, with a Liberal increase to 32 percent and the NDP stagnant at 21 percent. The real question is whether this represents normal election-time slippage, or a true, significant, and continuing alteration in feeling. I take the more positive view.

Breakfast, and then down to the St. Lawrence market (in my red jacket) to meet David Peterson. There is a good, though not overwhelming crowd of Liberals present. Our St. David signs arrive and they are much more dominant in numbers than those of the neighbouring riding, St. George.

Shelley and David get off the bus with the three kids. They are really an attractive family. As we go into the market, I walk with Shelley. She is terrified of these great scrums of reporters, photographers, and cameramen, and her eyes dart about constantly counting the three children. I suggest I should take one in hand and do so during the tour.

It is amazing how the leader manages to function in the middle of this mob through which he can barely move. But both he and Shelley are quite relaxed, really, as they move in directions established by the advance crew. From time to time, they break out of the scrum to move to a meat counter, where a pound of meat is bought, or to a fish counter, where a great fuss is made over the tentacles of squid being offered for sale (some of which is purchased).

As we exit the end of the market (where David has — several times — offered to debate Frank Miller, who will arrive in half an hour) I have a quiet talk with David. He is confident and buoyant and really makes a wonderful candidate. If only the people of Ontario could get to know him personally.

On the way back to the car, I see the Tories massing to meet the Miller bus, which is expected within minutes. Their crowd is no bigger than ours. Julian and Susan Fish are there. I catch Julian's eye and he comes over. We talk for two or three minutes until we are surrounded by photographers, who take our picture shaking hands and we both leave, rather embarrassed.

Julian is very affable and friendly as usual and I am glad to see him and shake his hand. He is every bit as attractive a personality as his bio suggests, and indeed, I could have written a number of the endorsements of him myself.

He seems very concerned about me, asking, "Are you all right?" several times. This I take to be a sign either that I look dreadful or that he feels my campaign is in tatters. Or maybe it is just the way ex-Edmonton Eskimos talk to each other.

Tuesday, April 16, 1985:

The big difference between this campaign and the last one is that last time, our campaign was dominant over the Conservatives. This time, the Conservatives clearly dominate us and it is difficult to know how the ballot can be sustained over the long run.

A small item in the paper today: Margaret Laurence has objected to Porter's inclusion of her name in his pamphlet and he has had to write her a letter of apology.

Mr. Libel and Slander indeed.

Harold Nicholson writes in his diaries of meeting Ramsay MacDonald, briefly a Labour prime minister of Britain, at a train station in London. MacDonald was about to embark on a five-hour train ride so that he could address a large crowd in Scotland later that day. MacDonald told Nicholson that he was running a temperature of 105 degrees. When Nicholson expressed surprise that he was continuing with the engagement despite his illness, MacDonald replied that he had discovered that the chief requirements for a politician were energy and stamina. Without those, no other qualities would allow success. The following diary entry shows what one day of campaigning was like, and how right MacDonald was.

Thursday, April 18, 1985:

The bus stop today is at Parliament and Dundas, with Helen Keely. It is not very busy, but there are many interesting people here . . . I talk to a young black man named Winston, a graduate of George Brown College who has been out of work for six months. I decide to use his story during this morning's interview on *Metro Morning* with Joe Coté, which is on for 8:40 along with Julian and Barbara.

At the CBC studio on Parliament St.: At 8:40, I meet Julian and Barbara. We are all nervous, and I notice that Julian's hands are shaking as he rifles through his briefing book.

I am getting to like Barbara more every time I meet her. She is the best sort of person, very low-key. She is probably not very successful at the oratorical level but obviously a hard worker with real concern.

Julian is glib and polished and tries to "old Boy" me in the seven-minute debate. But I think I get the better of the discussion, which concerns jobs (I talk about Winston) and environmental concerns.

Next stop is the Environmental Assessment Board where Linda and I have an hour with the board. We talk about judicial review and then for twenty minutes I talk to these Conservative appointees about politics and youth unemployment. I think I am persuasive — I even get a little round of applause. But what am I doing here? It has nothing to do with St. David.

Back to the Committee Room for a meeting with three representatives of the Canadian Jewish Congress – Ontario Region. We retire to the back of the room and have a discussion about the three issues that concern them: deinstitutionalization of mental and other hospital patients, racial hate prosecutions, and education grants for private schools. I am with them on two of three issues and I think I make a showing that is satisfactory.

Direct from this meeting to the corner of Gerrard and Parliament where a number of the people from the office are gathered with signs and we are to meet David Peterson's bus. It arrives and we march up Parliament Street visiting a variety of stores, dipping our fingers into pastry at one location and posting a sign in the bakery window (upside down as Mile points out) all for the benefit of a horde of photographers. I am wearing a microphone in order to assist the CBC, who are doing a candidate profile in the riding, and I am very wary of it. I point it out to Peterson and he nods an acknowledgement, which means we will not talk privately.

The half-hour event is fun and I admire David's ability to perform so informally and so effectively in this kind of environment.

Then directly back to the committee room where I see Dan Reisler has come in and I do an interview with the CBC, which will be shown later on as part of their film clips. I am getting tired and I am sick of being asked how I am different than Julian. As the front-runner I do not suspect that he gets this kind of question.

Then we move directly to Castle Frank High School where Jean Chrétien and I are to speak. It turns out to be an ordeal but I think in the end successful. In any event, I get a lot of compliments on it. I am introduced by the principal, a very nice fellow, and speak for ten minutes about the charter in a non-political way. Chrétien is supposed to then arrive at the back of the hall and I will introduce him as he marches down the hall to the stage. The problem is that he does not arrive for thirty-five minutes and I am left to amuse a very raucous but basically good-humoured class of about 400 for that period of time. I decide with the principal's assistance that we should do a question-and-answer and happily the questions, some of them amusing and entertaining, are forthcoming. The kids want to know why I am doing this, what an MPP is paid, how the money is raised, how I have time for a sex life.

Chrétien then arrives, very late, quite unruffled, and speaks for about five minutes. He has obviously not been coached that this is a non-political event. He therefore does not speak about the charter at all but exhorts this audience to tell their parents to vote for Ian Scott. Happily he remembers my name. I do not know how he manages this. We finally drag Chrétien away. He is spending a lot of time signing autographs for the kids and (very nice) many of the kids come up to me and say quite sincerely that they enjoyed the afternoon.

I think obviously that some of them were very conscious of the difficulties that I had and were being sympathetic. The principal tells me that notwithstanding the criticism of the school and the fact that these are dropouts from other places, he finds the kids essentially non-abrasive but very direct in expressing their views. They do not accept or give BS.

Down to Gerrard and Broadview, where we do eight or ten shops, restaurants, etc. Chrétien is marvellous. He just comes into the shop, pinning my buttons on everybody and introducing himself and me. Many seem to recognize him but it does not make any difference to him whether they do or not. Many of them are elderly Chinese ladies doing their shopping and are quite taken aback but I think in the end pleased by the little bit of excitement that we create. Chrétien does a short interview with Colin Vaughan. I should say that Colin was covering the Castle Frank High School and I heard him accosting Chrétien about the political nature of his speech. I hope that this does not make the news as it will not be very well received in Rosedale and Moore Park that we have used school facilities for this purpose.

Back to the headquarters and then on with three research assistants from the caucus to Sick Kids, where a press interview is given with respect to the minister's budget allocation for hospitals and the effect of this on Ontario hospitals in light of a survey conducted by the OHA. I think I do the press conference very well. The reporters ask very direct, straight-line questions, which are very easy to answer.

There is one exception, a CBC reporter who knows how to ask follow-up questions and knows the subject well. She is most effective, and after it is over I search her out to congratulate her. I point out to her that I think she should be a lawyer. I do this in part because I think it is true. I do it also because I want her to be friendly so that any gaps in my statement can perhaps be minimized. There is no end to this kind of manipulation and I presume if I am elected I will get more expert at it in time.

Then back to the committee room and up to 45 Balliol with Jeff to do an apartment lobby. The reception is friendly enough but there are not very many people, probably less than 100. I am getting very conscious that we have done the usual bit of running through apartment halls and I wonder if this is a mistake. Our secret weapon will, I hope, offset this. Then back to the house for an hour.

I am really very tired and an all-candidates meeting at Jackman School is tonight. I turn up at about 6:40 p.m. It is not in the assembly hall but is rather in a smaller room with probably 150 seats. I note the Porter signs are all stacked outside as are ours (in my car and in the van). There is an unwritten understanding that signs will not be used unless the other side starts it but we have both come prepared.

I think from our point of view the meeting goes very well. Julian has the disadvantage of speaking first and he talks about making an inventory of jobs and small businesses in the community. I think it is a rather inane speech, but it is well received by his supporters.

I am next and I speak very directly and as forcefully as I can about Miller being the issue. (Peter later tells me that I am too direct, at least for the Leaside meeting, and I must soften the tone.) Barbara is sincere but not terribly effective in her prepared remarks.

The questions that are asked later produce more fun. Julian, very early (I think too early), begins an *ad hominem* on my pamphlet for not mentioning Peterson. The point is that he should have indicated that I did mention Liberal. It is an attack not well received by the audience and I reply that Margaret Laurence's endorsement of him has been withdrawn so nobody's pamphlets are perfect. I am able to get a few laughs from the audience in response to some of the questions. With respect to the pollution issue, I get angry and say that enough is enough. This government must go. It is the one spark of legitimate feeling that I allow to come through.

I am satisfied with it and I think the reception is good. Bob Hawkins later tells me that he is sitting next to an old couple and the lady indicates that she is prepared to vote for me. Her husband says "Don't be silly. Remember it is the party, not the person, you vote for."

[Journalist] Ron Haggart and his wife are in the front row, smiling and friendly. If I cannot win their votes I of course cannot win this election but I think I have done so. A question is asked about intercommunicating telephones for the deaf. Julian in this question (along with other questions) says he doesn't know anything about the issue. Happily I do, as a result of my work with the United Way and the Canadian Hearing Society, but the fact that I know about it makes it seem that the question is a plant.

The president of the association is a rather pompous little man who is rude to some of the questioners. They are, however, probably not members of his association.

In the entire crowd I do not suppose there are more than ten or fifteen independent voters. The only people I see from the old campaign, for the Tories, are Frank Roberts and Michael Callaghan. All the other Tory supporters seem to be Rosedale matrons with rich blonde hair and young kids dressed in designer sweaters. Someone in the audience makes an attack on the liquor issue because it will produce fourteen-year-old drunks, an absurdity if ever there was one. I indicate that the fourteen-year-olds I know aren't like that and I hear later that Mile and his group are absolutely thrilled with my response. I am glad to be able to do something for them.

We leave at 9:30 (Julian is eager for a deal to quit at 9:00, which I reject) and I rush to Alick Ryder's where there are about sixty people including a good number of people from the office. John Evans, Ned MacAuley, etc. I speak for five or ten minutes with the basic pitch being jobs for young people. There is no question and answer period, which in a way is too bad because I do best at those sorts of thing but it is a friendly meeting and Mary tells me we got three or four sign locations and a couple of workers, which is more than we usually do, so I am content.

After everybody has left, we sit around Alick's dining room table (Leslie, Alick, Peter, Ken, Tom Ryder's young son and a couple of others) and tell jokes and laugh and have a wonderful time. I am elated and feel that the day has been worthwhile though I have not done any actual canvassing. I recognize that this weekend is going to be a heavy ordeal with blitzes beginning on Friday night through Sunday afternoon and I hope I can physically prepare myself. My lip is a mass of cold sores but this is simply something that must be borne. I reassure myself from time to time that I am doing this not only to win but because it is important to do it for the values that I think are significant, and that this should be its own reward.

As I leave, Bob Hawkins drives up and comes running over to me. He has already been to my home. He has been absent all day after the fuss the previous day and he wants to indicate that he is back onside. He has had a day of sulking and he is now going to deliver himself full-time over to the campaign. That is good news.

Home to bed by 11:30. I do not yet know whether any of these frenetic activities have made the national news or any of the other news broadcasts. I sincerely hope so because what we do require is some sense of profile particularly in Rosedale and Moore Park. I speak to the *Toronto Sun* by telephone at Peter's urging about the hospital issue and a 6:40 a.m. telephone call with CKO has been arranged for the following morning.

Friday, April 19, 1985:

The floppy disc record has arrived and I play it. I think it will be rather hokey for the more sophisticated people. I hope my sense of convictions about what I say, bland though it is, comes through. No one has any sense about the effect it will have in the apartments or the other residential parts of the riding. Eddie Goldenberg, who has turned up and is full of ideas, says at least it won't cost any votes.

Because it is a novelty I fear it. I hope it will not appear too slick. It was not intended to be. The picture backing is absolutely dreadful.

Saturday, April 20, 1985:

Before the blitz Hawkins calls. He and Ross Wells have heard the record and think it is wonderful. He is concerned that there should be some kind of press conference to announce the release of this innovative material. He is also concerned that it says "Made in the USA." One of the political realities is the technology to make a record of this type does not exist in Ontario. Where was the IDEA Corporation?

Hawkins also reminds me that the tenor of the campaign and the zeal of the workers is very much dependent on my attitude and that I must begin to be extremely positive and indicate (as we may be) that we are winning. He says the importance of this is evidenced by the effect on our workers of the Jackman School meeting, which was apparently electric. It is very hard for me to do this.

. . . I am extremely tired. The weather is warming up. The sun has come out after an early morning rain at 8:00 a.m. and it is humid. I get very steamed up running from house to house and I wonder how I look appearing on these front porches drenched in perspiration.

There are occasions when I have difficulty speaking because I am so winded but I do the best I can. I remind myself that I am two years older than Julian. I keep telling these people that we are even in the race with Porter, which I think to be true because many of them feel that the result of the election is a foregone conclusion. His name recognition factor is very high. I have hardly met a voter in the entire four weeks so far who did not know who he is.

. . . We decide to do the second blitz in Moore Park and start off shortly after 2:00 p.m. It is initially devastating in the sense that there are very many Porter signs and people do not seem at all interested in us and quite clipped and formal in their response. At the first two houses I am confronted by angry ratepayers who say that I have lost their votes. It turns out that this is not a personal accusation. What they are concerned about is public school funding. It seems to me ironic that I, as a Liberal, am about to pay the price for a Davis-bungled initiative. There was no debate in the House because no bill has yet been introduced and somehow our party is held responsible for this. I attempt my constitutional qualification to modest effect.

. . . We do some of the streets in Moore Park and then drive over to Julian's cul-de-sac. There are a number of signs on the street. Happily it is a short street and we will not be long. The band starts to play. Julian's house is about the fifth in and he comes out onto the veranda before we arrive there. A large hedge frames the walkway at the street line. I see Julian and immediately go up the steps. I notice that the kids have formed a sort of barricade at the entrance waving placards. Julian looks uncertain. He undoubtedly feels that there is going to be some kind of demonstration which of course is not what I intended and would be inappropriate . . . I shoo the kids away and I speak to Julian.

He keeps saying that we have been friends for twenty-five years and I introduce myself to his daughter Katherine, a pretty girl of eight or nine. She not unnaturally has already formed an unfavourable opinion of the man who is against her daddy, which I can see framed carefully in her eyes. Julian begins to explain to her the intricacies of political democracy assuring her that I have to do what I am doing. It is really quite touching and I admire her for her loyalty and Julian for his openness and tolerance in this small family vignette. In fact I like him very much. We move on up the street, go down one other street and work our way back to St. Clair, running into some more personal friends of Julian's who indicated they are committed to him.

Back to the campaign headquarters. I am almost beyond exhaustion at this time and am walking around in a state . . . it is terribly hot and I am determined to canvass in a jacket for reasons which escape me.

At one doorstep on Geneva I recognize that I am going to faint and I grab the lintel and lean against it in the most casual way I can manage, mouthing my piece. What must these people think of the sight of a sweaty, physically bleached candidate who stumbles on their doorstep to mutter incoherently his four or five sentences . . . I see Annie MacDonald with her Julian Porter sign on the lawn and all the trendies are of course with him. It has already been pre-announced that he is the winner.

Monday, April 22, 1985:

The Leaside all-candidates debate. Julian Porter has announced that he will not attend any event outside the riding's boundaries.

Barbara Hall speaks first. She is forthright, direct and attractive as usual and I quite admire her. I speak next and attempt to heap ridicule on Miller and take a jab or two at Porter, who has not been present. If he is not present before the election, will he meet after the election?

Bob Elgie speaks next and he is a model. He has a little fun to begin with at my expense and rather puts me down by suggesting that I am humorous and witty. (The assumption is that I am shallow.) But he does a masterful job talking about the importance of compromise, direct dealing, and frankness. He is a most admirable man.

Tuesday, April 23, 1985:

We begin at the St. Clair subway station south with Barry Leon and Paul Pape, who are willing and eager. I suppose I probably meet 100 people, perhaps more, at this stop. The interesting thing is only one of them announces that he is voting PC and most of them are extremely friendly and many of them seem to know me from previous occasions. I get the sense from a lot of them that they will be voting for me. It is a positive, exhilarating experience in a very Tory area . . . At this bus stop, I get the sense that the election can be won.

Thursday, April 25, 1985:

Gwen hands me a "secret" note, which is apparently a report of Allan Gregg's poll in St. David. It shows that at present we will win by 1,700 votes and this is before the record is out. A moment's elation is followed by a report of a poll from Lissman, which shows that we will lose the riding by 3,000 votes. I secretly believe the latter to be more likely. I keep thinking that there are 8,000 votes in Rosedale and Moore Park and I cannot believe that we can achieve a 5,000 to 3,000 division. If we can do that, however, Julian would then get 30 percent at least of the remaining 16,000, which will give him a total of about 10,500, enough to win unless the NDP vote collapses, which is unlikely.

Friday, April 26, 1985:

At a coffee party arranged by Mary Kiervin, the separate school issue again causes a lot of trouble. These people are really not talking about Grades 10–13 but about the whole separate-school system. Bishop Garnsworthy has already branded Davis a Hitler. While everybody seems to recognize it was imprudent to say this, the spirit of his remark typifies the attitude of very many people. I have not even yet met a separate school supporter who has congratulated us on our stand.

Miller's teleglobe performance of the night before has not been particularly well received. Apparently it was preceded by three lengthy, windy speeches by Miller, Davis, and Mulroney and there was time for only nine questions. This has heightened the recognition that he was unwilling, perhaps afraid, to debate.

Saturday, April 27, 1985:

The Gallup Poll is out and the figures are 43, 33, 23. Not nearly good enough it seems to me. We must get Miller well below 40 to win this riding. I am told that there is a south-end poll that shows him at 40 and us at 34.

... The Summerhill Gardens poll effectively ends at a house where a single late-middle-aged lady confronts me as a black cat runs into her home. She screams in horror. The cat is not hers. She has spent weeks trying to keep it out of the house.

I go up the stairs to remove it. She then gives me a long harangue about how single people are over-taxed because they do not use public facilities. All I can say is that I understand her position and make my way to the door. The cat enters again and she chases it all over the house, which of course frightens the cat, and it runs under a chesterfield. Again, I have to spend about five minutes getting it out.

Will she remember me as the candidate who got the cat out of her house? And if she does, what will the effect of that be?

... I look forward to May third more than I can say. A week goes by so fast, and it will soon all be over. I am, however, very anxious to win if only to satisfy the gang of four and others who have worked so desperately hard with such imagination.

Also, if I win, it will probably be easier to pay my bills. But I am impressed really for the first time, as the rumours begin to grow, with the responsibility that I am taking on, particularly in the south end of the riding, where the conditions are so desperate and where so much needs to be done.

An issues committee system is formulating in my mind. I tried it on at the Bowden St. coffee party. It is something that could be workable and would be a great resource for a sitting member.

I cannot bring myself to make any promises to the people of the south end at all. They have heard all of this so often and are naturally cynical about it, although they remain good-natured. I cannot feed their cynicism further. I simply say that I will do my best and be in regular contact with them, open an office in the area, and try to bring about some changes. Indeed I think that the most effective role a member can play is to be a kind of resource person to the community associations.

One thing we will find out in this election is whether it is true that Mrs. Scrivener was well respected in this area. In fact, what we have to do is see to it that Julian gets as few votes here as possible.

I stopped keeping the diary at this point, one week before the campaign ended, for two reasons. First, there were glimmers of hope that I would actually win, in which case it would not be such a good idea to publish the book. Second, and more prosaically, I was tired. All the early-morning bus stops and the three-a-day canvasses had taken a toll. We had covered all the bases. Now it was important to keep up the momentum.

We took a leaf out of Margaret Scrivener's book and held barbecues, with free hot dogs and balloons for the kids, in spaces close to the advance polls in Regent Park and Deer Park. These events attracted fairly big crowds, and we got many of the attendees to vote at the advance polls while they were there. The band was omnipresent, lending a festive air to our campaign.

As the campaign wound down, we thought we had done everything we could to maximize our vote. David Rubin and his committee had raised lots of money: we ended up spending $140,000. We needed the money in part to pay for our "secret weapon" — the floppy disc recording used for the first time in any political campaign in Canada. It had required an enormous amount of volunteer labour to package. A backing picture had to be stapled to each of the 35,000 records we had ordered. Then, each record had to be inserted in an envelope, which then had to be inserted into the third pamphlet. A team of Sri Lankan volunteers from St. Jamestown had taken over the task, and they did a wonderful job of it.

Thanks to our fundraisers, we had enough money to buy advertising space on the message boards in the TTC subway system. As usual, there had been a spirited debate in the committee rooms about what the pixelled messages should say. Ken Rosenberg was in charge of the operation, and he and his team had come up with nineteen different statements of where I stood on the major issues of the day.

They had cobbled together uplifting statements like "Ian Scott believes in world peace." When Ken took these inspiring but vague messages to the man who sold the advertising space for the TTC, he found enlightenment.

"You have an interesting and challenging approach," the man said. "Have you ever considered going with something a bit simpler and more direct? I might suggest something like: 'Ian Scott, Ian Scott, Ian Scott, Vote for Ian Scott, Vote for Ian Scott, Vote for Ian Scott, Ian Scott, Ian Scott, Ian Scott.'"

We took his advice.

On election day, we put in the ritual appearances at polling places and coped with the task of getting inside and outside scrutineers in place for the vote-mobilizing and the vote-counting. So much of politics depends on volunteers, and by the end of the campaign we had a solid core of committed and enthusiastic workers.

When the polls closed, there were some early indications that we were going to win. First, we had won the advance polls by a considerable margin: the barbecue technique had worked well. Second, as Dawn Potts, one of the best of the volunteers, noted in the poll in Rosedale where she was inside scrutineer, the Tory vote had dropped considerably from the previous election and the Liberal vote had gone up. So even in the polls that the Tories won, they did not get enough of a cushion to offset our gains elsewhere. Third, we won Regent Park by a wide margin.

When it was clear that we had won by some four thousand votes, we paraded from the committee rooms in triumph along the Danforth and up Broadview to the hall we had rented for the election night party. I thanked all the people whose hard work had made it possible and we had a joyous celebration.

It was sweet. Peter Lukasiewicz had helped hoist me onto his shoulders to carry me into the hall. The *Sun* ran a photo of this the next day over the caption, "Scott derails Porter in St. David."

SIX

The Romance of
Government

ACROSS ONTARIO, the unimaginable had happened. The Tories had lost seats they had held for half a century, including my riding of St. David. The election was on a Thursday. Doubts lingered about the outcome in some close ridings, so it took until the weekend for it all to sink in. Frank Miller had been a hard sell in urban areas, and the notion that it was time for a change had ultimately, if unevenly, worked its way across the province. David Peterson took advantage of Miller's refusal to debate to portray him as someone afraid to deal directly with the people, a candidate under the influence of "handlers," who were the real powers in the province.

Besides my St. David win, other Toronto seats were won by Liberals Elinor Caplan, Monte Kwinter, and Greg Sorbara. Gerry Phillips and Alvin Curling won in Scarborough. London, Ontario, the base for many years of John Roberts's dominant political machine, produced three Liberal members — quite a change from the London once characterized by Peterson as so conservative that the Tories could run a yellow dog and win. Liberal successes in the election were real, but Liberal seats were rather lumpily distributed. René Fontaine was the only Liberal to win one of the fifteen northern seats; the Tories and the NDP split the rest.

The Liberals had won the biggest share of the popular vote, but the Tories had obtained the most seats. They had fifty-two, we had forty-eight, and the NDP had the balance of twenty-five seats. There had been many minority governments in Ontario in the 1970s, but never one with such a small Conservative plurality. There were no certainties about how the scene would unfold.

In the meantime, I had to get organized for my new role as the representative for St. David. My first decision as an elected representative of the people was relatively easy. I got a phone call from Stu Houston, who had run Margaret Scrivener's office for five years. He was interested in keeping his job. I was interested in providing good service to my constituents. So I hired Stu, initially for six months. He and I hit it off, and he stayed for my whole term in office.

We also decided to take over the lease on the existing constituency office, which was on the second floor of a small building on Gerrard Street, east of Parliament. It was not accessible to people with disabilities. It had no street presence. If one were cynical, one would say that its location and ambiance were effectively designed to discourage visits. When the lease expired, we moved to a much more visible and accessible ground-floor location on Parliament.

It was important to master the mechanics of a good constituency office. When I was running for election, I was struck by the number of people I met on doorsteps or at subway stops who had problems in their dealings with the government. I shared their frustration: the intransigence of the provincial government in the Pickering lands expropriation case had helped to push me into politics in the first place. In setting up the office, then, I selected people who I felt would be responsive to the needs of the community, people who were efficient in cutting through red tape. I had a good start in Stu Houston. Later on, I was also fortunate to have Lesley Yaeger, a lawyer, working for me as well.

Throughout my time in politics, I tried to maintain a balance between meeting face-to-face with constituents and getting done my work as a minister. Stu and Lesley were good at sorting the demands coming into the constituency office into those they could handle and those where my intervention might help, if only to keep the constituents aware that I worked on their behalf. As much as possible, I set aside Friday afternoons and early evenings for constituency meetings.

I enjoyed the hours I spent meeting with people from the riding. I have always liked meeting people whose backgrounds differ from my own. St. David, and later St. George–St. David, has one of the most diverse populations in all of Canada. The north end of the riding, in Rosedale and Moore Park, is home to some of the most prosperous people in the country — in the case of Ken Thomson, make that the world. The south end of the riding, on the other hand, houses some of the most desperately poor people in Canada. There are immigrants from all over the world, and a substantial aboriginal community. People used to say that the aboriginal population in the riding would make the second biggest reservation in Canada, but this was an urban legend, which, like most urban legends, turned out not to be true.

An MPP must function like a poor person's lawyer. I was encouraged by how skilled Stu and Lesley were at helping people cut through red tape. But I was discouraged by the intractability of so many of my constituents' problems. There were people down on their luck, who needed to get plugged into a social service agency. There were people who had trouble speaking English who needed someone to intervene on their behalf with some government agency. Certain problems tended to recur, but individual quirks and peculiarities made each case interesting. I loved the variety of it all. There were some cranks, of course, and lots of people who needed help from the federal as opposed to the provincial government, but the door was always open, and we all tried to do what we could for them.

There is a limit to what any representative can do to solve social problems. It is gratifying, however, when I was able to do something for a family in need of accommodation or having trouble with OHIP, or welfare, or any of the whole range of government services and departments. And the hours that Stu, Lesley, and I spent may have saved my political hide in the riding in the 1990 election, though I'll never know that for sure.

My second decision as an MPP was also straightforward. I would bring Pete Milner with me from my law office to Queen's Park. She was competent and unflappable, and knew how to anticipate what I needed.

At Queen's Park I shared an office with the newly elected Monte Kwinter, soon to be in the cabinet with me. Over our years together, I had a lot of fun with Monte and his charming wife, Wilma. The best thing I did for Monte was to recommend that he hire Ken Rosenberg, who had worked on my campaign, as his executive assistant. This was one of the rare occasions when Monte took my advice, and I don't think he ever regretted it.

My third decision was that Peter Lukasiewicz would be my executive assistant. I am still not sure whether I made this decision or Peter made it for me. But with Peter, Marilyn Hood, Mike Cherney, and the others who came on board after it was clear we would form a government, I had the nucleus of the team that would serve me well in office.

With these organizational matters out of the way, I could concentrate on playing my role in the complicated chess game that resulted in the accord between the NDP and us.

After a brief period, while everyone got over their shock about the election results, preliminary negotiations began between the Liberals and the NDP. At the beginning of the process, relations between David Peterson and Bob Rae weren't much better than those between Miller and Rae. Before the election, most people probably would have said that Rae was more likely to upset the Tories than Peterson. So there were tensions in the initial contacts.

According to Ted McGrath, who was with Peterson at the time, the first phone call started with Rae complaining about Peterson's remarks that Rae was a tool of the big union bosses. Peterson apologized, and then thought that he should have a grievance as well, to put things on an even footing. So he stated that he didn't appreciate

Rae's comment that Peterson's main campaign poster, which pictured him running in a reddish-orange track suit, made him look like a big Cheesie. Mutual grievances aired, the two agreed to talk about how to end forty-three years of Conservative government in Ontario.

It was clear that the period ahead would be dynamic. Historically, the NDP had supported the Conservatives in the Davis minority governments. There was a natural sympathy between the two parties; the relationship between Davis and Stephen Lewis was still remembered in each party's history. And so, there was every prospect that if the Conservatives played their cards right, the NDP would do what they usually did and support the Conservative government in a minority setting.

I think, however, that the personal rejection of Frank Miller by the electorate made it extremely difficult for the NDP to support him. Certainly, Miller's performance as premier during the four months leading up to the election did not encourage the NDP or anyone else to believe that he would be the kind of progressive figure that the Conservatives have traditionally presented. It's odd, but all the way back to George Drew, the Conservatives have always selected the most conservative of leadership candidates. This was true of Miller, Davis, and Robarts. As soon as the leader is elected, however, he immediately moves to the left of the party, and then becomes a progressive premier who astounds, confounds, and upsets the delegates who voted for him. Before Mike Harris's time, Miller was the single exception to that rule of which I am aware, and I think it cost him the election.

Miller was under a lot of pressure. He was being blamed for the defeat of the government. Ed Stewart, Davis's right-hand man, apparently advised him to make any concessions in order to retain power. But Miller vacillated between his hope that something could still be salvaged from the election and the resolve to stick to his principles. His indecision did not improve his relations with the NDP.

When the NDP first negotiated with the Tories, the latter were reluctant to enter into a written agreement. They changed their minds when it became clear that there would very likely be a written accord between the NDP and the Liberals. But this change of mind came too late in the day, and was regarded by the NDP as opportunistic.

Ross McClellan and Michael Breaugh, both MPPs, and Hugh Mackenzie, a policy person, made up the NDP team. I was part of the Liberal team, along with Bob Nixon, the party's former leader; and Sean Conway, the MPP from Renfrew. Hershell Ezrin, Peterson's chief of staff, popped in and out of the talks as needed.

I think I was probably put on the negotiating team because I was a lawyer and had done a lot of negotiating in my time, acting for trade unions, the Ontario Medical Association, and various other organizations. Peterson probably saw me as a negotiator. He might also have seen — and this would be fair — that, unlike Sean and Bob, I was an elected person who represented the new part of the party. That party was now going to represent urban as well as rural Ontario.

When it was clear that there were going to be negotiations, the accord team immediately got all kinds of advice about how to behave. I got the most astounding advice from some very senior political figures in Canada who knew all about politics and government. I respected them. I was inexperienced. I had never been elected to anything except president of the student council. But I was surprised when they advised us that we should not make a deal with the NDP. Instead, they said, we should allow the NDP to support the Conservative government. Then, in a year or two, the Tories would be defeated; we would be the natural successors, and get a majority. In other words, we should not go through a minority period relying on the support of the NDP.

I was astonished at this advice. It was counterintuitive, as far as I was concerned. I mean, I had got into politics to get rid of the Tories and here I was being advised by very senior people to let them stay. And I remember thinking to myself, "You know, the Tories know how to run politics in Ontario. If you let them stay for six months they'll get rid of Miller. They'll pick Timbrell or someone and they'll be in for forty more years, and that isn't what you got in here for." My colleagues felt the same way and, I think, so did David.

Our formal negotiations with the NDP started on May 13. They were very straightforward. The NDP's greatest fear was a snap election call. We were afraid that they would join with the Tories to vote against tax measures and for more spending. After some jockeying for position, we agreed to co-operate for a two-year period during which we promised not to call an election. On their side, they promised not to treat a defeat in the house as a confidence measure. We also agreed on a shopping list of policies that had been in both parties' manifestos.

This isn't well understood by the public, but we decided that we would not in the accord promise to undertake any initiative that was not in our 1985 campaign manual, and we didn't. We made no variations from that principle, so I get a little irritated when people say that we accepted a whole bunch of NDP policy initiatives. In fact, as it happens, when you have two progressive opposition parties, there tends to be an overlap in policy proposals, so it was fairly easy to work out a list.

The sticking point was the question of the budget and how these proposals would be paid for. The NDP didn't care about funding. In effect, they said, "These are the things we want you to do. Raising the money is your problem." I asked, "Well, if we need new taxes, are you going to support that?" They replied, "Well, of course not," and behaved as if finances weren't a matter that concerned them. The key feature of the agreement we made was that our commitment to initiate proposed policies would be consistent with our understanding of what was fiscally responsible. We spent a lot of time trying to develop a formula to flesh that one out; that was the most significant role I played. We didn't, contrary to accepted wisdom, undertake to institute all proposals, plain and simple. We simply undertook to do them when we could do so consistent with fiscal responsibility. We weren't in office yet; we didn't know what the fiscal situation was.

All in all, it was a relatively uneventful negotiation. It wasn't difficult when we saw that the NDP were not, in fact, going to support the Conservatives. We saw that on day one, and then we had it. When we knew they weren't talking to the Conservatives seriously, and that they wanted to talk to us seriously, we were home free.

It's interesting. Had they played their hand a little more drastically, the NDP might have said, "We want some seats in your cabinet." Now, I think that David would have had grave difficulty in doing that, but on the negotiating team there were at least three members who would have looked at that prospect. Conway, Nixon, and I were so determined to end Conservative rule in Ontario that we would have been quite comfortable with a coalition cabinet. But the NDP never raised the matter. On the last day of negotiations, Mike Breaugh said, "Instead of doing all this, what would you say to having a coalition?" We said, "Mike, it's too late: you've given the store away."

On May 28, the accord was signed. From that point on, we knew that we had the votes to defeat the Tories, should they persist with their plans to meet the legislature and carry on as if the election had not occurred. It was only a matter of time.

One of the major benefits of the accord was that it gave us a chance to prepare for the first session of the legislature with the knowledge that we would be coming to power. The Tories were still in something of a state of shock and denial. They were badly split on their campaign plank of extending full funding to Catholic secondary schools, and they solved this internal problem by not bringing forward any bills about how to carry out this promise. We were committed to bringing in a bill to provide full funding for Catholic schools for the next school year, so we knew that we would have to be ready to act on that and in other areas. Before we could act, however, we had to find out what the new cabinet would look like.

There was much excitement at the prospect of forming a government, and much speculation about who was going to hold what portfolio. I wanted to be attorney general, as that was the office I knew the most about, and where my legal experience would be most useful. There were rumours, however, that Peterson was considering me for the minister of health, to help with protracted negotiations with the province's doctors about our pledge to ban extra billing. We thought that there would be a doctors' strike if the negotiations failed.

There were also some concerns about my sexuality. Only a few years earlier, a whole series of raids had been conducted on bathhouses frequented by gay men, and some members of the caucus expressed the belief that a homosexual should not be attorney general on that account.

People in my law office knew about my sexual orientation, as did a wide circle of friends and acquaintances. I did not, however, want the issue to be a distraction for the new government. As I was a political neophyte, I thought I should discuss the matter with Robert Nixon. He was a former leader of the party, the son of the last Liberal premier in the province, and the man who, by all accounts, would be given the finance portfolio by David Peterson. I told Bob that I was homosexual, and asked him if he thought there would be any problems with my being attorney general on that account. He thought the matter should be cleared with the premier, so I arranged to discuss it with David. His response was "So what?"

A measure of the concern I felt before the appointment was made can be seen in a memorandum I drafted before David announced who was in and who was out of cabinet:

Memo to: David Peterson QC
From: Ian Scott

I thought I should record some of my views about cabinet so that you will have them when you come to make your decisions.

There are a number of reasons (which I very much hope will commend themselves to you) why I should be appointed attorney general.

1. Perceptions: I believe that the perception of the government formed by the "movers and shakers" in Metropolitan Toronto is critical in the early months. The view that the leaders of the professional and business community of the government have is to a very substantial sense (at least in Metropolitan Toronto) the initial public image of the new government. They will be looking for signs of the government's strength or weakness. They will focus (as they always do) on two principal portfolios: treasury and attorney general. I am confident that if

Bob Nixon is appointed treasurer and I attorney general the appropriate signal would be sent to that community and will lead it to believe that a strong viable government was established. I am not confident that the appointment of any other lawyer available to you will have the same effect. No doubt all of them are able but equally all of them are young and little known in the important communities to which I refer. The appointment of any of them as attorney general would be a matter of considerable surprise, if not alarm.

2. Importance of the Portfolio: While there may be times when the portfolio has reduced significance I am firmly of the view after three weeks in government that the position of attorney general is critically important in at least the first six months of your administration. It is, I think, increasingly obvious (and I think Kirby, Conway and others will confirm this view) that the heat on separate school funding is going to be taken not only by the minister of education but by the attorney general. You are entitled to have the best advice from these two ministers as to how the project is to be managed. Less than the best advice will only get us into very serious trouble. Within days of assuming office, crucial legal issues and significant questions of legal tactics will have to be analyzed and determined in order that the matter proceed expeditiously, properly, and without sinking us in a morass, thereby derailing the rest of our program over the summer. I think therefore that what you need is the strongest attorney general that you can find. I don't believe you can leave these questions in inexperienced hands. The situation may be different nine months from now but at the present time I do not think the importance of the office can possibly be underestimated.

3. Extra Billing: I share your view that the question of extra billing is the second most difficult question that the government faces. It is important to have a strong minister in the health portfolio. I simply emphasize the following facts:

(1) While negotiations may commence at any time it is perfectly clear that the extra billing fight should not take place until

education matters have been effectively dealt with. It is therefore some way down the pike.

(2) The extra billing "negotiations" are sensitive but not likely to be critical at an early stage. There will be protracted exchanges of view between the parties, which will continue indefinitely until the government decides that action must be taken. At that moment, it seems to me that it will require all your cabinet resources including a resourceful lawyer (the attorney general) to bring the issue safely through. Whether you decide to change the minister of health before this ultimate stage is reached I leave entirely to you. In any event, I think you will need a strong attorney general at that time who, as the government's lawyer, can participate effectively (and perhaps as a fresh face) in the ultimate negotiations.

(3) I would have thought it would be useful to appoint an able, conscientious, and consensus oriented member like Murray Elston to take charge of health. The preliminary negotiations over the next six months or so may show (as I believe) that he will be enormously effective in which case you will have made the right choice. If your nominee, however, turns out to be not particularly effective there will be plenty of time to shuffle your cabinet before the ultimate stage is reached and the battle finally drawn.

4. Politics: If I "carry the can" as Minister of Health I will not survive the next election. While extra billing is a matter of principle to most doctors it is a matter of dollars and cents to the specialists. Probably a third to one half of the specialists in Metro who will be vitally affected in their pocket book, live in St. David. The riding has more doctors per capita than any other. I am confident that if I am the minister of health and engaged in this exercise they will band together and defeat me. There is a political advantage in passing the task to a member who is not quite as vulnerable in his constituency as I am.

A copy of this memo was found in my desk drawer when I was cleaning out my office at Gowlings. I did tend to write memos and letters that

I never sent, so I cannot remember whether I actually sent this memo to David. In any case, he gave me the job; I was thrilled when David appointed me to the office of attorney general. It was the best job I ever had.

Because the number of Liberal MPPs was somewhat limited, David also made me minister responsible for women's issues and minister responsible for native issues. Though I lobbied him to get control of the Ontario Human Rights Commission, he decided to leave it with the Labour ministry. It was practically the only thing I ever asked him for that he did not give me. Perhaps it was because the first line of the memo I sent to him about the commission began with these words: "The Ontario Human Rights Commission is a joke."

During the interregnum, when I was pretty sure that I would be attorney general, I went to see my old friend Roy McMurtry, who had been Bill Davis's attorney general before quitting politics to become Canada's high commissioner to the United Kingdom. Roy told me two things. First, he had been back in the ministry recently, and found that it was still reeling from the changes introduced by the brief but intense Miller experience.

"Don't worry about your reception in the ministry," said Roy. "They'll treat you like you were the Allies entering Paris."

Second, Roy told me not to hire lawyers for my staff, so that I could get some independent advice about how to run the department. I thanked him for the advice, but told him that it came a little bit late, as I had already decided whom I wanted on my staff, and they were all lawyers.

The Conservatives met the legislature, brought in a Throne Speech, and attempted to govern. They faced a vote of confidence on June 18, 1985, and they lost. Frank Miller resigned, and the lieutenant-governor, John Black Aird, requested that David Peterson form the government.

It had been so long since the last change of government in Ontario that a number of mix-ups occurred. At one point, the Great Seal of Ontario, needed for all the swearings-in, was temporarily lost. It was found in time for us to be appointed formally to our offices. I had been working as a lawyer in private practice for as long as I could before the ceremony: I argued a case in the Court of Appeal in the morning and was sworn in as attorney general in the afternoon.

After the formal swearing-in ceremony, conducted in public for the first time, we threw an informal public reception and picnic on the grounds of Queen's Park. Everyone was invited. It was a hot day and the grounds teemed with people. The crowd reflected the diversity of the new Ontario. A sense of excitement was in the air — people couldn't believe that Tory rule had ended. Everyone felt that things were going to be better, that the new government would be open and accountable. David Peterson served hot dogs to small kids, working the crowd with his considerable political skill.

In addition to excitement, however, there was also a lot of pressure. We had to prove to the people of the province, and probably to ourselves as well, that we were capable of managing the province.

My first mistake, though, was quick in coming. Sometime in that first week, our triumphant team was scheduled for a formal portrait. No one had told me about the event, or if they had I forgot all about it in the excitement of getting down to work in my new job. While everyone else in the new cabinet was assembled for the picture-taking, I was in my office, blissfully unaware that anything was amiss. I was hastily summoned, and arrived half an hour late. The newly sworn-in David Peterson was not amused by my tardiness: several pictures had been taken without me. But we all survived that mishap and got set to take on the task of governing.

I assembled a wonderful team of assistants. Peter Lukasiewicz became my first chief of staff. Pete is bright, articulate, and able to get things done, even if it means stepping on a few toes on the way to achieving the goal. Throughout my career in politics, I could count on people like Pete, or Chuck Birchall, who became my next chief of staff, to give me blunt advice. Often, I rejected their advice in the morning, and came round to accepting it later in the day. Shelley Spiegel was my chief adviser on aboriginal issues. On constitutional issues, I retained my friend Ian McGilp to do special projects. I was also able to obtain the services of people like Neil Finkelstein and later, Pat Monahan, both respected experts in constitutional law, as constitutional advisers. I wanted to be sure that my ideas could be translated into action.

Someone once commented that I ran my ministry like a graduate seminar on legal issues. It was not quite as free-flowing as the comparison implies, but I was determined to get the best possible advice from the widest circle of advisers. Over the years, I enjoyed the challenge of working with a collection of bright, energetic people, some of whom left to go back to the private sector after a year or two, but all of whom I respected and encouraged to state their views forcefully.

Our first project was the Freedom of Information Act. When I broached it in the ministry, I met with some resistance. The Davis government had managed for a long time without such an act, and the ministry favoured study before the bill came into being. We did not, however, have any time for study. Bill Davis had promised to bring in full funding for the Catholic schools for the next school year. Our government was sworn in on June 26, and we were committed to holding public hearings on the full-funding bill and to have something in place by the start of the school year. We convened the legislature on July 2, which did not leave a lot of time for leisurely meetings on other matters.

My response to departmental caution was that I had been elected to make laws, not study things. Over the long holiday weekend, Ian McGilp, Steve Goudge, and I worked up a Freedom of Information Act as Bill One, the first legislation of the new government. I had the privilege of speaking the first words in the legislature for the new government when I rose to introduce the bill on July 2, 1985.

Introducing the Freedom of Information Act made a statement about what kind of government we hoped to have. It certainly made a statement about the refusal of the previous Tory regimes to give the public access to the public record and the decision-making process. The act was in our accord with the NDP, so in one sense we were committed to introducing it sometime in the first two years of government. But we brought it in first because we believed it was the right thing to do: in a democracy, citizens have the right to know what information the government uses as the basis for its decisions.

David Peterson's transition team had done its work well. For the ten days the legislature was in session, we acquitted ourselves without any major gaffes. Then the legislature recessed, and we had some breathing space in which to get to know our departments and make our plans for the next session.

Practically the first thing that Peterson did as premier was to assemble all the deputy ministers and ask for their co-operation in making the new government work. He started off this meeting by making a few jokes about Archie Campbell, my deputy in the attorney general's department, who had been his roommate in law school. This broke the ice. It also made it clear to the deputies that Peterson's would be a very different government than either Miller's or Davis's.

Frank Miller (like Mike Harris after him) had been deeply suspicious of the power of the bureaucracy. He had sought, in his short time in office, to change dramatically the way decisions were made, by bringing in a group of right-wing advisers to supplant the Big Blue Machine that had dominated Ontario politics for a generation. Bill Davis had operated through Ed Stewart, his right-hand man. Stewart, a likeable former teacher, had been his deputy when Davis held the education portfolio. Though a civil servant, Stewart was quite comfortable in taking part in the strategy and brainstorming sessions Davis held with his political advisers at the Park Plaza Hotel over breakfast. Civil servants dealt with Stewart, who then dealt with Davis. Some deputies had never been inside the inner sanctum of Davis's office.

David Peterson was determined to change the way the system worked. When he wanted information, he picked up the phone and called. He wanted to get the best possible advice before he made a decision, and he didn't particularly care whether it came through the "correct" channels.

I took something of the same approach. When I became attorney general, I wanted to reform the process through which provincial court judges were appointed. I wanted to reform the structure of Ontario's courts. I wanted to make sure that all Ontario laws and regulations conformed to the letter and the spirit of the Charter of Rights and Freedoms. Finally, I wanted to open up the legal and judicial system to ensure that different voices and viewpoints could be heard.

Any incoming minister faces a difficult challenge: to establish good relations with public servants and at the same time get those public servants to embrace new ways of doing business. During my first few days in office, as we discussed drafting the Freedom of Information Bill, it became clear to me that I would have to deal with some vested interests within if the ministry was to reflect my sense of priorities.

To an outsider, the ministry was structured like a collection of independent law firms. Chief among these sections was the policy branch. Within the ministry, the policy branch had the reputation of being quite radical. To me, they were quite traditional in their approach to law and legal issues. The ministry was further divided into the civil-law side and the criminal-law side. In addition, there were a number of agencies, like the Public Trustee. Sections of the ministry also performed such tasks as preparing regulations for self-regulating professions, like engineers and accountants.

Some of the departmental systems I inherited were strange to me. For example, all correspondence that came into the department was filtered through a central office, which sometimes meant that letters got stuck in a kind of black hole, from which it took a lot of energy to extricate them.

The ministry bureaucracy, naturally, was content with the way things had always been done. They prepared enormous briefing books for me on the way the ministry operated, and suggested that my first task as attorney general should be to go on a grand inspection tour of it for several weeks. The tour would give me a chance to absorb the briefing books, and, presumably, to come round to the traditional view of how the ministry ought to operate. I resisted their recommendation. I had my own agenda, and a sense that I, unlike the Tories, might not have forty-three years in which to implement it.

Certain routines, as a practical matter, had to continue. Cabinet meetings were on Tuesdays; caucus met on Wednesday mornings; priorities and planning met on Thursday mornings; and the Cabinet Committee on Justice met on Thursday afternoons. If the house was sitting, I had to be there for question period, and for other times at the whip's discretion. Regular times were set aside for meetings on regulations and other matters. In addition to my official duties, I had a whole series of speaking engagements. It was not uncommon for me to put in fifteen- or sixteen-hour workdays. I had a lot on my plate.

The best thing about being a minister is that the position comes with a car and a driver. Wayne Hawke, my driver, had been around government a long time. He saved me lots of that most precious commodity, time. My own record of driving left something to be desired. I once got a ticket for leaving my car running at the corner of Bay and King while I ran into the law office for some documents I needed for an appearance in the Court of Appeal. Unfortunately for me, the car was not pulled up high enough on the sidewalk to prevent its rear end from obstructing the King streetcar. More unfortunately, once inside the firm, I accepted the offer of a ride to the courthouse from someone else. Only after we had pulled out of the parking garage in his car did I remember my own. Fortunately, I managed to retrieve it before it was towed away.

But wait, as they say on the infomercials, there's more! While I was working on the Singh case, I had been getting a lot of calls from a Mr. Singh. I assumed he was one of the clients I was representing, and I really had nothing much to say to him about the preparation of the appeal. So I ignored the calls, until the stack of pink telephone slips from Mr. Singh teetered over on my desk. I got McGilp to call to see what the fuss was about. It turned out that this Mr. Singh was not connected with the immigration case at all. He ran a car-impoundment lot, and my car had been there for three weeks. I had not even noticed it was missing.

But now such troubles were over. Wayne picked me up before seven every morning and dropped me at the King Edward Hotel for breakfast. I had breakfast meetings most days. Often, Peter or Chuck would join us. My breakfast guest could be someone from a lobby group, someone I was trying to persuade to undertake some task for the ministry, or someone with special knowledge of some matter that the department was working on. I always had two poached eggs with bacon and toast, a high-cholesterol special.

The breakfast meetings gave me a chance to organize my day, and to catch up on the morning papers in case I needed to do anything as a result of some story in the press. They gave the people I met the chance to pitch me on some idea or other, or to find out privately what I thought about issues of concern to them. The breakfasts were an excellent way of meeting people in a quasi-private setting, away from the fishbowl of my ministerial office. After breakfast, if I had to go somewhere for a meeting, Wayne would be there to take me. If I was just going to the ministry, I walked.

It was quite a transition for me to go from a relatively small and informally run law office to a department that was large, rather staid, and set in its ways. From cases I had argued, I knew many people in the ministry, especially those on the civil side. Those on the criminal side I knew less well, because it had been many years since I had practiced much criminal law. I had appeared in court against ministry lawyers because of my extensive work on behalf of clients opposed to policies of the provincial government.

One woman on the civil-litigation side, for example, had appeared against me on an administrative-law matter before a full panel of the divisional court. Before the judges came in, she had explained that it was her first appearance in the divisional court and she was nervous. She asked me if I had any advice to give her. I pondered the question, turning over sage legal advice in my head. Finally, I said, "If you're nervous, don't keep your water glass so close to your papers."

In another case before the divisional court in which I had opposed the same woman, the only evidence I put before the court was a long affidavit prepared by a lawyer in my office, who claimed, as is the custom, to have knowledge of the matters under consideration. She moved to strike the affidavit on the grounds that it was not proper evidence. In the face of her objection, I told the court that I withdrew my reliance on the document. When the court ruled, however, it was obvious that they had relied for the factual evidence on the disavowed affidavit. Some months later, she appeared before the court on a similar matter, this time opposed by my partner Steve Goudge. This time, she relied on a long affidavit of the kind that I had used earlier. Steve objected. When she cited the divisional court ruling in the previous case, he said, "Oh that's bad law. You can ignore that." She felt she had been whipsawed by the two senior litigators of Cameron, Brewin & Scott.

Another member of the civil-litigation department had represented the government in some of the cases I took on for clients aggrieved by the government of Ontario. In one case, in which the government wanted to seize a fisherman's boat for alleged licensing infractions, this litigator had furnished the court with all the required affidavits supporting the government's position. When he got to court, he found that I had not filed any material, having been only recently retained for the case. My client, the fisherman, was out on his boat on Lake Erie, talking to my office on his ship-to-shore phone. He awaited instructions from me on whether it was safe for him to bring his boat into port.

The first words out of the judge's mouth were "What do you think we should do in this case, Mr. Scott?" I then proceeded to outline my case for an injunction against the government's seizure of the boat, as well as a whole series of other measures. None of my recommendations was backed up by any piece of documentation. The judge accepted most of my recommendations, my client was able to bring his boat into port, and the opposing counsel, now working for me in the ministry, learned that paperwork was not the key element required for winning cases.

The person I knew best on the criminal side of the department was Doug Hunt, whom I had first encountered when I appeared at the Grange Inquiry on behalf of the Hospital for Sick Children and he appeared on behalf of the Crown attorneys. According to him, at the first five meetings I had as minister with the Crowns, I told them the story of my defence of Muggsy Dean, as if to reassure them that

I had actually spent some time in the criminal courts. I am sure that this is an exaggeration.

Whatever my methods of breaking the ice, I needed all the people in the ministry to be onside if I was going to be able to do what I wanted to do within it.

I had weekly lunches with all the assistant deputy ministers for input on what they regarded as the important issues. Once a week, I had brainstorming sessions with the entire policy branch. I was interested in ideas and feedback, whether it came from the most junior member of the department or one of the seniors. It is my understanding that no attorney general before or since has held such sessions.

When David Peterson consulted Bill Davis before the formation of our government, Davis apparently told him that the two most important appointments were the treasurer and the attorney general. Both of these ministries are important in a policy sense, but in terms of the resources they deploy they are relatively minor. Ministries such as Education or Health consume governmental resources on a scale unimaginable within the attorney general's department. Within the latter, for example, more of the budget allocation went to underwriting legal aid, an expenditure of funds over which the department had no direct control, than to the office of the Crown attorneys. People in the department hoped that I could get more money for them, but I had slightly different priorities. I tended to think that there might be better uses for public funds than building more courthouses, for example, a belief that later got me in some trouble with members of the judiciary.

Shortly after we assumed office, I achieved one of my greatest triumphs in terms of getting more money for a cause I believed worthwhile. I met with representatives of LEAF, the Women's Legal and Educational Fund. They wanted funds to be able to represent women's voices in assorted legal and constitutional challenges. The impetus for the group had come from the opposition to the patriation of the Constitution in 1982, when they felt that women's interests had been excluded from the bargaining table. They came to the meeting expecting to be referred to some study group in the department. I agreed on the spot to get them one million dollars. They were shocked and pleased in equal measure.

We met with the department. The bureaucrats wanted to study the issue. I told them that I had already made the decision; their job was to find out how to set up the program so that it would work. This incident sent shock waves through the ministry. Prior to that meeting, the ministry had held the view that everything should be done through its own staff lawyers. The idea of outsourcing to a small, inchoate legal organization with no track record of handling money was then a novel one.

We were able to get the funds for the grant through before the central-funding-granting authorities knew what hit them. We regarded ourselves, in those first days, as the vanguard of a shock troop movement; we figured if we got to Management Board first with demands for money, we would be more likely to be successful. Trace amounts of that seed money still support the work of LEAF, which has done a commendable job of protecting the interests of its constituency. The members of LEAF regard it as one of the best investments I made.

At the same meeting at which I announced funds for LEAF, I also announced that I had decided to withdraw the ministry's objection to Justine Blainey's case for being allowed to play hockey with boys. As I later reflected about this case in an essay on the role of the attorney general:

Very early on in my career as attorney general a young woman who wanted to play on a boys' hockey team said that she believed the section of the Ontario Human Rights Code that prohibited complaints of sex discrimination in sports was unconstitutional and should not bar a complaint she wished to make to the commission. She alleged there had been discrimination in the league's refusal to permit her to try out for the neighbourhood hockey team made up entirely of boys. We reviewed the matter carefully, and we came to the conclusion that she was right and the provision of the Human Rights Code was unconstitutional and in breach of her charter rights. We told her that that was our view, and said that we would ask the legislature to repeal the section. But repealing a section in the legislative process, even one that has to do with sex discrimination, takes a good deal of time. She couldn't wait. She commenced proceedings notwith-standing our undertaking to repeal the offending section. We joined with her in court, and the attorney general of Ontario made the submission that the statute was unconstitutional. The court did not agree; Mr. Justice Steele said that not only was Justine Blainey wrong but, more embarrassing for me, the attorney general of Ontario was wrong — the section was constitutional. Happily, Justine Blainey decided to appeal the case to the Court of Appeal, and we were both vindicated.

I also indicated that I had no problem in general terms with negotiating native land claims on the basis of aboriginal titles. The ministry's position had previously been that there were no legal grounds for upholding such claims against the government of Ontario.

Most public servants grasped quickly that my tenure as attorney general would not be a continuation of the old ways. Some were a bit more difficult to convince. Once, for example, I intercepted at the last moment a factum prepared for an intervention on a constitutional case. The problem with the factum was that it intervened on the wrong side. This incident, however, was very much the exception that proves the rule. Once I set out my expectations, I was well received in the ministry. People were excited to be part of a new direction for the department. Things were happening.

In one unwelcome development, however, I found myself as the defendant in a jury trial. I had acted for a lawyer who faced disciplinary hearings at the Law Society of Upper Canada. I had, with his approval, entered into a plea bargain with the Law Society. Some of the more serious charges he faced were dropped in exchange for his agreement to cease practicing law. After the deal was struck, and he was struck off the rolls of practicing lawyers, he felt that he could have got a better deal. So he sued me. I retained a lawyer to represent me. Then the plaintiff requested a jury trial. This was unusual, but certainly within his rights. The problem was that my lawyer had never done a jury trial.

Although I was confident that I had represented the man competently, and that the deal I had struck was a good one for him, I was nervous. Because it was a jury trial, I had to be in the courtroom for the whole proceedings. I put my ministry briefing books on the floor, and tried to read them unobtrusively while the trial proceeded. The jury found for me, but it was an experience I could have done without.

While this was going on, letters and phone calls poured into my office concerning who would be appointed a Queen's Counsel in the list put out each year over the Christmas and new year period.

In England, where the title of QC originated, there is a major distinction between barristers and solicitors in the legal profession. Barristers are the lawyers who appear in court, and solicitors are the lawyers who look after wills and real estate conveyances, and who retain barristers to look after their clients' interests should the need arise. Within the rank of barristers in England, only a select few become Queen's Counsel. It is a mark of professional distinction that carries with it risks as well as benefits. Queen's Counsels are entitled to wear silk robes with quaint little pockets into which the instructing solicitors slip fees, to be attended by junior counsel, and to charge more for their services. But they have to be good enough at what they do to ensure that clients will retain them at their higher rates. Thus, there is a kind of built-in check on their fitness for holding the title.

In Canada, there is no such sharp dividing line between solicitors and barristers. Consequently, the title of QC had degenerated into a political patronage plaything. People got to be QCs because they supported the right political parties, not because they were superior courtroom lawyers. I did not like the existing practice of appointing QCs, even though I had one myself. Roy McMurtry had also questioned the wisdom of appointing QCs. He had sent Eddie Goodman, the quintessential political lawyer, over to Osgoode Hall to ask how the lawyers would react to a decision not to appoint any more. In particular, he wanted to find out if the lawyers who already had QCs would stop using them on their letterheads and cards. Eddie apparently returned with a blunt message for Roy: "If you do that, they'll sue your ass off."

Roy took the threat seriously, and continued to struggle each fall with the pleas from his caucus colleagues for their friends and supporters to be made QCs. Unfortunately, I only heard this story of his attempt to reform the system many years after I had left politics.

I decided, with Peterson's enthusiastic support, to abolish the title of Queen's Counsel. In so doing, I managed to ruffle a lot of feathers in the legal profession. There were angry protests that I could not reclaim the honours already given out, that retrospective legislation would be unconstitutional, that a refusal to appoint more QCs would set up an artificial distinction between those (like me) who already had them and those who would never get them, thanks to my draconian measure. I paid little attention to most of these protests, but I did listen to John Robinette on the matter. When we were waiting for the judges to come in so we could argue our respective briefs on Bill 30, on full funding for Catholic schools, he said he found it ironic that he had written a letter for me so I could get my QC, and now I was trying to take away his. It was clear that he didn't want his title taken away. And it was doubly clear that he had earned it many times over.

Robinette was a great advocate, and on this occasion he persuaded me that it would be wrong to take QCs away from those who truly merited them. As it would be impossible in practice to separate out different categories of worthiness among people who had QCs, I decided to drop the attempt to take away existing honours.

My solution was to refuse to recommend anyone new for the honour, which, given a long enough time period, would amount to abolition in any event. In recognition of this feat, the Hamilton Bar Association kindly presented me with a vanity license plate that read "AN-EX QC." No subsequent Ontario government has seen fit to bring back the title.

I also took steps to eliminate another long-entrenched area of political patronage. The appointment of judges was part of a patronage system that had remained largely unchanged since the days of Sir John A. Macdonald. When party A was in power, it appointed as judges people who tended to be active party members of long standing. When party B came to power, it filled the bench with party B members or sympathizers. Over time, this system resulted in a bench that was sometimes used as a repository for retiring politicians, or for people who had run for the party, lost, and were looking for their reward for services rendered.

Some of these people were wonderful judges, and some were not. Once they were on the bench, however, it took moral culpability of a staggering nature to get them removed. It almost never happened. As a result, the provincial bench reflected small-town Ontario as it used to be. Judges were middle-aged, mostly white, mostly men. Ontario had changed, but the process of appointing judges had not.

I instituted a new appointments system that had a different focus. Instead of inquiring about party affiliation, I looked for two things: I wanted judges to be appointed on merit, and I wanted them to reflect more accurately the diverse Canadian population. In the new system, anyone who wished to be appointed to the bench had to make a formal application, and had to be recommended by the local bar association. This put a kind of quality-control check on the beginning of the process. Next, hopeful judges had to apply to an appointments committee headed by Peter Russell, whose expertise in judicial and constitutional subjects was universally acknowledged. The people on this committee were selected to represent different communities and viewpoints. The committee itself had a built-in affirmative-action edge; it was eager to have the courts represent the diversity of modern Canadian society. They recommended a short list of candidates to me, and I made my selection from that list. This took old-style politics out of the process. The new appointments system was an important breakthrough. It helped to recruit many women judges, and it helped to make the bench more professional and competent.

Taking stock at year-end, after our first six months in office, I was struck by the ups and downs of fortune. At the beginning of the year,

I had thought it was hopeless to run for election again. I did it in part because I did not want to appear to be yet another person running away from David Peterson. When the election was first called, as my diary clearly shows, I thought I had no chance of winning. When we negotiated the accord that brought us to power, I had obtained the best job that any lawyer could have: being attorney general in an administration that was inclined to give me a free hand with the department. I loved being in the legislature. I loved being in cabinet.

Then, the bottom dropped out of my world.

Kim went to the doctor to see about some swollen lymph glands in his neck and throat. He was tested for HIV as a routine precaution. He tested positive. It was devastating. I rushed off to be tested. I was negative.

AIDS had been recognized as a disease only a short time earlier. Not much was known about it, except that it was fatal. To this day, I have no idea of how Kim was infected. Given the sexual lives that we, and many other gay men, had led, it was almost pure chance that determined whether one was lucky or unlucky with respect to exposure to HIV.

Kim was so young to be so afflicted. He was doing his bar admission course at the time of his diagnosis. He wasn't out of the closet. His father didn't know he was homosexual, and it didn't seem right to break the news to him about the medical complications. We decided to keep very quiet about it. I thought about resigning, but Kim persuaded me not to.

It was unclear how much good time he would have before fully developed AIDS would appear. Every little cold became a worry. Nothing would ever be the same again.

SEVEN

First-Term
Challenges

WHEN THE NEW LIBERAL CABINET was sworn in in 1985, the members shared a distinctive feature: none of us had been in government before. You would probably have to go back to the United Farmers of Ontario government in the early 1920s to find such a lack of government experience. We did, however, have one advantage over that government, and indeed over the NDP government that replaced ours in 1990: we had a two-month gap between the election and our assumption of office. David Peterson used this time to prepare by setting up a transition team that made a number of recommendations about how we should govern. Those recommendations set the stage for the entire government.

All premiers or prime ministers in a parliamentary system have to decide whether to have a centralized or a decentralized decision-making system. The transition team looked at this question and came down on the side of decentralized. I was happy about this. In my mind, the differences between the two approaches could clearly be seen in a comparison of the governing structures of the Pearson and Trudeau governments.

It's hard to remember now, but Pearson went through minority governments and all the rest of it, yet when it came to policy-making his government was enormously progressive and imaginative. A lot of people might have thought that Pearson wasn't up to the job, but when you consider the things his government did, from the flag and health insurance to pensions, it's clear just how productive a period it was. The Trudeau period, I believe, was not as productive. True, it was more charismatic; Trudeau outdistanced the more bumbling Pearson in the headlines and newsreels. But Trudeau's achievements, in my opinion, pale in comparison to Pearson's. And they had two different systems of government.

The Pearson model permitted a decentralized system as long as it was safe to do so. The theory was that you had real ministers who had real initiating capacity. Now, they had to take their proposals to cabinet, but they were expected to initiate change. A Pearson minister was supposed to go back to his office and develop some ideas. The Trudeau system — and Davis was a follower of that system — was quite different. I'm exaggerating slightly, but in effect no one was supposed to initiate an idea until it had been approved by some central agency, either the Prime Minister's Office or the Privy Council Office. The same kind of thing happened in the Davis regime with Ed Stewart in control. No minister would bother to expend the time and energy necessary to work out a proposal if he hadn't run it by Stewart first.

The decentralized Pearson model left its legacy. You can remember the names of ministers in his cabinet: Robert Winters, Walter Gordon, Judy LaMarsh, and Eric Kierans. You can identify who the people were and what they stood for. It's much tougher to remember the individuals in a Trudeau cabinet. I think this caused friction between John Turner and Trudeau. Turner had come out of the Pearson years and, by that stage, was the only person of real seniority who remained in the Liberal cabinet following Trudeau's election. He found the Trudeau regime foreign: it didn't account for him as an individual or as finance minister.

Peterson, having adopted the Pearson model, assembled around him a group of ministers who were expected to initiate ideas even if he didn't like them. He wanted debate. He did control the debate, but he took his ministers' ideas seriously.

Once, early in our term of office, when I was bringing something to cabinet for debate, I was told by the bureaucratic central office, "Minister, we don't think that matter is ready for cabinet yet, and we don't want it to come to cabinet this week, so we're taking it off the list." I put up a fight. "You can't take it off the list," I said. "The only people who can take it off the list are the premier and me. This is our cabinet, not yours." A horrendous fight with the bureaucrats ensued. They said, "Oh well, no, the central bureaucracy always decides what's ready for decision-making and what's not." I told them, "Well, that's not the way I intend to behave in this government. If I want to put a proposal before my cabinet colleagues, I'm going to put it before them, and if they don't like it, or if the premier doesn't like it, it can be rejected. But I'm not going to be deprived of the opportunity to make my case."

I won the issue, and I won it in Peterson's office. He said that we did have the right to bring proposals to the cabinet without prior approval. It didn't mean those proposals would get through cabinet, but we had the right to argue about them. As a result, Peterson had a core of ministers who were an aggressive and an important influence on him. And you can name them: Sean Conway, Bob Nixon, Elinor Caplan, Murray Elston, and me, for example. Things weren't done that way in the Davis government, or the Rae government, and they're certainly not done that way in the Harris government. And I wouldn't have wanted to serve in any other kind of government. I hadn't got into politics to say, "What do we do now?"

One of Peterson's best qualities as leader of the government was that he was open to listening to a variety of views. He believed in the virtues of an open government, and was comfortable reaching out to people to find out their thoughts on the issues of the day. He was not overly concerned with the proprieties of departmental pecking orders: he wanted the best possible information on which to base decisions.

Our initial cabinet meetings were full of discussion. Most of us so-called powerful ministers in this decentralized government took a pretty broad view of our responsibilities, and we didn't censor ourselves. I had lots of ideas about issues that had little, if anything, to do with my mandate as attorney general. For example, I had a ton of ideas about housing. And I was not shy, as many of my colleagues could tell you, about expressing them. In fact, Alvin Curling, and later Chaviva Hosek, got sick of hearing from me on the subject. Sometimes my ideas made a difference; often, they were ignored. But they were always listened to, and it was understood that I was not expected to confine my interests to my own department. Some of my colleagues would say that they faced more effective cross-examination on new policy initiatives from me in cabinet than they did from the opposition when they brought the legislation into the house.

As cabinet members, individually and collectively, we thought that we would make better decisions if the public had an opportunity to make informed representations to us. So we funded all kinds of groups — some of which ended up giving us a hard time — on the theory that truth emerges best from the competition of ideas. Our informal motto was "a government without walls or barriers, open to the people." To this end, we brought people together for consultation before we made major policy decisions.

Because the caucus was so small, and we were, after all, in a minority position in the legislature, a small group of ministers formed an informal "inner cabinet." This group usually met every five or six weeks or so at a downtown steakhouse, like George Bigliardi's, to discuss upcoming issues and decisions. In such a small, informal setting, we were able to get through a large number of issues in a relatively short time. The group who met most frequently included Peterson, Bob Nixon, Sean Conway, Murray Elston, and me, as well as any other ministers who might be most affected by the policy decisions taken. It was a highly effective means of coordinating policy and of reaching agreement without involving the whole panoply of cabinet and cabinet officials. After the big election victory in 1987, however, this practice of inner cabinet meetings ceased absolutely. This was a mistake.

When we started to govern, we faced an unusual situation. On the surface, we appeared to be a very weak minority government. The Tories had more members than we did. Our salvation was that both opposition parties knew that public opinion since the election had moved strongly in our favour; the public now believed that we should be given a chance to govern. We also had the accord, designed to last for two years, as a relative guarantee of NDP support. An advantage of the accord was that our legislative agenda was tightly focused. A disadvantage was that the details or content of any bill based on the accord had to be worked out from scratch. This made for some lively debates in cabinet.

Seven big issues had to be settled in our first term in office: the Darlington nuclear-power plant, the banning of extra billing by the province's doctors, the extension of full funding to Catholic schools, abortion and abortion clinics, pay equity, aboriginal rights, and the Meech Lake Accord.

Darlington presented a huge problem. Ontario Hydro had already spent a considerable sum on the facility. If we cancelled it, all the money would all be lost. In addition, there would be a lot of ancillary closing costs. At the end of the day, we would have nothing but red ink to show for it. We were also acutely aware of the jobs that depended on the construction of the plant and on Hydro's nuclear division. Environmental concerns were forcefully raised, but we were assured that there was no need for worry.

Such are the economics of the nuclear power–plant business that estimates of how much Hydro had already committed to Darlington ranged from $2 to $4 billion. We were assured that it would take "only" another $4 billion to complete the plant, and that it would ensure a supply of electricity into the foreseeable future. We decided to authorize completion. This was undoubtedly the worst decision the government ever made.

Darlington ended up costing some $15 billion, not including the decommissioning costs, which lie somewhere down the line. The annual interest costs alone on the money borrowed to finance its construction probably total more than all the money invested by the province in the SkyDome, a project often cited as the most extravagant public spending of the prosperous eighties. Yet, at the time, the opposition parties applauded our decision to complete Darlington.

The Darlington decision typifies the problems in exerting control over a large, entrenched bureaucratic organization. It is by no means clear that the information the utility provides is complete. This is one of the reasons that, while I was attorney general, I drafted the Freedom of Information Act to include Ontario Hydro in its ambit, and why the Harris government's recent decision to exempt Hydro's successor corporations from the Freedom of Information Act is a mistake.

The problem of "extra billing" also consumed a lot of energy. We were committed to banning the practice whereby doctors could charge patients fees in excess of what the provincial health insurance plan would cover. The doctors, not surprisingly, were determined to keep it. From the time of our election, therefore, we were on a collision course with the Ontario Medical Association, the professional organization of Ontario's doctors. Negotiations broke down. The doctors went on strike. There had been an earlier doctors' strike in Saskatchewan, when the CCF government first introduced medicare in Canada, but it was thought unlikely that Ontario's doctors would ever strike. Traditionally, the Tory governments maintained a cosy relationship with the doctors; the Robarts government had even attempted to keep Ontario out of the first national medicare plan.

As a left-leaning member of the Liberal party, I regarded the commitment to abolish extra billing as a basic ingredient of my kind of Liberalism. I saw extra billing as a first step toward an American-style health system, with one system for the rich and insured, and another, much less adequate, for the poor and those without medical insurance. Indeed, in the period between my defeat in 1981 and my decision to run again in 1985, I had determined I would leave the party if it did not adopt a policy banning extra billing.

I had nothing against doctors, *per se*. In my previous existence as a lawyer, I worked on a whole series of disciplinary matters for the College of Physicians and Surgeons, and I had represented the college in many disciplinary hearings. In fact, it had retained me to suggest a new structure for such hearings. I recommended that the investigative and judicial functions be separated, a recommendation the college ultimately accepted. My experience meant that I knew many of the officials of the college. This did not, however, render me particularly sympathetic to the demands of the OMA.

While the strike was on, a small group of ministers and advisers met each morning in the premier's office to discuss strategy for the day. Murray Elston, the minister of health, was there, as was Hershell Ezrin, Peterson's chief of staff. Bob Nixon showed up occasionally, and I tried to be there every day. We had to make decisions about how to deploy resources to ensure that basic emergency facilities were available to the public. It was exhilarating.

A certain number of doctors thought that no government in Ontario could take them on and win. They were wrong. I think that the leaders of the OMA made two basic miscalculations. First, they thought that the public had a basic sympathy for doctors, and that public opinion would be on their side. But the public perception of doctors had shifted, from the kind of small-town reverence expressed in Norman Rockwell's *Saturday Evening Post* covers, to one that saw doctors fighting to protect a position of economic privilege. Second, the doctors seriously underestimated our determination as a government not to yield on a point of principle.

Feelings ran high in the dispute. Some doctors, notably Michael Rachlis and Philip Berger, supported our position. The latter's statements opposing the OMA's position provoked some phone calls, one of which came to Berger's office from David Peterson. Dr. Berger's secretary took the call, asked who was calling, got the response "David Peterson," and then said that she couldn't put the call through because Dr. Berger was seeing patients.

"Well, then," asked Peterson, "could you have him call me when he's free?"

She replied, "I don't know who you are. Are you a patient of Dr. Berger's?"

Long pause, then: "I'm David Peterson. I'm the premier of the province. Please have Dr. Berger call me when he's free."

Dr. Berger made an appointment to see me at my constituency office on Parliament Street about some other phone calls he had received. He was quite alarmed when he came into the office. He said that he had been getting death threats on his home phone line, an unlisted number. My response to his revelation surprised him: I just laughed and said, "Oh that's nothing. I get those all the time. Don't think anything of it." The advice was a bit cavalier, but it was true that once you were involved in politics, you were a target for all kinds of disaffected people. You just had to accept that as one of the prices for your involvement.

The doctors' strike was a huge test of the government, and we passed it. We faced the doctors down, and we won a new deal. There would be no extra billing for doctors in Ontario. In the process, we undoubtedly antagonized a lot of doctors, but we did what we thought was right, and we held firm in the face of their opposition.

The third big public issue we faced was the extension of full funding to Catholic schools. This question had long hung over Ontario politics. It was also an issue with historic resonance for me. My great-grandfather, Sir Richard Scott, had brought in the legislation that established the nature of religious schools in Canada. His solution to the vexing question of religion and language in Upper and Lower Canada was to hive off the question of religion from that of language of instruction. Hence, he proposed a system for Protestant schools in Quebec, and Catholic schools in Ontario, with local ratepayers allocating the education portion of their local taxes to support the school system of their choice. At the time, the Protestants in Quebec, of course, were almost all anglophones. The Catholics of Ontario, however, were just as likely to be of Irish as of French-Canadian origin.

Sir Richard's principle was incorporated into the British North America Act of 1867. The difficulty in later generations was that the principle applied only to primary education. At the time of the BNA Act, most secondary schools were private, fee-paying institutions. My grandfather, W.L. Scott, had in the 1930s failed to win a number of court challenges to extend the tax base available to separate schools. In Ontario, a test case on extending funding to separate high schools, *Tiny Township*, had gone to the Judicial Committee of the Privy Council in 1920. That august body had decided that separate schools could only be funded up to Grade 10, the end of free public education at the time of the passage of the BNA Act.

The confessional nature of the separate Catholic schools made them a subject of hot political debate in a number of Ontario provincial elections. As previously noted, for example, they had been a big issue in the 1971 election, when the Tories opposed full funding and won. This issue didn't come up on the Tory agenda again until Bill Davis's surprise announcements in 1984 that he was getting out of politics and that he would bring in a full-funding bill.

I had lunch with Davis after my stroke. He told me a story about an audience he and his wife had with the Pope. They had been informed when they went in that audiences usually lasted for ten or fifteen minutes. Fifteen minutes passed; Davis could hear the sounds of officials scurrying around in the background. He got nervous, not knowing whether he should end the audience, or wait for some signal from the Pope. While he was pondering what to do, the Pontiff suddenly leaned forward and asked, "You're not really going to close the Catholic hospital in Sarnia, are you?" Davis, stunned, was still contemplating his reply when the Pope added, "And what about full funding for Catholic schools?"

Davis never told me whether the Pope's questions influenced his decision. More likely, Emmett Cardinal Carter's annual entreaties at banquets played a role. Either way, there is little doubt that his promise caused major repercussions.

For one thing, the details of the bill had to be worked out. For another, the promise of aid to the separate-school system touched off a pent-up demand for aid for other private schools, both confessional and non-confessional. As the election campaign had demonstrated, the issue still carried nasty overtones, with echoes of former Orange anti-Catholic crusades, and Anglican Archbishop Lewis Garnsworthy's comparison of Davis to Hitler. That the separate-school system had existed for more than a century at that point did not seem to make much difference to the opponents of the scheme. We had to draft a bill that would meet the needs of the school systems and withstand a charter challenge.

In our first months in office, we convened a series of meetings to find out what the public thought about full funding. As usual, there was not one public, but several, all with differing opinions on what should be done. The bill to fully fund Catholic separate schools was drafted, passed, and immediately referred to the Ontario Court of Appeal for a ruling on its constitutionality. As attorney general, I argued the case before the Ontario Court of Appeal, and then before the Supreme Court of Canada. It was the only case I argued as attorney general, and I had to think long and hard before I did so. I did not want to be seen as grandstanding on a hot political issue. I also did not want to sit on the sidelines on an issue that had involved my family for more than a century.

In my office, I had two pictures. One was of Sir Richard Scott, my great-grandfather who had brokered the separate-school funding deal in the first place. The other was of Oliver Mowat, premier and attorney general of Ontario, who had argued many of the most important cases in Canadian constitutional history while he was in office. As I prepared to argue the case, I felt in some ways that I represented both of my distinguished predecessors.

Many accomplished counsel were retained to represent the various interests in the case. John Robinette was one. In the thirties, he and my old mentor Andrew Brewin had appeared as junior counsel in a case that my grandfather W.L. Scott took to the Supreme Court of Canada. W.L. had for many years been a legal partner of Mr. J.S. Ewart, who had in his lifetime articled with Sir John A. Macdonald in Kingston, been Oliver Mowat's partner in Toronto, and worked with Macdonald's son in Winnipeg. For me, the case represented the culmination of my family's contribution to Canadian constitutional law.

The case would not be won, however, by invoking names from the past. It required careful research, in which I was immeasurably aided by Ian McGilp. The arguments had to be shaped into a coherent story for the judges.

On January 29, 1987, in the coffee shop of the Supreme Court of Canada, I borrowed Pat Monahan's copy of the *Consolidated Constitution Acts, 1867–1982*. On the back of the copy, I sketched out my oral argument. This is what I wrote, in its entirety:

Process — Amending the Constitution
Formalistic Arg.
    s. 53 is not a head of power
    s. 29 guarantee — doesn't analyze the purpose
1. Revolutionary Result
    1. completing a system
    2. every prov. remake Const. Educ. System
        amend the Constitution
        funding for grades 10–13 in non-denom schools
Pentecostals

From these somewhat cryptic notes, I made my argument. When James McPherson, a former dean of Osgoode Hall Law School, was invested as a member of the Ontario Court of Appeal, he was kind enough to mention my argument on the full-funding act as the finest courtroom performance he had ever seen. In their decision, the Supreme Court of Canada decided that the bill was constitutional.

I was elated. I was no longer a practicing Catholic, nor a believer, in any of the accepted senses, of the teachings of the Christian church. But I thought that there were elementary issues of fairness involved in the case, and I was happy that the court agreed with my analysis.

The Catholic Church also figured in the fourth big issue our government had to contend with in our first term of office: abortion and what to do about the abortion clinics operated by Dr. Henry Morgentaler and associates.

Abortion was clearly outlawed in the Criminal Code, which was a federal responsibility. Just as clearly, juries were refusing to convict Dr. Morgentaler, in spite of evidence that he was performing abortions.

There was little I could do about changing the laws on abortion, as it was a federal statute, part of the Criminal Code. In the United States, the Supreme Court decision in *Roe* v. *Wade* had made abortion a private issue between a woman and her doctor, unless she was in the last trimester of her pregnancy. Canadian groups advocating freedom of choice for women often invoked *Roe* v. *Wade* as the appropriate model for Canada. Anti-abortion groups were equally adamant that the American jurisprudence would not be imported into Canada.

The public was badly split on the issue. Women's groups, for the most part, supported the right of women to have an abortion when the health of the mother, including her emotional health, was at stake. Anti-choice groups, including the Catholic Church in which I was raised, opposed abortions, and painted Dr. Morgentaler as a kind of murderer.

All kinds of demonstrations were directed against Morgentaler's clinic, which was eventually firebombed. People on both sides of the issue were angry. In my first few weeks in government, a group of women invaded my office, demanding a halt to prosecutions of Dr. Morgentaler. As if to balance them, Ken Campbell, an anti-abortion crusader, once tried to perform a citizen's arrest on me in my office for failing to prosecute Dr. Morgentaler more vigorously. As for the doctor himself, I used to see him working out at the YMCA from time to time, but I was not otherwise acquainted with him.

The stark legal dilemma that Morgentaler posed was that juries refused to convict him, and disregarded judges' instructions that the doctor's defence of "necessity" was not available to him. The case eventually proceeded to the Supreme Court of Canada.

While we awaited the judgment of the Supreme Court, violent demonstrations took place outside Morgentaler's clinic. The police chief of Toronto, Jack Marks, came to see me to say that Morgentaler should be charged again, to stop him from performing abortions while we waited for the Supreme Court decision. He was tired of having to put policemen on the line between the pro-choice and anti-abortion forces.

I was alarmed at his request. I did not want to give in to the pressure tactics of the anti-abortion groups. On the other hand, I did not want it to appear that I endorsed the deliberate challenge to the law made by Dr. Morgentaler. I went to see David Peterson to explain my dilemma. From his comments, it was obvious that Chief Marks had been in touch with him as well. I told him that if it were decided to proceed with more prosecutions of Dr. Morgentaler, then I would certainly have to think about resigning as minister responsible for women's issues.

David, to his credit, said he would support whatever decision I made. All he asked of me was that I inform John Sweeney, the minister of community services and a strong pro-life advocate, what my decision was. After a somewhat tumultuous meeting with policy advisers in the ministry, I decided that the correct course of action was to allow the police to prefer charges against Dr. Morgentaler, and then to have those charges stayed, pending the decision of the Supreme Court.

The charges were laid and stayed, and Dr. Morgentaler continued to perform abortions. Anti-abortion groups then took out their anger on me by picketing my house. My neighbours were even less amused by this than I was.

As I explained in a paper written at the time:

Before laying the charges, the police consulted the attorney general and his agents, and were advised that any charges laid would, in the circumstances, be stayed. Notwithstanding this advice, the police concluded that it was their duty and responsibility to lay charges that they believed on reasonable and probable grounds were warranted. The attorney general, while acknowledging the role of the police that entitled them to take this action, did what he believed the administration of justice required. To some observers, it may have appeared that the right hand did not know what the left hand was doing. In my view, that difficulty does not offset the importance of the principle of separation.

Eventually, the Supreme Court struck down the provisions in the Criminal Code regarding abortions, and those provisions have never been reinstated.

The fifth big issue from our first term was pay equity. This was one of the items in the accord. I was minister responsible for women's issues, so I had primary responsibility for designing a pay equity policy.

The Women's Directorate had been created in the last years of the Davis government. It combined the section of the Labour ministry responsible for monitoring the working conditions of women in the government, and a policy unit charged with developing new policies for matters of concern to women. Glenna Carr was the first deputy minister of the Women's Directorate. She had decided to move on. A public-service competition was held to fill her job. The board conducting the interviews could not decide between two excellent candidates, and they decided that I should make the final choice. I knew one of the candidates, Elaine Todres, who was the director of policy research at the directorate. The other candidate, Naomi Alboim, worked for the federal government in Toronto. I was going out of town that evening, and I had only one hour available that afternoon to interview Naomi.

She was at work dressed in her casual clothes, complete with Birkenstock sandals. She did not want to be interviewed before she had a chance to change into something more formal. The officials arranging the interview assured her that I would not care what she wore. So she came to the interview in her casual clothes. I rather ruined the impression that I didn't care what she wore by pointing to her sandals and asking her if she was indeed wearing Birkenstocks. Then I laughed.

It was not the last laugh I would have with Naomi. I told her at the interview that she was qualified for the top job, but that I was leaning to giving it to Elaine because she had been working on the Green Paper on pay equity. I also told her that if she would start by taking Elaine's old job as director of policy, I could guarantee that she would have the top job within a year, as I was sure that Elaine would be moving on to another ministry. She accepted, and Elaine did move to another department after the pay-equity bill was drafted. Both Elaine and Naomi later served with distinction as deputy ministers in a number of other ministries through the Rae and into the Harris government. I was lucky to have them work for me. My work at the Women's Directorate occupied only a small portion of my ministerial time, but I probably had more fun there than in any of the other portfolios I held in government.

One advantage of being minister responsible for women's issues was that it put me in touch with many of the provincial premiers. In the smaller provinces, premiers like Joe Ghiz, Richard Hatfield, and Frank McKenna tended to have the women's portfolio. The position thus helped me establish good connections with people with whom I would deal on Meech Lake and other matters. There is no doubt that the conferences on women's issues were much more fun than most federal-provincial conferences: I was great friends with the federal minister of women's issues, Barbara McDougall, from our university days, and we tended to have a convivial time at conferences.

The Women's Directorate existed because women as a group had been systematically discriminated against, if one judged by earnings potential and workplace experience. All kinds of glass ceilings within and without the public service showed the results of past discrimination. Some of the discrepancy in earning power reflected the fact that most women with families did not spend as much time in the workforce as most men. Some represented outright discrimination: historically, professions like nursing, which were dominated by women, paid less than other medical professions where most of the members were male.

Opinions differed on how to rectify the situation. Groups like the National Action Committee on the Status of Women had a very different perspective from REAL Women, for example. Some women's groups argued for better child-care programs, while others argued for tax breaks for stay-at-home moms.

Deciding how to respond to these competing claims was a problem. Within the Women's Directorate, we worked on getting the government's act together first. We set about implementing a number of reforms that cut across other government departments. One of the key issues was equal pay for work of equal value. There were all kinds of pink-collar, low-wage ghettoes in the provincial government workforce. I thought that this was unfair, as well as short-sighted. We released a Green Paper on pay equity in November 1985. In that paper we canvassed the reasons that women were still being paid significantly less than men, even when factors like education and full- or part-time employment were taken into account.

We convened a number of public hearings on the question of how to implement pay equity. The business community feared the whole notion. My cabinet colleagues were uneasy about what pay equity meant. The Women's Directorate was split about whether we should attempt to bring in employment equity instead of pay equity.

I embarked on a speaking tour, talking to women's groups, chambers of commerce, Rotary Clubs, and the like, trying to make sure that what we meant by pay equity was clearly understood by the people who would be most affected by our decision to support it. As I explained to one such group:

> Just what does the Green Paper on pay equity say?
>
> First, the definition of pay equity chosen for the Green Paper is that, excluding non-gender-related factors which influence pay, work performed by women which is equivalent in value to that performed by men in the same establishment is to be paid the same.
>
> Possibilities covered by "non-gender-related factors" include seniority, performance rating systems, and labour market conditions. But once such factors have been taken into account, it is the value of the work, not the gender of the worker, that counts.

I sent a memo to my caucus and cabinet colleagues, explaining to them what I was doing to promote understanding of pay equity, and asking them to consult with me before they embarked on attempts to explain it to their particular constituencies or audiences. In it, I began with the crass political observation that "52 percent of the Ontario voting population is made up of women. A majority work. They are a natural constituency for us." I then outlined some of the fears of the business community, and set out some points that caucus members could use in discussions with their constituents. One of these was the following:

> Equal pay for work of equal value is simply an extension of equal pay for equal work, which has been the law of Ontario since 1951. It has already been implemented in the private sector federally and in Quebec as well as in some European jurisdictions. Nobody is dying there. We intend to learn from those experiences.

I found it difficult, however, to explain to my cabinet colleagues what pay equity would mean in practice. I felt that the concept of employment equity, which looked beyond pay to a whole series of factors difficult to quantify, was just too hard to sell. After a number of discussions within cabinet, Peterson told me that he trusted me to devise a bill that would satisfy the interests of women's groups while not scaring the business community out of its tree.

I set aside a weekend to do this. Elaine and Naomi joined me, as well as Chuck Birchall and assorted experts in legislative drafting and translation. At a series of meetings, we hashed out the details. I disappointed some of my staff by opting for pay equity instead of employment equity. On Sunday afternoon, I brought in some food and drink for the assembled crew and we finished bashing out the draft bill. I did some of the drafting myself, an unusually hands-on move for a minister.

When we finished the content, we had to assemble it for distribution in both French and English versions, together with the requisite press releases and synopses that accompany such bills. This required a lot of paper. To our horror, we discovered that there was not enough white paper to print all that needed to be printed. It was Sunday. The stores were all closed. The only colour of paper in stock in sufficient quantity to print all the documents was pink. So the pay equity legislation came out on pink paper.

Drafting the bill was challenging. Greater challenges awaited its implementation. The difficulty lay in amending existing statutes, regulations, and union contracts, and changing long-standing practices in workplaces, in ways that would bring about the desired changes without inducing paralysis. I was reminded of the difficulties inherent in the government's commitment to bring all existing statutes into conformity with the Charter of Rights and Freedoms and the Ontario Human Rights Code. To amend all the legislation, the government created an Omnibus Equality Bill. As introduced, it amended no fewer than fifty-eight statutes. More were added over the course of the process.

The Pay Equity Act enshrined the principles of equal pay for work of equal value in the statutes of Ontario. By the time the act was proclaimed, I was no longer minister responsible for women's issues, as it was thought that responsibility for the implementation stage more properly belonged in the Ministry of Labour. The portfolio was transferred to Greg Sorbara, minister of labour.

The sixth and seventh issues we had to deal with, the conferences on aboriginal rights and Meech Lake, both involved constitutional change. They both proved to be more intractable than any of the five issues set out above, absorbing endless amounts of energy without showing any concrete results.

One of the reasons that bureaucracies are conservative is that they have to operate through many different regimes, and serve ministers with widely differing policy agendas. One of the reasons that politicians are impatient is that they are aware that they may not be around for very long. It is also true that in Canada politicians are often tempted to make an indelible mark on the body politic by arranging for a new constitutional deal. Successive generations of provincial and federal politicians are drawn to this goal like moths to a flame, and like many moths many politicians end up getting singed.

For many years in Canadian politics, the Ontario government had played a balancing role in constitutional affairs, with something of a smug assurance that what was good for Ontario would be good for Canada, and vice versa.

Ontario had played a key role in the political and constitutional conferences leading up to the patriation of the Canadian constitution in 1982. In the *Reference Case on the Constitution, 1981*, the Supreme Court of Canada had made an unusual ruling. The federal government wanted to be able to make a unilateral request to the British Parliament to amend the Constitution. This kind of request had been granted on several previous instances, and expectations were that the federal government, whose case was argued by John Robinette, would win.

Things would not be so easy this time. The Supreme Court, in a judgment written by the chief justice, Brian Dickson, stated that although on a strict reading of the Constitution the federal government had the right to request such an amendment, political conventions of the day suggested that the government should attempt once more to enlist the support of the provinces before going to Westminster with such a request.

The ruling is reputed to have infuriated Pierre Trudeau, who thought that the court was well outside its jurisdiction in ruling on political conventions instead of black-letter law. Whatever Trudeau's private opinion, the Supreme Court ruling touched off another round of constitutional negotiations. As it got underway, it was clear that Bill Davis and New Brunswick's Richard Hatfield were the only provincial premiers who supported Trudeau's position in the initial bargaining. Ranged against them were all the other provinces, with Quebec a rather improbable bedmate of the other provinces in the so-called Gang of Eight.

The deadlock was broken in the famous meeting in the kitchen between Jean Chrétien, then federal minister of justice; Roy McMurtry, the attorney general of Ontario; and Roy Romanow, the attorney general of Saskatchewan. The Gang of Eight disintegrated, leaving Quebec a disgruntled outsider. The Constitution was patriated.

The document was a curious kind of political compromise. There was a Charter of Rights and Freedoms, but it was hedged with provisions that rights could be overrun in certain situations. The provinces were also given the right to use a "notwithstanding clause" to take designated provincial legislation out of the provisions of the charter for five years. Echoes of Mackenzie King's "Not necessarily conscription, but conscription if necessary" seemed to linger in the very idea of a notwithstanding clause — "Not necessarily rights, but rights if necessary." The notwithstanding clause was inserted at the request of the NDP government in Saskatchewan, and Saskatchewan, under a later Conservative government, became the first province to invoke it, in order to remove its Essential Services Act from the ambit of the charter.

The document also contained a promise to work out the details of native land claims and rights by holding a constitutional conference on these issues within five years of the adoption of the charter.

Before the Supreme Court's ruling, participation by interest groups in constitutional discussions had been limited to giving papers to assorted royal commissions examining the question of "Whither Canada?" The process set in motion by the ruling raised expectations of many groups with constitutional agendas. Two groups in particular were energized by the constitutional discussions: native groups and groups espousing the rights of women. As the minister responsible for women's issues and for native matters for the government of Ontario, I had to deal with the increased expectations on at least two levels.

The first level was the mundane one of finding a better way to deliver government services to the affected populations. The second level was to reshape the constitution to reflect their concerns. The first task was manageable, as the saga of the Pay Equity Act demonstrates. The second task, almost by definition, was something that could be accomplished only in short, sharp bursts of negotiation with other governments, followed by months of often rueful attempts to put the intended results of those negotiations into constitutionally acceptable language.

From the time our government was formed in 1985, it was clear that the constitutional expectations of women's groups and native groups would be an ongoing concern. It was also clear that a kind of constitutional conference fatigue had set in. Certain constants inevitably arose in the process. For example, whatever the government in Quebec, separatist or federalist, it pressured the federal government for constitutional change. The separatists always wanted to show that the existing system could not work, while the federalists always wanted to show that they were capable of delivering the constitutional goods through co-operation. Hence, any Quebec government was reluctant to discuss other constitutional issues until the Quebec ones got settled. In the West, most of the governments still resented the way that the federal government had handled mineral rights at the turn of the twentieth century, and they saw Trudeau's National Energy Policy as an unfair transfer of wealth and resources from the West to the East. Each region of the country had its own particular axe to grind and, until that axe was honed to the requisite degree of sharpness, was not particularly inclined to be helpful on any other issue.

Nothing illustrated this collective attitude more clearly than the constitutional conference on aboriginal rights mandated in the 1982 amendments to the Constitution.

Federal and provincial governments continued the ongoing discussions on how best to conduct the conference. Two huge obstacles stood in our way. First, the Quebec government refused to talk about aboriginal rights until its own constitutional demands were met. Second, the western provinces did not want anything to do with native self-government of any of their territories; self-government, on the other hand, was something that all the native groups thought should be the minimum starting point for the negotiations.

The whole process was delicate. Within the government of Ontario, there was little infrastructure for dealing with native issues, as they were clearly a federal responsibility under the terms of the Constitution Act, 1867. At my first briefing within the ministry on the matter, it was stated categorically that, in the opinion of the ministry, no legal obligations arose from the assorted treaties that had been entered into with native bands in Ontario. The prevailing view within the ministry was that these were friendship-only treaties, devoid of any real content.

We had, then, to build up in-house expertise on native issues. We also had to develop a policy to take to the constitutional conference scheduled for February 1987. In this, the Ministry of Intergovernmental Affairs helped immeasurably. Over time, we co-operated closely with them to produce a proposal to take to the conference.

At the same time, we set about negotiating land claims within the department. The most pressing of these was in Temagami in northern Ontario, where a hold had been placed by the courts on all land transfers within an area claimed by the aboriginal people there. In an effort to resolve the dispute, I would meet from time to time with the native leaders on their home territory, a practice I had first encountered in the days of the Berger Commission. Sometimes we sat in a meeting place for more than an hour before anyone said anything. I was the guest, and so it would have been rude for me to say anything until I was invited to speak. My experience with Mr. Justice Berger was invaluable here. He taught me a lot about respecting the customs of the groups I met with. Keeping silent for an hour was not, as many could testify, my natural state.

We pursued several different strategies, then, to meet the real needs of Ontario's aboriginal communities. While the individual negotiations went on, we also tried to work on a proposal for the constitutional conference on aboriginal rights that had been promised in 1982. As I studied the matter more, I came to believe that some form of native self-government was the answer. The problem was developing a strategy for achieving self-government in the face of both considerable skepticism on the part of many provincial governments, and the absence of Quebec from the bargaining table.

Native self-government stepped on sensitive toes in Quebec City and Ottawa, and was anathema to the western provinces. Even native organizations were suspicious of it. But I was convinced it was the right policy. How could you ensure self-reliant and self-confident aboriginal groups without granting them the right to make mistakes just like the rest of government?

Eventually, Ontario did present a formal and complicated proposal to the constitutional reform meeting. It set out native self-government as the end goal of the proceedings, but recognized that the meaning of self-government would have to be negotiated in several stages.

In the end, only the federal government, Manitoba, and Nova Scotia supported our proposal. The four native organizations did not. Had we been able to draw seven of the ten provinces, I think they might have gone for it, for the consent of seven of the ten provinces was needed to amend the Constitution. The proposal constitutionalized an inherent right to self-government, but required a period of negotiation during which the terms of self-government would be worked out before being constitutionalized. But the native organizations didn't think that went far enough.

In some ways, the most useful part of the whole exercise was that it contributed to building the sophistication and bargaining skills of the native organizations. On the whole, they didn't have the stability and the resources to make tough choices. To be effective as a politician you have to be able to say no to your constituency without worrying that your organization will self-destruct.

The worst part of the process was that natives linked the failure of the conference on aboriginal issues with the success of the first two rounds of Meech Lake. The native people were embittered when they compared their failed proposals to the success of Quebec's. And that bitterness, of course, surfaced during the third round of Meech negotiations, contributing, in some measure, to its defeat. Thus, the attempt to reach an agreement at Meech Lake must be seen in the context of both the earlier difficulties in reaching agreement on aboriginal issues and the recognition that if too many topics were on the table all at once, nothing would be accomplished.

At a first ministers' meeting in Edmonton in 1986, the premiers and prime minister decided that it would be impossible to get agreement on a wholesale constitutional change that would address the needs of native organizations and other groups, like women. Instead, it was decided that the federal and provincial governments should attempt to reach consensus on how to meet the constitutional needs of Quebec. This decision, it must be recalled, was made in the aftermath of the defeat of the PQ government and the return to power of Robert Bourassa, a wily crypto-federalist, or crypto–Quebec nationalist, depending on which way the wind blew at the time.

The Quebec government presented a list of five points that were its requirements for going back to the constitutional table. Various discussions were held over the next eight months about Quebec's list, but not much progress was made. Officials from Ottawa, Queen's Park, and Quebec City met informally to see if we could work out a united front for the Meech Lake negotiations to come. I took a number of people with me to Quebec City the week before the negotiations began for consultations with Guy Rémillard, the justice minister of Quebec.

The next week, when we got to Meech Lake, it was somewhat surprising to note that not all the provincial premiers had even bothered to bring their constitutional advisers. I think that this shows how low the expectations were heading into yet another round of constitutional negotiations on Quebec's desires.

The physical surroundings of the first set of negotiations were quite important. Brian Mulroney, as an experienced labour negotiator, used a strategy of isolating the participants in the negotiations. Only the first ministers were present, and he kept them in the room for a long time. The rest of us didn't have much to do while we waited for the first ministers to take a break. Several games of hearts went on in an effort to relieve the tedium of waiting. During breaks, we had the chance to confer. But as there was no set agenda for the issues under discussion, the talks moved around. This made it a little difficult to give advice, as we on the outside didn't really know what trade-offs the first ministers were making inside the room. Until quite late at night, there did not appear to be any chance of success. But Mulroney kept working away, and in the end an agreement was produced.

It was, in some respects, an agreement to reach an agreement. Many of the terms were not very well defined, at least as these things are understood in constitutional-law terms. There is an old saying that the devil is in the details, and details were lacking in the first Meech Lake agreement.

The key to the agreement was the recognition of Quebec as a "distinct society." This was a difficult bone for many of the western premiers to swallow. To get around their reservations, the term had been put in the preamble. Traditionally, in legal terms, a preamble is not legally enforceable. The first round of Meech Lake thus raised the big question of what "distinct society" meant, especially as the term was contained in the preamble.

Initial reaction to the accord was mixed. Trudeau criticized it on the grounds that Mulroney had given away the shop, that he had failed to protect the interests of the federal government in his eagerness to get a deal done.

Once the accord was made public, it became the subject of intense scrutiny and lobbying. Because the aim going in to the negotiations had been narrow, that is, to focus on the Quebec demands in the Edmonton meeting, the accord was open to criticism that it did not meet the needs of aboriginal groups or other groups seeking more constitutional protection. Of course, no agreement could have been reached had the negotiations not focused solely on the Quebec demands. This fact seemed to escape most of the critics of the accord.

During the next month, intense consultations were held about how to spell out the terms of the accord. It was by no means certain that this could be accomplished.

My own reservations centred on the meaning of the "distinct society" clause in the preamble. My position was clear. Either the statement meant something in judicial terms, or it was an empty throwaway, a meaningless sop to the nationalist forces in Quebec. If the clause meant something in terms of interpreting the Constitution, what was it? I had the greatest respect for the members of the Supreme Court of Canada, but I thought it would be better to include the expectations for the phrase "distinct society" in the text of the agreement, rather than the preamble.

The physical arrangements for the second round of Meech Lake negotiations were quite different. They were held in the Langevin

Block in Ottawa, across from the Parliament Buildings. This time, each province brought a full complement of constitutional advisers. In Ontario, we had supplemented the resident talent in my department and Intergovernmental Affairs with such legal luminaries as Peter Hogg, the author of the leading legal textbook on the Constitution; Rob Prichard, a former dean of the U of T law school; Jamie Cameron, a leading feminist legal scholar; and a host of other constitutional experts.

This meeting with the first ministers was much more structured than the previous one. Again, they went into the negotiations on their own, with only a federal official to act as recording secretary. But they had an agenda this time, and they came out at regular intervals to report on what was going on inside, and to be briefed on what positions to take on the coming issues.

It became apparent that Ontario stood alone in its position on "distinct society." Peterson was isolated. Mulroney had persuaded all the other first ministers to go along with the wording that had been worked out. In a sense, Trudeau was right: Ontario in fact represented the traditional viewpoint of the federal government, while Mulroney and Bourassa encouraged everyone to sign on the dotted line, and to trust them that it would work. I was unhappy with this approach.

Feelings began to run high. At one point, I got into a shouting match in a corridor with a very old friend of mine, Frank Iaccobucci, then the deputy minister of justice for Canada, now a distinguished member of the Supreme Court of Canada. Pat Monahan, my constitutional adviser, joined the fray. The discussion became so heated that fisticuffs almost broke out between Frank and Pat. Peterson suggested that Monahan leave for a cooling-off period.

Back in the negotiating room, when Peterson persisted in his objection, essentially stating my concerns, Bourassa and Mulroney began to become annoyed with him. They suggested that they should hear my objections in person. So I was marched into the room full of first ministers, along with Ian McGilp, Patrick Monahan, and Peter Hogg, and invited to state my position. I did so, but felt hostility coming from Robert Bourassa in particular.

The problem, which my questions crystallized, was that Bourassa needed to have it both ways to be able to sell the accord in Quebec. That is, he needed to be able to tell the nationalists that he had obtained recognition from the rest of Canada for Quebec's distinct status, and he had to reassure the western provinces that they could sell the accord as not granting any special powers to the province of Quebec.

I made my points, but I could sense that my target audience, Robert Bourassa, was not amused by what I had to say. We were dismissed somewhat icily. Eventually, Peterson came out to say that he felt totally isolated, and that he did not think that he could be the one to pull the plug on what he thought was the best chance to buy constitutional peace for twenty or thirty years.

So the deal was made. When it was done, I felt a deep malaise. I was full of misgivings about the wisdom of what we had done; anything, I thought, that rested on a fundamental ambiguity was doomed to failure at some point or other. Either the clause meant something or it meant nothing. If it meant something, then the other provinces would be upset when the courts explicated its content. If it meant nothing, then the deal would be forever criticized in Quebec.

I remember that after the deal was done, I called my friend and adviser, Chuck Birchall. He was back in the hotel, having been deemed by others not to be needed at the heated constitutional conclaves that went on whenever the first ministers took a break. I told Chuck I was so distressed that I wanted to resign. I thought my advice had been rejected and that I should go.

He pointed out the difficulties that a resignation in such circumstances would pose. It would certainly give the opponents of Meech, who for the most part were not friends of my government, a weapon with which to beat Meech participants. It would be a rebuke to Peterson, who had after all represented my views for some time in the face of considerable disapproval from his colleagues. Finally, it would remove me from any possible influence on the future course of the Constitution.

I spent a restless night wandering through the streets of Ottawa, ending up for no particular reason at Dow's Lake, thinking about what I should do. Eventually, I decided to accept Chuck's advice and stay.

The initial reaction in the press to Meech was quite enthusiastic. It looked as if old wounds had been stitched up. David Peterson was widely perceived to be a nation-builder. His personal popularity, and the popularity of his government, soared.

By the summer of 1987, the Ontario Liberal accord with the NDP was nearing its end. The government was riding high in the polls. The public liked the new style of openness, and the fact that we did what we said we were going to do. One of the few 1985 campaign promises that we did not deliver on was to let Ontario variety stores sell wine and beer, as they did in Quebec. Once in office, we felt that implementing this initiative would have been more trouble than it was worth. It seemed a relatively insignificant matter compared to all we had accomplished.

We spent more on education. We started to take the environment seriously. We took on the doctors as part of an attempt to ensure that public health-care spending went to the resources that would improve public health the most. We annoyed the lawyers but, I think, pleased the public, by taking away the prospects of more QCs. We spent more money on public housing and co-operative housing. When we were criticized, it was not for our priorities, but for not doing enough to implement them.

As a government, we had responded quite well to the challenges of office. We also had our share of minor political brushfires. For many of these, as attorney general, I was called in for damage control.

Elinor Caplan, for example, got in some difficulty as chair of Management Board, when there was an appearance of conflict of interest over a contract that her husband's company had bid on. She stepped down, and then came back to serve ably as minister of health after 1987. It wasn't surprising that ministers made mistakes; lots of Tory ministers over the years had made mistakes as well. But it was surprising that there were so few of them, considering that no one in the cabinet had ever held office before.

We also brought television in to cover the proceedings of the legislature. One of the great strategies that the Tories used over their extended period in office was to prorogue the house whenever any scandal broke. In the absence of a sitting, the print media were deprived of the blood sport of question time, and no electronic media covered the legislature on a province-wide basis. In putting television cameras in the legislature, we opened ourselves up to more public scrutiny than any previous Ontario government had. If the legislative sitting was adjourned, then the media had lots of video clips to run to keep issues alive. As a government, we didn't think we had anything much to hide from public scrutiny, though there were occasions when it might have been more peaceful to go back to the pre-TV era.

As I look back now, our initial period in government seems to have come from some other world. Some would argue that our activism was the result of our accord with the NDP. This, however, was part of a myth that suggested that the worthwhile policy initiatives in the accord came from the NDP, and that we were only interested in carrying out political reforms during the minority period of our government. In reality, all policy initiatives in the accord were already in the Liberal party platform. To say that we got our ideas from the NDP is simply not true.

A second, more complicated, myth grew up around the Ontario Liberals. It suggested that once the accord was behind us, we became an arrogant and out-of-touch government. For the period of the accord, both opposition parties were muted. The NDP was effectively silenced because of the terms of the accord; if they did not support us, we would have called an election, and the numbers strongly suggested that we would have won a majority. They couldn't get much political mileage out of any other course of action. The Tories, on the other hand, were still in a state of shock about losing power. Frank Miller had resigned, and Larry Grossman became the leader of the party. Unfortunately for Grossman, who appealed to urban and suburban but not rural segments of the voting public, David Peterson had emerged as the natural spokesperson for all those areas. Grossman was also having some marital difficulties that affected his ability to campaign. So, during the period leading up to the election call in the summer of 1987, the opposition was effectively hamstrung. In our second term, Bob Rae in particular was extremely effective in criticizing us.

The accord expired at the end of May 1987. At the end of July, we called the election. Within the first week, the committee rooms for St. George–St. David were flooded with volunteers. More than 700 people came in. It was a pleasant problem to figure out what to do with them all. Sign locations flowed in abundance. Canvasses produced astoundingly favourable results. In a sense, given the tough battles I had before in the riding, it was hard to believe that everything could go so well.

Provincially, the election was a love-in for David Peterson and the Ontario Liberal party. Canvassing was a breeze. It was not difficult to get volunteers. A happy glow seemed to emanate from Peterson that summer. It was infectious. He went from barbecue to barbecue, finding adoring crowds in areas where the Liberals had had difficulty for years. In Timiskaming, for example, David Ramsay, first elected in 1985 as an NDP member, had crossed the floor and was now the Liberal candidate. In 1985, in contrast, the Liberals in the riding had been able to recruit only Dale Woods to run at the last moment, and he did it only as a favour to his friend Bill Murray, one of the party's key organizers. Woods had not found the constituency particularly responsive. But by 1987, at one barbecue Peterson attended outside New Liskeard, there were, he estimated, more people than he saw during the entire 1985 campaign.

A redistribution had changed the nature of my riding quite substantially. For one thing, it was now called St. George–St. David. For another, all my former territory across the Don Valley was now in the riding of Riverdale, and my riding had gained some territory to the west, taking in St. Jamestown and the so-called gay quarter around Church and Wellesley. This helped me in electoral terms, as the area across the Don Valley was not great terrain for a Liberal. But this was a small matter; in 1987, it was not hard for a Liberal to get elected in Toronto.

We swept the city. Bob Rae hung on by some 400 votes, running against Alan Tonks, the chairman of the Board of Control of Metropolitan Toronto. Larry Grossman lost his seat and his appetite for politics. The Liberals won a large majority: ninety-five seats. No one in 1985 could have predicted that this would happen. Some excellent new members of caucus were elected; the next government would not have to rely as heavily on the services of Nixon, Conway, Elston, and Scott. When the caucus assembled for its first meeting after the election, however, Peterson issued a warning:

> Your job is to work as hard as you can in government, and to work as hard as you can in your ridings for the people you represent, because a time will come when you will not want me to come into your riding. A time will come when I am so personally unpopular that you won't want help from me, let alone be able to get it, and then at that moment, when I'm not able to help you, your chances of being re-elected are going to depend entirely on your own efforts.

Now, this was 1987. No one believed that this was possible. They were talking about this man as a future prime minister of Canada. But Peterson's was a wise prediction. It was part of his strength that at a moment of triumph it would occur to him to reflect on the inevitability of defeat. I don't think many people would have opened a victory caucus with that kind of observation. It was a remarkably human and understanding thing that he even thought of it, and quite remarkable that he said it. It should have been a caution to everybody.

Second-Term
Blues

◆

THE FIRST TERM OF OUR GOVERNMENT was marked by the excitement and novelty of being in power. Much of that term was dominated by carrying out the reforms we thought necessary to correct the drift of the last few years of Davis's government. As we embarked on the second term, we were buoyed by the public adulation demonstrated in the election, and cheered by the knowledge that we had time to carry out systemic reforms.

Elinor Caplan was the new minister of health. She brought in Martin Barkin as her deputy minister. Together, they embarked on a program to change the philosophy of the health-care delivery system to one that promoted less reliance on hospitals through better community health organizations. John Sweeney, the minister of community and social services, commissioned a report, *Transitions*, that proposed sweeping changes in the social welfare system, trying to provide better services to single mothers, more retraining opportunities, and more programs to break the bonds that kept people in the welfare trap. My big systemic change was court reform.

What these approaches had in common was a need to talk to the stakeholders affected by the changes and to consult with experts about how to structure reform. We were all conscious of the fact that the changes would produce short-term pain — a small price to pay, we thought, for long-term gains. We had no inkling that we wouldn't have enough time to implement all these changes.

As the second term began, I realized again how much I loved being in politics. Every day brought new challenges, some predictable, some completely out of the blue. Whatever the day's plans were, the front-page story in the morning paper could completely change the agenda. The most boring day I had in politics was ten times more exciting than the most exciting day I had in law.

The adrenaline flow was addictive. As attorney general, I was drawn into any controversy arising from legal issues. If a judge made a contentious remark or decision, or if one of my cabinet colleagues overstepped the bounds of propriety, then I would be dragged, willy-nilly, into the controversy.

In addition to dealing with crises, I had a set of long-term goals for the department. Juggling it all was difficult, but the very difficulties made it so exciting. Granted, there were excitements — like the Patti Starr affair, discussed below — that I could have done without. But once you're in politics, you deal with what comes along. It's like being on the bridge of a ship: icebergs may appear unexpectedly, and it often takes a lot of effort to avoid them. But, also as with icebergs, nine-tenths of the political battles take place out of view of the public eye. It is this submerged activity that has the biggest potential to affect the lives of citizens, who for the most part are blissfully unaware of the struggles for power underneath the surface.

For example, in our second term, I wanted to improve access to the justice system by expanding funding for legal clinics. At Cameron, Brewin & Scott, I had worked for Mr. Justice John Osler on the inquiry that established the basic legal-clinic system in Ontario. I believed in it then, and I believed in it while I was attorney general. Clinic lawyers worked for salaries. The clinics built up expertise in different areas of the law, and they helped ensure legal representation for people who could not afford it. I had trouble convincing the people in charge of the purse strings, however, that increased funding to clinics was desirable.

In the first budget after our re-election, the funding for clinics was flat. Murray Elston had been moved from his post as minister of health to chair of the Management Board, and he refused my entreaties to increase the funding for clinics. So the clinics took matters into their own hands and launched a picket line outside his office at Queen's Park. Elston thought that I had instigated the whole protest as a way of getting more money. He called me up to bawl me out and to tell me that my pressure tactics would not work.

I was out of town when Elston called, and so he spoke to Chuck Birchall, my executive assistant. He expressed his belief that I had orchestrated the whole demonstration. "Scott couldn't orchestrate the opening of a car door," Chuck told him. Eventually, Murray calmed down. Then he said to Chuck, "You know what really pisses me off is that is that they've all got my name spelled wrong on the signs. They've got 'Elton' instead of 'Elston.'"

In the next go-round of negotiations, I managed to get the clinics a 30-percent increase in funding, much to their astonishment. This was not an example of a government being extravagant, but rather of a government putting resources where they would produce a good return.

I tried to be careful with public money. For example, John Sopinka had represented Susan Nelles at the Grange Inquiry, which recommended that her legal fees be paid. Sopinka started his negotiations for payment with Roy McMurtry, but by the time they got serious I was attorney general. Sopinka complained that I was "tight" with public money, and a tough negotiator. In connection with this incident, I capped the fees that counsel could recoup from the public purse in commissions of inquiry. This led to much complaining by lawyers in the Kaufman Inquiry on Guy-Paul Morin's wrongful conviction, but I believed that lawyers engaged in such quests should be willing to serve the public for less than their normal rates.

I tried to take a broad view of how my government spent its

money, rather than working to increase the budget of my own department. In some respects, this reflected my unconventional approach to the role of attorney general. It is safe to say that past attorneys general had had cosy relationships with judges. Judges probably regarded the AG as their spokesperson within government. Judges, as we all know, are above politics, but they are not devoid of views on how the system should operate. I found this out when I set about trying to reform the structure of the courts in Ontario.

The existing structure of the courts in Canada was a kind of hodgepodge, dating back to colonial times. England was a unitary state, and its court system was therefore not troubled by any federal division of powers. This is not to say, however, that the English system was completely straightforward, with its divisions into Chancery and common law, its complicated rules stemming from the ancient writs of action, and a host of encrustations and peculiarities stemming from centuries of practice.

At the time of the British North America Act of 1867 (now renamed the Constitution Act, 1867), a division had to be made in Canada between federal and provincial powers, and between federal and provincial court systems. The Criminal Code was federal, but its enforcement was provincial. Section 96 of the act conferred on the federal government the power to appoint judges to the superior courts. Judges appointed to those courts had the powers and rights of English superior court judges as they existed in 1867. At a later date, a number of district and county courts were created. The incumbents of these courts, also appointed under s. 96, did not have the full panoply of powers enjoyed by their judicial brethren on the superior courts. They did, however, occupy a niche above the provincial court judges, who were appointed by the provinces, and whose powers were fixed by statute.

Provincial court judges were the ones most citizens were likely to brush up against. They handled most criminal charges and many matters arising out of marital breakdown, though only s. 96 judges could issue divorce decrees. This division of powers was inconvenient for people caught up in marital disputes, who obviously had more important things on their minds than which level of court they needed to be in to pursue their remedies. I thought that the solution to this was to have a unified family court. I started a pilot project to this effect in Hamilton.

I was also forcefully reminded that provincial court judges deserved the same respect, and the same salary, as federally appointed judges. Ted Andrews, the chief judge of the provincial courts, surprised me by raising the issue at a public ceremony. My response was as follows:

> I also want to emphasize that I am conscious of the concerns of the members of the Provincial Court Bench about remuneration. I very much regret that the representatives of the Provincial Judges have not seen fit to reappoint their nominee to the statutorily established Provincial Courts Committee. I have met with representatives of the Provincial Judges on a number of occasions and will continue to do so in order to ascertain whether a more suitable mechanism for examining issues of compensation cannot be devised. I must make it plain, however, that it is the position of the government that no mechanism can be established which removes or reduces the authority of the government of the day to control or determine the expenditure of tax dollars to be allocated for judicial remuneration.

Supreme Court of Ontario judges disagreed with Chief Judge Andrews' view on levels of remuneration. Some of the provincial court magistrates were not lawyers: this proposal would have the effect of elevating them to the same level as other judges, who were all lawyers, an outcome not popular with the Supreme Court of Ontario judges.

Even within the courts staffed entirely by federally appointed judges, there were complications. There were monetary limits on the actions that could be brought in the district and county courts. The court costs for the Supreme Court were higher, a fact that led to complicated decisions about whether the higher costs were justified in cases that were just over the threshold of the district and county courts. Lawyers and judges were comfortable with the existing system, but it set up artificial distinctions about which court had jurisdiction to hear which cases, adding uncertainty to a process that was already too expensive and too hard for most laypeople to understand. I proposed that the courts should be reorganized and streamlined. It had been done without much dispute in Alberta, but Ontario turned out to be different.

I appointed Mr. Justice Thomas Zuber to make a report on the matter, and explained my rationale for his appointment to an audience of somewhat skeptical judges in the following terms:

We have, I think, over the last few years come to realize that many of the most fundamental problems that confront the operation of the system are in fact structural. We have indeed learned that the provision of more judges and more courtrooms (an exercise in which we have been engaged for a quarter century) does not solve our problems but often merely exacerbates them. It is for this reason that the government has appointed the Honourable Mr. Justice Thomas Zuber with terms of reference of the widest scope to deal with any question that arises in the area of organization, structure, jurisdiction or workload of any court of Ontario from a Justice of the Peace to the Ontario Court of Appeal. Mr. Justice Zuber's inquiry is not intended to be a mere tinkering with the existing system but rather a fundamental re-thinking of all the assumptions on which our courts have operated since 1792 when they were first established on the creation of the Province of Upper Canada.

When Mr. Justice Zuber reported, I accepted only some of his recommendations. The changes I made produced a surprising amount of resistance nonetheless. As it happened, the chief justice of Ontario was William Howland, who had supervised my articles, and who had caught me sneaking out of the movies when I was supposed to be at the Registry Office. He was a charming and affable man, but I could not help feeling sometimes that he wished I would just go away with my proposals for changing a system that had endured for more than a century. Frank Callaghan, the chief justice of the Supreme Court of Ontario, was even more opposed to change. At one point, we even had a battle over using a room in a courthouse for a meeting I called. "It's my courthouse," he said, rather melodramatically. I replied, "No, it's the people's courthouse." We held the meeting there. Eventually, I got his somewhat grudging support for the court reform proposal by threatening to get my friend, Ray Hnatyshyn, then the federal justice minister, to appoint someone to the Court of Appeal whom Mr. Justice Callaghan did not want there. The threat worked.

Despite the fact that I considered it to be in their best interests to have a much more streamlined court system, some judges did not like having their wings clipped. The judges undoubtedly thought of me as something of a legal pariah. They thought my job was to go into cabinet and get more money for the judicial system. That was what attorneys general had always done. I, however, thought that my job as a cabinet minister was to assist the government in spending its total budget in the best possible way. I also thought that it was more important to spend money on health care than on the administration of justice.

This rather idiosyncratic belief was not widely shared within the legal community. Chuck Birchall recalls that each time I met Mr. Justice Howland, I would ask him the same question: "What do you think is more important — a new courthouse or a new hospital?" Each time, Bill Howland would reply, "The courthouse." And I would always tell him that he was wrong, that the correct answer was "The hospital."

Many people in my lifetime have accused me of being cheap, always bumming cigarettes, or letting other people pick up the tab for lunches. Whether these charges are true of me personally remains to be decided; what *is* true is that I was careful with the people's money. I wanted to reform the court system without pouring a lot more money into it. I thought that reorganization was the answer. My critics within the judicial system thought that my responsibility was to get more money from the Management Board, and then talk to them about changes.

I proposed to support the changes to the court system by insti-
gating a reorganization of the Ministry of the Attorney General. The
ministry was thus changed to reflect the new judicial regions that
were part of my court-reform proposals. Each judicial district had a
full range of court services available within its jurisdiction, and no
longer needed to rely on circuit-court judges from Toronto.

While my proposals for reform and reorganization were being
worked out, the number of cases for the courts to hear surged. A long
backlog developed, especially in rapidly growing areas like Brampton,
west of Toronto, where there was considerable pressure for more
courtrooms to be built and more judges to be appointed. In my view,
there was no point in throwing money at the existing system for temporary patches. I preferred to set up the new system, and then put
money into making sure that it worked.

This approach got me into trouble with judges. I was pressured
on issues ranging from court security to the length of time it took to
get a hearing in certain jurisdictions. It must be remembered that at
the time I became attorney general, the first of the charter cases were
just being resolved. *Singh*, the immigration case I argued and won,
for example, was decided while I was out campaigning in 1985. The
charter conferred new procedural safeguards for Canadians, but it
also introduced the notion that excessive delay in coming to trial was
enough to have charges dismissed. Judges wanting more money and
more courtrooms took a kind of grim pleasure in pointing out to
me at each year's opening-of-the-courts ceremonies just how many
cases in each jurisdiction had been stayed as a result of excessive
delays. The first time such remarks were made, I felt sandbagged.
I wanted to make sure that delays were eliminated. I also wanted to
be prepared to address the judges' complaints on future occasions.
Unfortunately, I discovered that there were no statistics in the
department about how many stays had been granted in each jurisdiction. Without such information, it was impossible to respond with
comments like, "There is a problem there, but the statistics show that
it is getting better, and it is all well under control." I made sure that the
department began to collect such statistics.

It took a certain amount of fortitude to put up with the complaints of judges who insisted that the system would work better if they had more funding, and the squeals of outrage of the popular press, which found dramatic examples of accused people having charges stayed for excessive delay. In the opinion of the papers, many of these people ought to have been in the slammer, due process or no due process.

Regional judicial districts were created, and the offices of the Crowns were correspondingly reorganized, according to my proposals. The courts were restructured and renamed The Ontario Court of Justice (General Division) and the Ontario Court of Justice (Provincial Division). Many judges disliked the new names. Some judges still resent having had to swear a new oath of allegiance to the Queen on their appointment to the new court. But judicial feelings were not my main concern. I wanted a system that would work. I thought it important that Provincial Division judges be on an equal footing with the General Division judges. This attitude was popular in the former provincial court, but its popularity there did not make up for the odium with which it was regarded in the former Supreme Court of Ontario.

A measure of the resentment within the judiciary at having these changes forced on them can be seen in the recent change of name of the court system. Where I had amalgamated the district, county, and high courts into the General Division, that court has now been renamed the Superior Court of Justice. Strangely, Ontario is not part of the official title of the court, and the name, in my opinion, seems to beg the question, "Superior to what?" The underlying reforms have remained, in that the district and county courts are still part of the Superior Court, but the name change indicates the strength of judicial feelings regarding judicial pecking orders.

We also made access to law easier through legislation that permitted class actions. Historically, one of the big differences between the American and Canadian legal systems has been that contingency fees were allowed in the States. This meant that lawyers could sign up clients who were willing to give a percentage of the awards in successful lawsuits to their lawyers. In exchange, the lawyer would underwrite the cost of getting the matter to trial. If there were no awards for the client, then the lawyer was out of pocket.

The advantage of the system is that matters could be litigated regardless of whether the plaintiffs had any money. The disadvantage was that lawyers quite naturally looked for cases where the defendants had deep pockets. Matters of principle that lacked a reasonable probability of a big payoff might slip through the system.

The Canadian legal system had always opposed contingency fees. There also was no common-law mechanism for permitting class actions. If, for example, a group of people had each incurred a loss of $5,000, they could not pool their cases to present a united front against the organization or individual who caused the damage. Unless the damages were substantial, individuals might not pursue their rights in court because of the risk that their court costs would be more than any damages they could collect.

The class-action bill I set up contained a number of tests to ensure that a commonality of evidentiary facts could be established. Once that hurdle was overcome, lawyers who received certification from the courts could proceed on a contingency-fee basis. These safeguards prevented frivolous actions, but allowed worthy class actions to proceed. Examples of the latter are the lawsuit brought against the Canadian Red Cross and other blood agencies by people infected with HIV or hepatitis C as the result of transfusions with unsafe blood products. In the long run, the legislation allowing class actions may be the most important legacy of my time as attorney general.

While my efforts were concentrated on systemic reforms, political issues would bubble up, sometimes in quite dramatic form. As if it wasn't enough to have riled lawyers by abolishing QCs, and judges by amalgamating the courts, our government also brought in a system of no-fault auto insurance. The NDP was all for a publicly funded system of auto insurance, like the ones instituted by NDP governments in Saskatchewan and British Columbia. Peterson had stated in the 1987 election campaign that whatever system of auto insurance was brought in, there would be no increase in rates.

Our concern was not so much with who owned the companies

TOP: With Kim, early eighties, and with Irish lamb, 1983.

BOTTOM: The band, Mary Kiervin, and me in front of chartered streetcar, 1981 campaign.

TOP: My staff at Queen's Park. I am flanked by "Pete" Milner and Peter Lukasiewicz.

BOTTOM: Opening our new constituency office with Lesley Yaeger, Stu Houston, and Angela Langmead.

Top: With young constituents.

Left: Phone slip recording call from payphone by Chief Justice Howland, notifying me of bomb threat at Osgoode Hall Court House.

Right: At Queen's Park.

Top: My cabinet colleagues, 1985, without a tardy me.

Bottom: Smoking a peace pipe.

TOP AND MIDDLE:
A perennial bed and
the patio, at the farm.

BOTTOM LEFT & RIGHT:
With Kim; My sister
Martha in my Toronto
backyard.

TOP: With Frank Iaccobucci.

MIDDLE: With David Peterson at University of Toronto Convocation.

RIGHT: With Ray Hnatyshyn, after Order of Canada ceremony.

TOP: With David Peterson (left), Hal Jackman, Roy McMurtry, and Bill Davis.

MIDDLE: Happy times: Martha, me, Ian Roland, and Christopher Cossonnet.

BOTTOM: My brother David (left) and Chuck Birchall at my 65th birthday party.

TOP: Circa 1996.

BOTTOM: Visiting Kim's
hometown, 1997.

administering insurance policies as with the legal costs of the liability system. A huge legal industry was based on litigation of relatively minor accidents. The costs of the litigation were eventually recouped through higher rates charged by the insurance industry to the public. In a kind of seepage from the American legal system, tort awards in Canada were rising, though they never reached the level they attained in the United States.

Our solution was to apply no-fault provisions to accidents not involving serious personal injury. We defined serious personal injury in the legislation, leaving some room for judicial interpretation of what it might mean. But the act took most accidents, involving as they do only property damage, out of the litigation framework.

This angered litigation lawyers. They believed we were restricting access to the courts and depriving them of one way to make a livelihood. Their anger was palpable: when I was first elected to the legislature, David Rubin organized a fundraising dinner for me. More than a thousand lawyers paid $150 each to attend. After the no-fault legislation was introduced, we could have had a fundraiser in a telephone booth, such was the antipathy in the profession.

The NDP was upset that we did not opt for a system of non-profit, public ownership. They accused Peterson of misleading the public in the previous election. Peter Kormos, a maverick NDP MPP, filibustered in an impressive manner. Rhetoric ran high. The legislature became acrimonious. We had to cut off debate by invoking closure to get the bill through the legislature. We got it from both ends of the political spectrum: from the right for restricting the right to sue for certain kinds of damages, and from the left for not going far enough in curbing the powers of insurance companies.

Despite all the brouhaha, we must have done something right, because even the NDP did not essentially change the system we put in when they assumed power in 1990. Kormos, running true to form, filibustered his own government on the issue, but to no avail. It is safe to say, though, that the passions engendered by the auto insurance issue went some way to poisoning the atmosphere in the legislature for the rest of our second term in office.

Another issue generated a lot of political heat and much political ill will: Sunday shopping. In the United States, Sunday shopping was the norm. This led to a loss of sales for Canadian stores near the border. It is difficult now to believe, but there was not at the time much difference in purchasing power between the Canadian and American dollars; thousands of Canadians made trips across the border to the big outlet malls in places like Buffalo, New York.

The Supreme Court of Canada increased the political heat in Ontario with its decision throwing out the federal statute, the Lord's Day Act, which had still been the law in Alberta and British Columbia. Alberta decided not to bring in new legislation. This meant that shoppers in Ontario had not only the American example of Sunday shopping, but the Canadian example of Alberta as well. No one could really say that Alberta was any worse off as a result of its decision not to replace the former federal Lord's Day Act with provincial legislation.

In Ontario, the public as well as the Liberal caucus were split. On the whole, urban members favoured Sunday shopping and rural members did not. The existing situation was a patchwork in any event. Local municipalities had the power to declare certain areas of historic or tourist interest. Shops located in such areas could open on Sundays. So could bookstores. The legislation was unclear: what about stores that sold other things besides books? What percentage of a business had to be devoted to books to qualify it as a bookstore?

In Toronto, the most persistent challenger of the status quo was Paul Magder, a furrier on Spadina Avenue, in the heart of downtown Toronto. He stayed open, paid fines for staying open, and pointed to some of the glaring inconsistencies in the existing laws. Four or five blocks north of his place of business, for example, stores could open legally on Sunday, in the designated tourist areas of Kensington Market and Chinatown. Magder's point was that it was unfair to force him to close shop on the days when the area was full of tourists, while his competition in a so-called tourist area could remain open.

It might have been simple to adopt the Alberta strategy and abolish the Retail Holidays Act altogether. The problem was that this solution was not uniformly popular. To my mind, there were some similarities to the "wet or dry" controversies in the nineteenth century. It is perhaps not widely appreciated how much of Canadian constitutional law revolves around the regulation of, and the control of the revenues derived from, the sale of alcohol. My great-grandfather Sir Richard Scott, a teetotaler who did not mind if his guests drank from his extensive wine cellar, had faced this dilemma in drafting a liquor-control act in the nineteenth century. Parts of the country were strongly prohibitionist; parts were not. Sir Richard's solution was the "local option" feature of the Canada Temperance Act, allowing municipalities to decide whether they should be "wet" or "dry." I proposed something of the same as the solution to the problem of Sunday shopping. I brought forward a bill that amended the existing act by providing for local votes by municipalities on whether they wanted Sunday shopping. Hence, a city like Sarnia, bedevilled by the sight of cars going over the Blue Water Bridge en route to Port Huron or the bigger malls in Troy, Michigan, could allow Sunday shopping, if it so chose. Other cities, like Woodstock or Brantford, for example, could choose to keep their stores closed.

I was savaged for the proposal. The NDP was of the opinion that I was doing nothing to protect the right of workers to choose to spend quality time with their families on Sundays. It was suggested strongly that the time for such piecework measures was long past.

A few years later, the president of the Bay department store announced that he was going to keep open his stores on Sunday whether the government liked it or not. Bob Rae, by then the premier, who had strongly opposed my local-option measure, reluctantly agreed to most of the changes demanded by the big stores.

Today, no one seems to care one way or the other, to judge from the number of people in the stores on Sundays. The whole issue stands as a prime example of the short life of some political issues. Unlike the abortion issue, this one went away.

Another issue that I fervently hoped would go away, but didn't, was the Patti Starr affair.

Patti Starr initially worked as a volunteer with the National Council

of Jewish Women, a charitable organization. She came in contact
with the provincial Liberals through the agency of Heather Peterson,
David Peterson's sister-in-law. Heather's husband, Jim, was the
member for the federal constituency of Willowdale, which has a large
Jewish population. When Jim lost in 1984, it created something of a
vacuum for Starr's redoubtable political energies.

Starr's first contribution to politics was in mobilizing people to
attend political fundraising dinners. Tickets for these dinners would
be sold to corporations or to law firms, who might feel that writing the
cheque was the end of their political commitment. There is nothing
more dispiriting for a politician than facing a room full of empty
chairs, even if some non-attending corporate sponsor has paid for
each one of them. As Heather Peterson said, "Patti could put people
in the seats for you."

Starr switched to provincial politics after Peterson's win in 1985,
and soon took on a prominent role in organizing events for the
Liberals. Her charity, meanwhile, was interested in co-operating with
the Del Zottos, a family of prominent real estate developers, to build
a retirement/nursing home for older Jewish women, on a development where the Del Zottos would build condominiums. In the end,
the zoning laws for the condominium project were waived in
exchange for the construction of the old people's home.

By 1989, Starr had become the head of Ontario Place and was
busy reorganizing that venue to her satisfaction. Then, a series of stories began to appear about irregular campaign contributions that she
had orchestrated through the charity for which she worked. (After
I left politics, I discovered that she had sent my campaign a cheque
in 1987, but that David Rubin had prudently sent it back without
cashing it.) It was then reported that Gordon Ashworth, the political
organizer who ran the Liberal party for Peterson, had had some work
done for free on his house. Bob Nixon heard that Ashworth had also
received a free refrigerator, allegedly from the Del Zottos, through
the agency of Patti Starr. Nixon went to Peterson with the story. I
was called in to see an angry Peterson confront Ashworth. The latter
resigned forthwith.

All that summer, there had been speculation that Bob Nixon would retire from politics to go to England as Ontario's agent general. There was also speculation that a major reshuffling of cabinet was in the works. My staff had heard rumours that I was going to be asked to become the minister of housing. In the wake of the Starr revelations, however, Nixon decided to stay, and I remained attorney general. Peterson moved quickly to appoint a commission of inquiry into the allegations being raised in the press about improper links between the Liberal government and the building and development industry. Housing was a huge issue in the 1980s, as the baby-boom generation moved through the family-formation stage. A whole raft of stories suggested that developers made campaign contributions to Liberal members of the legislature in order to get developments approved.

Within twenty-four hours of the story breaking, the premier's office had drafted the terms of a public commission, to be headed by the respected judge Lloyd Houlden, to investigate the allegations about improper dealings between the government, Patti Starr, and the Del Zottos. I did not participate in the drafting of those terms, though Machiavellian motives were later attributed to me when the Supreme Court of Canada threw out the inquiry on the grounds that its terms of reference invaded the ambit of the Criminal Code.

Many previous judicial inquiries, including the Grange Commission into the deaths at the Sick Kids Hospital, had also intruded into criminal matters, and no one thought much of it at the time. The Houlden Commission started its work, but came to an abrupt halt when the Supreme Court of Canada said its terms were too broad. Patti Starr served time. She sued me and other members of the government, but the suit was settled after several years. Although much was made at the time of supposed links between the calling of the election and the beginning of Patti Starr's trial on charges of fraud, in the end I do not think that this scandal had much effect on the election outcome.

The case illustrated one of the problems that all attorneys general must face. As the top law-enforcement officer, the attorney general must be able to enforce the law without fear or favour. This entails a certain separation from one's cabinet colleagues, especially when their actions violate, or appear to violate, the standards for proper action.

For example, someone took a picture of the solicitor general, Ken Keyes, a former mayor of Kingston, serving alcoholic drinks while on an OPP boat in the waters off Kingston Harbour. In my view, this was a trifling offence, but at the same time it was one that raised questions of preferential enforcement of laws. So I took over the office briefly until a replacement solicitor general could be found.

I also found myself the cabinet member responsible for race relations for a very brief period of time. I called in Dan McIntyre, the head of the government's race-relations unit, and told him, "You know, I'm probably not going to be in this office for very long, but give me your wish list, and I'll see what I can do for you." He gave me his list, and we brought in a new race-relations policy based on his recommendations.

The office of attorney general is also intensely political, as there are political dimensions to practically every decision. At the end of the day, if you are to be effective, you have to be above politics. You cannot be effective, however, if you try to operate in a political vacuum. This conundrum was often painfully clear to me during question period in the legislature. I had not spent any appreciable amount of time in opposition, just the brief interregnum when Miller tried to govern and we had negotiated the accord with the NDP. Most of my legislative experience, therefore, was as a government minister, often on the spot for something that someone else had done. I enjoyed the cut and thrust of parliamentary debate, even if I did not particularly enjoy the circumstances of some of the debates.

From my days at Ashbury, through my time in the Senators debating club at St. Michael's College, I enjoyed debates. In the House, I could heckle, something that few of my ministerial colleagues did, and I could have fun. For the first two years in office, the years of the accord, all sides of the House had been relatively restrained. For the last three years in office, however, the gloves were off.

Bob Rae was a very effective opposition leader. He had nothing to lose, as for most of the period from 1987 to 1990, he thought that he would be getting out of politics after the 1990 election. On issues such as auto insurance and housing, as well as on Patti Starr, Rae chastised us enthusiastically. With television now in the legislature, however, issues could be kept fresh simply by replaying clips from before an adjournment. The Opposition could wring considerable advantage out of them.

Similarly, the advent of television in public inquiries, as in Grange or Houlden, gave the public — or, more accurately, the news directors of assorted news shows — the opportunity to replay key moments of testimony, reinforcing the notion that where there was so much smoke, there must have been some fire.

When the legislature was in session, I prepared for the worst each day, trying to anticipate likely lines of questioning based on what was happening in the press. It was like preparing for a trial, except that the range of issues was wider and the consequences of a mistake might be greater. Knowing what questions I might ask on a cross-examination helped me to prepare for the opposition onslaught, which in certain instances could be quite taxing.

Glenn Hall, the all-star goalie, was reputed to have thrown up before the start of each hockey game he played, even though by the end of his career he had played in hundreds of them, and not all of them could have been of great importance. I did not throw up before question period, but I was always nervous. My adrenaline was definitely pumped. I tried to appear calm, and to use humour to deflect potentially serious questions, but once it all started I usually enjoyed it so much that I forgot all about being nervous.

There was a striking difference between our first and second terms in office. In the first, the Opposition had been relatively quiet. In the second, they were obstreperous and effective. A whole series of incidents arose involving ministers caught in situations in which they were vulnerable to attack. Joan Smith, the solicitor general, made a late-night visit to the Lucan, Ontario, OPP office when she got a call from the son of a family friend of long standing. He had been arrested. She responded as a friend, but she should have responded as a minister, and realized that there would be an aura of impropriety about such a visit. Chaviva Hosek was caught in a swirl of allegations about improper links to the housing industry before her appointment as minister of housing. The allegations turned out to be completely unfounded, but she was relegated to the back benches while they were investigated. And, of course, there was the Patti Starr situation.

Ontario governments had dealt with worse crises in the past. The government of Leslie Frost had road-paving contract scandals. There were allegations of improper land dealings by Conservative party members in both the Robarts and Davis governments. Those governments survived. We could probably have ridden out all of these incidents, except that the focus of the government shifted from the mundane world of politics as usual to the exciting world of constitutional politics.

The Meech Lake Accord was first signed in June 1987. It included a three-year ratification period for all the provinces and the federal government. I still had my reservations about the Meech Lake Accord, but I had come round to the view that it was the best deal that we were ever likely to get, and that it should be supported. At first, this was not very difficult to do. Most of the country was relieved that something was being done to end Quebec's unhappiness with the existing constitution. Then, some quirky things started to happen.

Premier Richard Hatfield did not bring the Meech resolution forward for a vote in the New Brunswick legislature, at a time when he had a majority, and it would have passed easily. Then, rather bravely — or pathetically, depending on your point of view — he campaigned for re-election when the polls showed quite clearly that he had worn out his welcome.

Frank McKenna, his Liberal opponent, keen to show the difference between himself and Hatfield, campaigned against Meech. McKenna won all the seats in the New Brunswick legislature, and though he subsequently came round and became a great supporter of Meech he put the process through which it had been negotiated into question.

Another new provincial premier then arrived in the person of

Clyde Wells in Newfoundland. He also questioned the process, and directed his legislature to reverse the ratification vote that his predecessor, Brian Peckford, had put through.

Meanwhile, in Manitoba, Gary Filmon had managed to extract an all-party agreement to support what was happening in Meech, by getting Sharon Carstairs, the Liberal leader, and Gary Doer, the NDP leader, to buy into the process.

Then the Manitoba agreement was rendered moot by actions in Quebec. Robert Bourassa faced threats from the nationalist forces in Quebec over language and education matters. Bill 178, a bill to determine the language on retail signs in Quebec, went before the Supreme Court of Canada. The court decided that the bill was contrary to the charter. Bourassa invoked the notwithstanding clause to remove it from the ambit of the charter, provoking outrage in the rest of the country, and in the English-language groups in Quebec. It seemed as if Quebec wanted the Constitution to work only if it favoured Quebec nationalist interests.

Meanwhile, Brian Mulroney, having won re-election after a bruising campaign in which free trade figured prominently, became more and more unpopular. People disliked the GST. People disliked Mulroney, though I, like most people who dealt with him in politics, found him a charming and considerate man.

Thus was the stage set in June 1990 for a third round of negotiations on Meech, with a vastly expanded cast of characters, and with a whole lot more, it seemed, riding on the outcome of the deliberations.

The Ontario delegation to the talks comprised some of the finest constitutional scholars in the country. We had been steeped in Meech and its aftermath, and we were committed as a government to getting it through and adopted.

The meetings this time were held in the convention centre in Ottawa — formerly the railway station in my youth in Ottawa — and they were televised, except for secret sessions. The stakes were high. Negotiations were intense. There were no threats of fisticuffs this time, but feelings ran high among the delegates. All the premiers were onside, except for Wells and Filmon. The latter was in a minority situation, but he had brought Gary Doer, the NDP leader, and Sharon Carstairs, the Liberal leader, as part of his delegation.

Deals were made. Deals were unmade. Tears were shed. Pressure to agree was intense. Discussions had widened from the five points of the Edmonton Declaration to include things like Senate reform. At one point, it looked as if the whole deal was going to collapse. James McPherson, then dean of law at Osgoode, and a member of the Ontario group of constitutional advisers, suggested that Ontario might offer some of its existing Senate seats as bargaining chips to ensure that a later round of negotiations would be taken seriously. If the later talks broke down, then Ontario would give up six of its existing twenty-four Senate seats to satisfy western demands for Senate reform. Peterson offered the seats at a point when the negotiations appeared to have broken down completely, although the rest of his advisers thought it was a mistake. It broke a logjam, and discussions continued.

Eventually, an agreement was reached, but it had to be ratified within a week or so by Manitoba and Newfoundland. Clyde Wells, having agreed to submit it to a free vote of the Newfoundland legislature, started to waffle about his commitment as soon as he got home. Connoisseurs of past constitutional deals that failed were reminded of Robert Bourassa and his change of mind that killed the Victoria deal in 1971. There was nothing new under the Canadian constitutional sun.

Gary Filmon bowed to the rules of the Manitoba legislature and allowed Elijah Harper to filibuster the approval to death. Native groups across the country thought this was an appropriate payback for the failure of the aboriginal-rights conference. A relieved Clyde Wells used the pending defeat in Manitoba as the excuse not to submit the agreement to a vote in the Newfoundland legislature, thus ensuring the defeat of the accord. For this act of breaking his word, those who opposed the accord hailed him as a statesman. To those who were in the room when he agreed to submit the accord to the legislature, he was seen as someone who lacked the backbone to do what he said he would do.

Meech Lake died on June 23, 1990.

Had it passed, it would have bought a decade or more of constitutional peace. Instead, it came to symbolize all that many groups
thought was wrong with the political system of the country. My experience with the aboriginal-rights conference had convinced me that
we could not get any progress on native self-government unless
Quebec was at the bargaining table. There was an almost spiteful
quality to the whole thing: if we can't get what we want, then you
can't get what you want.

I also think that Peterson would have won the election if Meech
Lake had passed. When I came back to Toronto after the agreement
was reached, but before it was killed in Manitoba and Newfoundland,
people in my riding were terribly enthusiastic about it. There was a
sense of relief that all the constitutional palaver was over and we
could turn our attention to the economy and other issues. When it
fell apart, people were angry at Mulroney and Bourassa, who were
very unpopular with my constituents. That anger spilled over to
Peterson, who was seen as hobnobbing with them. People in St.
George–St. David wanted Peterson to denounce Mulroney and
Bourassa. If he had done that, it would have been seen as a symbol
that he wasn't like the other two, that he could be trusted. But
Peterson couldn't denounce them, as there was every likelihood that
he would be dealing with Mulroney and Bourassa in the future.

The denouement to Meech Lake has always baffled me. It struck
me as extraordinary that the two heroes of the piece were two men —
Harper and Wells — who had prevented their democratic assemblies
from voting on the question.

NINE

Over and

Out

◆

ONE OF THE POWERS OF A PREMIER in the Canadian political system is the right to choose the date of the next provincial election. In the case of the 1990 election, this power may well have proved to be David Peterson's downfall.

At a caucus retreat in February 1990, our government debated the cases for calling an early election or holding on for a longer term. The retreat was run like a debate at my suggestion: Sean Conway and I were on one side and Bob Nixon and Steve Mahoney on the other. I think it is too cynical to say that those who were in favour of an early election were in favour of it because they thought it could be won, while a later election could not be.

A lot of people with long memories remembered the election of 1981. An election that occurs during a recession is a very unsatisfactory event because the economy and the community are at their lowest ebb. Opposition parties demand a response to unemployment or some other issue and you get into a bidding war. It doesn't lead to the development of sound economic policy; it doesn't lead to a fair price;

it leads to an auction. And that was the reason lots of people thought we should call the election before the recession, so that when the recession began we would have a mandate to take the very tough decisions it would be necessary to take. On the other side was the belief we should serve out a reasonable term. If we called an early election, the argument went, the people wouldn't understand.

Then, the recession came on a little faster than was predicted. By August, a recession that wasn't anticipated until November was on the boards. And with it, I learned something fascinating from watching my own constituency: the conventional wisdom that an election should be held before rather than during a recession is wrong. If it's held before a recession in the awareness that there will be one, everyone perceives himself to be a victim of it. If it's held during the recession — which isn't ideal either, of course — very often the victims of the recession are identified very early. There aren't any beneficiaries, but at least you can flush out those who will escape its effects.

The problem with the election of 1990 was that everyone knew some kind of a recession was coming. They didn't know how long or how deep or how tough or who would be hurt. So they assumed it would be terrible and that everyone would be hurt.

There was an air of unreality about our caucus debate as, for the most part, all participants shared the belief that we were so far ahead in the polls that we would win an election whenever it was called.

After the debate, I realized that the election might be called sooner rather than later. I wanted Chuck Birchall to run my next campaign, although he had retired as my executive assistant and was now working full-time at McCarthy Tétrault as an environmental lawyer. I took him out for dinner at the Corner House and plied him with much wine. He reminded me forcefully that I had always said that I would only serve for five years. According to him, I responded that I could not leave in midstream, as the public wanted me to carry through on court reform. To this, he replied, "That's bullshit and you know it. The only two people who care about court reform are you and Pat Monahan, and he just wants to write a book about it." Despite his misgivings, before the meal was over I had extracted a promise from Chuck to run my campaign.

In March, Peterson told the party to get ready for either possibility. Then, Meech Lake consumed most of the government's energy for the next two months. After the fact, Peterson told Neil McCormick, "If Meech Lake had passed I wouldn't even have thought of an election."

When Peterson first became leader, he had recruited a small group of advisers, including Hershell Ezrin, Gordon Ashworth, and Vince Borg. All three were capable of giving him blunt advice. By 1990, all three were gone from his immediate circle: Ezrin, who went to Molson's to make money; Ashworth, who had been caught up in the Patti Starr affair; and Borg, who left to head the Toronto bid for the 1996 Olympics. Their replacements were not as confident about saying no to Peterson. A whiff of the politics of courtiers hung about the office now; the environment was much changed from the days when Peterson languished in the political wilderness during the Davis years.

Peterson had handed control of the party's election mechanism to Beth Webster and Kathy Robinson. He gave Beth control of the day-to-day tactical operations, and brought her into the premier's office. Kathy, past president of the Ontario Liberal party and a prominent communications lawyer, was in charge of election strategies. Peterson announced this decision at a cabinet meeting as a fait accompli: he did not seek, nor did he get, input from the cabinet.

In the summer of 1990, after he got back from a vacation at Grand Bend on Lake Huron, David Peterson summoned the cabinet. He advised us that, later on that morning, he was going to see Lincoln Alexander, the lieutenant-governor, to request dissolution of the legislature. Of my cabinet colleagues, only Greg Sorbara openly challenged the decision, using a few choice profanities to express his reservations. Peterson ignored him, went to see Alexander, and set the wheels of the election in motion. His first press conference turned out to be a good predictor of what was to come in the campaign. Gord Perks, a Greenpeace activist, grabbed most of the attention by chaining himself to the desk from which Peterson was to kick off the campaign. Protesters would dog the premier throughout the next weeks.

Even though we were at 52 percent in the polls when the election was called, and even though the Tories thought that they would lose their status as an official party by dropping to fewer than twelve seats after the election, and even though Bob Rae was preparing himself for life after politics, I could sense on the streets almost immediately that we were in trouble. There were some very unhappy groups out there: lawyers unhappy about automobile insurance; environmentalists who felt that that we hadn't done enough on "green" issues; social welfare people unhappy that we hadn't moved faster on the recommendations outlined in *Transitions*, the Ministry of Community and Social Services' report on the social welfare system. What I could never have predicted was the extent to which all those issues became personalized in the name Peterson.

When the election was called, however, I saw it immediately. In a matter of hours, I had a very clear sense that my constituents didn't like Peterson. My colleagues in other parts of the province told me the same thing. The previous campaign, in 1987, had been the easiest in recent Ontario political history, a stroll from one enthusiastic campaign event to another. In 1990, as the caucus debate had predicted, people were angry with Peterson for the early election call. The anger lingered because he was unable to articulate any very good reason for the election.

Those running the campaign had made another major miscalculation. They had assumed that the key to members winning their ridings was to play up a close connection with the premier. The Liberal candidates had their pictures taken with him: they were to be featured prominently in the brochures that would be produced at campaign headquarters. But, as it would turn out, reminding voters of David Peterson was the wrong way to get re-elected in 1990.

In St. George–St. David, we did not have any recent pictures of me except for the one with Peterson. So we covered up his half of the picture, and ran off our brochures. We also stashed away some of the central party literature without actually distributing it, a wise move on the part of my campaign team.

The first challenge I faced in the 1990 election came when rumours circulated that the Conservative candidate, Keith Norton, a former cabinet minister in the Davis government, wanted to "out" me as a homosexual. This despite his having been in the closet the entire time he served in the Davis government.

When I first went into politics, it was rumoured that Claire Hoy of the *Toronto Sun* was intent on "outing" me. The *Sun* followed me around one day when I was campaigning. About the first person that I ran into was Toller Cranston, the flamboyant figure skater. The *Sun* published a picture of us together, something that apparently gave rise to an urban legend that Cranston and I were lovers. Eventually, nothing came of the stories. Many people in and out of government knew what my sexual orientation was, but they respected my wishes to keep my private life private.

But that didn't keep the matter from coming up in 1990. Early in the campaign, an all-candidates meeting was scheduled at the 519 Church St. Community Centre, which provided a wide range of social services for the gay and lesbian community. The community centre was located within half a block of the intersection of Church and Wellesley streets, the cultural crossroads of the Toronto gay community. I assumed that Norton would use the occasion to "out" me. Anticipating his move, I had a friend, someone well known in the gay community, begin the meeting by rising on a point of privilege and asking me, "Are you gay?"

I stated, "My private life has always been private. My friends know who I am and what I stand for." Thus, I was able to pre-empt Norton, while at the same time neutralizing some of the people in the raucous crowd who were chanting, "We're here, we're queer, we will not be denied." My response changed the tenor of the meeting. The matter was not raised in any substantial way in any of the other debates in the campaign.

That the issue of sexuality was raised so vociferously in the 519 debate demonstrated the increased visibility the gay and lesbian community in Toronto had achieved since my first days in the city, when discretion and secrecy ruled the public behaviour of so many homosexuals. It also showed that the gay and lesbian community, of which I was part, was beginning to assert its own political voice in ways that had not seemed possible a generation earlier.

In spite of the fact that I had amended the Ontario Human Rights Code to prohibit discrimination based on sexual orientation, I had angered a number of gay activists by my refusal to amend pension legislation to extend benefits to same-sex couples. I ruminated about this in an earlier article on the role of the attorney general:

> The government of Ontario at present is confronted by a case brought by a "same-sex couple" who live together and who want to receive OHIP benefits at rates available to those who live in a traditional spousal relationship. The straightforward legal issue is the definition of "spouse" in the health legislation — a narrow, superficially technical question. That narrow legal issue, of course, raises an important question of policy with major financial implications for the taxpayer and the administration of the provincial health insurance plan. When we prepared our response in that case, we identified some seventy-nine other statutes or tax-supported programs that would be affected in one way or another by the court's decision. Therefore, the section 1 charter argument can't be allowed to focus simply on the effects of a determination on OHIP; rather, it must focus on the wide range of government policies that relate to spousal entitlements.

I also thought that gay couples who wanted to get married were misguided. Perhaps it was my Catholic upbringing, but I regarded marriage as a church-sponsored religious ceremony that had little to do with the living arrangements that gay couples chose to enter. For gay couples to want to marry, I thought, meant that they were buying in to the values of the straight society that had for many years ostracized them and made them feel like pariahs. Personally, I could not imagine getting married. I had always defined myself by my work, not my sexual orientation, and I was old-fashioned enough to think that it was really nobody else's business.

In retrospect, I wish I had been more accommodating on the issue of spousal benefits for gay couples. It later became an issue in the two by-elections called to fill my seat and another vacant one. The new Liberal leader Lyn McLeod's apparent change of heart on the issue cost her dearly in the 1995 election campaign. At the time of the 1990 election, however, it was a relatively minor matter.

During the first stage of the campaign, support for the Liberals dropped, while the NDP surged to 32 percent in the polls, and then stopped. Peterson did reasonably well in the leaders' debate, and it looked as if the election was still winnable.

The next day, however, the brain trust at campaign headquarters decided that a dramatic move was needed to shore up Liberal support. Mike Harris, whose campaign for the Tories had been farcically badly managed, complete with lost buses and missed photo ops and all the other things that indicate a lack of political skill, had been portraying himself as the "Taxfighter." The Liberal strategists decided that the way to counter this Tory threat was to offer to cut a percentage point from the provincial sales tax.

When campaign co-chairs David McNaughton and Kathy Robinson first pitched the idea to Bob Nixon, who had just brought in the first balanced budget in many years, his reaction was characteristically blunt: "Are you nuts?" Nixon's initial instincts were correct, but he was persuaded that the tax cut was just the thing to put the Liberals over the top. Peterson was then sold on the same idea, and made a hasty announcement at a campaign stop later that day in a small eastern Ontario town.

It was a colossal mistake. When I heard about it, I very nearly decided to throw in the towel and stop campaigning. Chuck Birchall made me leave the campaign headquarters to discuss the situation. We stood on the street corner at Spruce and Parliament. Chuck was adamant that I couldn't continue to rely on the work of my devoted volunteers if I was so negative about the campaign. "There are a lot of people in that room who believe in you," he said. "You have to give them something to believe in." I resumed campaigning.

The proposed reduction in the sales tax led our government into its final slide out of power. The NDP had stalled at 32 percent, largely because the public thought that they would be fiscally irresponsible. Once the Liberals cut the sales tax, however, our image of careful fiscal management — Bob Nixon's hallmark — was shattered.

For the next ten days, NDP support soared, and Liberal support shrank. In St. George–St. David, we were locked in a tight fight with the NDP candidate, Carolann Wright, who lived in Regent Park. Chuck Birchall worked the phones and called in all the connections and favours he could to get the Liberal vote out.

As soon as the polls closed, it was clear that our government had gone down to a crushing defeat. Steve Goudge and I were fascinated and horrified by the provincial results. Peterson had lost his own seat. In six weeks, we had gone from being one of the most popular governments in Ontario history to the dustbin of history. Many of my cabinet colleagues had lost. I told Steve that if I couldn't be in government, I didn't want to be in the house. At that point, Chuck said to me, "If I'd known you wanted to lose the election, I could have arranged that two weeks ago. Don't be so negative in front of the volunteers. Shut up and let me get the poll results in peace."

Regent Park saved me. The people there voted for me in enough numbers to carry the seat by the magnificent total of seventy-two votes.

The phone rang. It was my former legislative assistant, Chris Ward, calling from Hamilton. He said, "Ian, I have unbelievably bad news. I lost by ninety-one votes."

I said, "Chris, that's nothing. I have even worse news. I won by seventy-two."

Wright requested a recount in the riding. John Ronson, one of the original Queen's Mafia, was legal officer for the campaign. He had asked for a reduced role at the beginning of the campaign, as he had young twin children and heavy demands on his time at Blake's, the big Toronto law firm where he worked. I had suggested that he act as legal officer, a job that usually entailed practically no work. The recount, however, meant he now had lots to do. He complained he could not get clear instructions from me on whether I wanted to win or lose the recount.

Two days after the election I dropped in to the premier's office at Queen's Park. It is safe to say that Peterson was depressed and discouraged. Sean Conway was also there, unable to look Peterson in the eye. Conway asked me what I was doing there and why I was looking so cheerful.

"I'm looking for thirty-six votes for Carolann Wright so I can lose the recount," I replied.

My flippancy aside, I felt terrible for Peterson. Without him and the changes he brought to the Liberal party in the dark days of opposition, I never would have won in St. David in the first place. He appointed me to the best job I had ever had. He supported all my major decisions. He gave me the independence to run my ministries the way I saw fit. Peterson paid a terrible price for the compromises he made for Meech Lake. He discovered that there was a distrust of accommodation and compromise in the country. But those are the tools of politicians in a highly pluralistic community.

It's not in the nature of the political process to always provide the kinds of answers that the people want. It's foolish to try. If you're lucky enough to win an election and to get into office as I was, you just do the best you can do and steel yourself for the reaction of those around you. Peterson's downfall happened more quickly than anticipated, and it happened in a particularly cruel and personal way; he was held accountable for a lot of things that I don't think he should have been held accountable for.

But he had five years in office. The real exercise is to look at his record and say, "How did he do?" And I think there were a lot of important successes in a progressive period that he can take credit for. In 1985, for example, for all practical purposes there was no ministry of the environment. It was a grossly underfunded place where junior ministers put in time. There were no programs of any significance to control or even to penalize environmental malfeasance. We changed all that. Then the Tories under Harris gutted the department and took it back to what it was before 1985, with predictably sad results.

I regretted the loss of office, as I still had lots of things I wanted to accomplish. But looking back, I was proud of the things I had managed to get done: freedom of information, pay equity, court reform, a completely new race-relations policy, intervenor funding for groups like LEAF, class actions, and all the rest. The realization that I would no longer be able to make policy was tough for me to accept, and it must have been even tougher for Peterson. But he bore up under the strain of a crushing defeat with his rueful sense of humour intact, and I admired him for it.

And in spite of my ambivalence about the recount, I won it.

The NDP had achieved a majority with a smaller percentage of the vote than we had when we formed our minority government in 1985. In a number of ridings, marginal parties, like the Family Coalition party or the Green party, got enough votes to sway the outcome. Mike Harris and the Tories had survived, to fight another day.

Popularity is a fickle mistress. We had it for a while, and then it went away. If we had to lose, I preferred to lose to the NDP than the Tories. In some ways, the Liberal-NDP accord changed the ground rules for politics in Ontario. During the Conservative's forty-three-year rule, their hold on power was sometimes tenuous. In the period leading up to the election in 1975, for example, the Liberals under the leadership of Bob Nixon actually had a substantial lead in the polls. That election saw a number of Liberals elected who would later play a prominent role in politics, including David Peterson and Sean Conway. But the Tories won enough seats to form the government, with the help of the NDP. They hung on for the election in 1977, and they won again in 1981.

It is safe to say that during the whole period of Conservative rule, the government had no concept of a contract between itself and the governed. The Frost and Robarts periods, in particular, were marked by a certain paternalism. This paternalism had a positive aspect, a sense that the government would look out for those least able to look out for themselves. The catch was that the government defined what it was that the unfortunate classes needed; it was all top-down, however well intentioned.

It is ironic that the Liberals under Peterson, in increasing public expectations about the role of government, helped pave the way for the Harris Tories, the most ideologically committed government in Ontario's history. It reminds me of H.L. Mencken's definition of democracy: "giving the people what they want, and giving it to them good and hard."

Despite my initial desire to lose the election, as so many of my colleagues had, at first I did not mind settling in to the routines of the House, sitting on the opposition benches. After two years in opposition, however, I found myself increasingly disenchanted. Opposition was not where I wanted to be, even though the first time I ran for election it was where I thought I might be if I was very, very lucky. I decided to resign my seat. It wasn't fair to my constituents to continue to represent them if my heart wasn't fully in it.

And my heart couldn't be fully in it. Other things in my life meant more to me. If I was prone to feeling sorry for myself, I had every excuse for feeling so at that moment. Kim had now developed full-blown AIDS. Unfortunately, doctors had not then discovered that a combination of anti-AIDS drugs could keep the infection in check. We all watched helplessly as he got thinner and thinner. His body, once so athletic on the tennis court or in the hockey rink, became an instrument of pain.

When I announced my resignation, I said nothing publicly about Kim's illness.

People in the legislature greeted my departure with some touching, funny speeches. Lyn McLeod remarked on my method of Socratic questioning while in cabinet. Ernie Eves, speaking for the Conservatives, emphasized how much money I had charged him when he had retained my services on behalf of a junior hockey team in which he had an interest. And Bob Rae spoke about how I taught him in law school, and wished me the best in my new endeavours.

I would not have missed my time in politics for all the tea in China. It was sad to leave, but what was sadder, in a way, was my sense that during my time in office, politics had become ever more like the Hobbesian state of nature, in which life was nasty, brutish, and short. I was through with that world. It had been quite a ride, but now it was time to get off the merry-go-round. Tim Murphy got the Liberal nomination in my riding and won the by-election. St. George–St. David was no longer automatic Tory turf.

James MacPherson, the dean of law at my alma mater, Osgoode Hall Law School, now at York University, kindly offered me the Bora Laskin Chair in Constitutional Law. I accepted, and got back into teaching law, something that I have always enjoyed. I also signed on as a commentator on provincial politics for "Fourth Reading," a weekly component of a new show, called *Studio 2*, on TVO, hosted by Steve Paikin. It paid me around $100 a show, a start to recouping all the income I had foregone for the thrill of politics.

The
Hardest Job

◆

MOST PEOPLE WOULD HAVE BEEN HAPPY TO TAKE A BREAK from the pressures of it all. I had maintained a blistering pace during my political career. When I started teaching at Osgoode, and practicing law again, it seemed as if my life had returned to normal. I could understand the need for a break intellectually, but emotionally it was a different story. I liked teaching, and I still enjoyed meeting the students and sharing ideas with them, but I missed the excitement of being attorney general. The adrenaline rush that had sustained me for my time in politics was gone.

Professionally, I felt between worlds. During my absence, Gowling and Henderson had merged with a much larger law firm, Strathy Archibald. When I went back to the firm, it seemed like a different planet. Everyone wore three-piece suits and spoke in reverential terms of the CIBC, Strathy's main corporate client. People kept precise time dockets, something I had never done in my entire career, and did not propose to start doing now. Even though most of my old partners from Cameron, Brewin & Scott were still there, and Steve

Goudge, who had engineered the merger, was running the combined operation, it didn't feel the same.

I was also beginning to pay a price in physical terms for the years during which I had operated on a flat-out basis. I had smoker's cough. Sometimes I found myself short of breath. I continued to smoke, though I made many attempts to give it up, as this undated list shows:

IAN SCOTT'S REASONS TO QUIT
1. No lung cancer
2. No fear of lung cancer
3. No stomach upset
4. No smell on hands
5. No emphysema
6. More energy
7. No pain in chest
8. Clean teeth
9. Clean tongue
10. No daily hacking cough
11. Better speaking voice — no gravel
12. No smelly ashtrays in bath / bedroom
13. Good kissing
14. Never having to give up smoking again or thinking about it
15. Garden better
16. Play tennis better
17. No burn holes in clothes, rugs, etc.
18. No confusion holding cigs, drinks, shaking hands at cocktail parties
19. No running out of cigarettes early in a.m. or late at night
20. Running better
21. Clear skin; no grey-green colour
22. Get the better seats in restaurants
23. Save $2,500 minimum / year
24. Can buy two CDs a week
25. No heavy phlegmy mouth in the morning
26. No embarrassment at meetings where I alone smoke.

I had been smoking since I was fourteen years old. Sometimes I managed to quit, but never for very long. I employed all sorts of strategies to quit, such as not buying cigarettes. But then I would just bum them from other smokers; when that became too embarrassing, I started buying them again. I took the Smoke-Enders course, a supposedly sure-fire program for quitting smoking, four times. Each time, I would cut out smoking, briefly. Then I would start again. I managed to get banned from further Smoke-Enders courses, an impressive accomplishment. Perhaps they were afraid I would set a bad example to their other clients. Maybe they were just tired of dealing with me.

Perhaps the low point of my smoking career occurred during my time as attorney general. The building was officially smoke-free, but I used to smoke at my desk all the time when people weren't around. I had just lit up one day when Dick Challenor, my deputy minister, ushered a delegation of visitors into my office. I stubbed out the cigarette in an ashtray, stuffed the ashtray into a drawer, and went around to the front of my desk to greet my visitors. Dick, who had accompanied the visitors into the room, could see that the cigarette was not out. Smoke started to curl up from crevices in the desk. He quickly asked the visitors to leave for a moment on the pretext that he had something important to tell me confidentially. Once the visitors were gone, we managed to extinguish the butt before it set the whole desk on fire.

The combination of my Gilmour genes and smoking was not a good one. I tried to stop smoking in the house so as not to bother Kim, but it was hard for me to quit. I also continued to drink. Drinking had always been a major part of my social life. It now became even more prominent, a development that did nothing to improve my blood pressure.

It was hard for me to deal with the fact that Kim was wasting away. He went through a number of medical travails. He developed cytomegalovirus, or CMV. This virus lies dormant in many, if not most, people, but a healthy immune system has no trouble keeping it in check. With the suppression of the immune system that AIDS induces, however, the virus can run wild. Its principal target is the eyes: Kim was virtually blind at the end. He also required an operation for an abdominal complaint. At the time, it wasn't certain that he would survive the surgery.

He also had to deal with the fact that James, one of his brothers, who had also been diagnosed with AIDS, committed suicide rather than face the decline he had witnessed in Kim. We tried to withhold this information from Kim, but one evening, he said, "You know, I've heard from all my brothers and sisters, except for James." This broke me up completely. If I kept the news from him, Kim would think that his brother didn't care about him. So I had to tell him that his brother had died, though I tried not to go into too many gory details. Kim had a horrible couple of days after I told him.

There were times when it appeared that dementia, a side effect of AIDS, was making an appearance. For the most part, however, Kim was alert, though weak. Despite his ordeals, he was always thoughtful of the people around him, both his friends and professional caregivers.

Kim and I both liked to cook, and throughout our relationship we had always split the cooking. Now I made special efforts to cook for him. We always ate at the dining table, with flowers and candlelight. Often, however, Kim couldn't eat much of anything I prepared for him. But I tried and he tried.

For some reason, Kim's metabolism could not tolerate the new AIDS drugs that his doctors prescribed. He simply could not keep them down, or they produced such severe side effects that it wasn't worth taking them in the recommended doses. As mentioned earlier, the doctors had not yet figured out that different combinations of drugs provided the best chance to put the disease into a chronic, but not necessarily fatal, state.

By the summer of 1993, it was obvious that Kim was dying. The only question was when death would come. Eventually, we set up a hospital bed in our bedroom for him. For some time, Kim had been taking a drug that took three or four hours to administer through an IV bag. He learned how to insert the IV needle himself. The drug was not working.

Mary Kiervin spent a lot of time with Kim, trying to make him comfortable. When she wasn't with him, she talked to him for hours on the phone. We hired nurses to make sure that he was as comfortable as possible under the circumstances. Billy, our black standard poodle, was a constant companion and comfort for him.

When I was first elected to the legislature, Kim's father was an opposition MPP. Kim had not wanted to come out of the closet any more than I did. His siblings were all supportive, but it would have been awkward for his father to deal with his homosexuality, and with his living with me. So as long as his father was alive, there was no acknowledgment of our relationship.

By the time Kim became ill, however, his father had died, though his stepmother was still living. There seemed to be no further reason for not publicly acknowledging our relationship. All of Kim's brothers and sisters came to the house to see him. I discussed our relationship with all of my siblings, except for David, who I thought would have the hardest time dealing with it. My sisters and my other brothers all indicated that they knew that I was gay and that they had no problem with it.

David and I had always been competitive. We both practiced law. We both built up successful careers doing litigation work. I did more appellate work than he did, but he did more intellectual-property law than I. It would be hard to find someone who worked harder at the law than David had over the years. We were both benchers of the Law Society of Upper Canada, but he was there because he ran for office and got elected by his peers, and I was there (very occasionally, it must be admitted) because I was an ex–attorney general. For all the similarities in our upbringing and our professional lives, though, there were some fundamental differences between us. On a political spectrum, David would have come down on the small-C conservative side, while I was to the left of liberal. We both liked to drink and argue, and we had many memorable evenings together when the words flowed with the vodka. Despite our respective propensities to talk a lot, I found it extremely difficult to talk to David about anything personal.

In the summer of 1993, David went on a camping trip to the Canadian Arctic with a group of people who regularly went off wilderness camping in some remote but beautiful spot. One night, he shared a tent with Peter Lukasiewicz, my old executive assistant. He asked Peter how I was doing. Peter said, "Not too well. You know, Kim is very sick." According to David, that was the first time he had heard Kim's name, although at that point Kim and I had been living together for a dozen or more years.

Once back in Ottawa, David wrote me a letter saying that we had to get together to talk. He had some meetings in Toronto. We arranged to go out for dinner on a Tuesday night. I knew that he wanted to talk to me about Kim and about my being homosexual, and I had earlier resolved to tell him about it.

Instead, we got drunk. Neither of us could talk about the issue. We booked another dinner for Wednesday night. We got drunk again, and again nothing was said about Kim. We booked dinner for the next night. David was going back to Ottawa the next day, so it was now or never. I said that I had to talk about "my lifestyle."

David said, "I know. How is Kim?" And that was it.

At that point, I was fifty-nine years old, and I had just told my fifty-eight-year-old brother, who moved in the same legal circles I did, that I was gay. Dr. Freud might have wished to explore why it was such a hard thing for me to do.

Six weeks later, on November 24, 1993, Kim died. The day before he died, he summoned Mrs. DeSousa, our wonderful housekeeper, to our bedroom, and asked her if she saw the angel in the corner of the room. The angel, he said, looked so much like his mother.

The obituary notice that I wrote for him was the first official acknowledgment of our relationship. Writing it brought home my sense of loss. It seemed unfair that Kim, with his quicksilver wit and his enthusiasm for life, should die so young.

And he was not alone in dying young. It seemed like a malign lottery. Of a group of ten of our friends who were roughly contemporary in age with Kim, seven are now dead of AIDS and two are HIV-positive. One, despite almost superhuman efforts involving intravenous drugs, unprotected sex with strangers, and other dangerous activities, is free of any trace of HIV infection.

I had been to many funeral services for many friends, but it was hardest for me to go to Kim's.

Leonard Woolf, in one of the volumes of his autobiography, writes that work is the best anodyne for pain. He wrote this in the wake of his wife Virginia's suicide. In England, Kim and I had visited Sissinghurst, the garden created by Virginia's lover, Vita Sackville-West. I keep a picture taken of Kim and me at Sissinghurst in my dining room. After Kim's death, I went on a trip to Florida with Ron Beck, one of Kim's best friends, to get away from it all for a while. Then I came back and threw myself into my work.

Some interesting legal cases had come my way. John Laskin, Bora Laskin's son, had been appointed to the Court of Appeal for Ontario and sent some of his files to me. One of them involved representing the landlords' association before the Ontario Human Rights Commission. On the day the hearing opened, I glanced around the room at the multitudes of representatives from tenants' groups and legal clinics who were on the other side and remarked, "You know, I see so many do-gooders in this room at this hearing, I doubt there's anyone left to be out doing good."

I was a regular on "Fourth Reading," Steve Paikin's show on TVO, talking about provincial politics. I enjoyed all the cut and thrust of debating with the cast of characters he provided. It kept me in touch with politics, without the messy business of actually being in politics.

I also appeared on Peter Gzowski's radio show, *Morningside*, several times. Peter and I had known each other since we were students at the U of T; he edited the *Varsity* while I was president of St. Michael's College student council.

Once, while I was on his show, my words would not come out in the right sequence. It was a live broadcast, so I was a bit embarrassed. Peter covered for me by saying that I made even less sense than usual. I now know the incident was an experience of temporary aphasia. It came back later, briefly, as I made an appearance at the Court of Appeal. For two minutes, I could not get the words out. The judges gave me a break, and when it was over I resumed my argument. I should have hauled myself off to a neurologist with all due speed, but at the time I shrugged it off. It was just one of those things, I reasoned, that could be attributed to too much work, or too much alcohol consumed the previous evening.

In March, I went on a trip with Ron Beck to visit our friends David and Jimmy in Mexico. As usual, the trip involved lots of sunbathing. One day, after a few hours of lying out in the sun, I couldn't stand up when it was time to go back to David and Jimmy's place. Something was wrong with my right leg and my right arm. I had to be helped to the house. The next day, my right arm was numb. A doctor was called. He wasn't sure what was causing the problem, as by the time he saw me most of the numbness was gone.

When we went back to Toronto, Ron wheeled me through the airport in a wheelchair, as I was still a bit unsteady on my feet. Once back in Canada, I felt better.

Mary Kiervin took these incidents seriously. She booked me an appointment with a neurologist, Dr. Marotta, who had just opened an office in Commerce Court West, the building where my law firm was now located.

During the second week of May, in 1994, I appeared in Ottawa before the Canadian Judicial Council on behalf of a judge who was being threatened with removal from the bench because he had been handicapped by multiple sclerosis. It was alleged that he was no longer capable of performing his duties as a judge, and that if he wouldn't resign, then he should be removed.

Each day that week, I made my arguments on my client's behalf. Late each afternoon, I flew back to Toronto for some event or other. I went to Chris Ward's nomination meeting in Hamilton, for example. Another night, as a member of the board of directors of the Toronto Symphony Orchestra, I was drawn into some labour negotiations with the TSO's musicians. The negotiations went on into the night, but the dispute was resolved without a strike. Each morning, I caught the shuttle into Ottawa and made my case for the judge with the disability.

On Friday, I made my final submissions at the Canadian Judicial Council in Ottawa, and flew back to Toronto. I was invited to Ron

Beck's for dinner that night, and I was going to my farm with Mary Kiervin for the rest of the weekend.

At Ron's, I told those assembled that I had been to see a doctor and that he had said that I would have to take an Aspirin a day for the rest of my life to reduce the possibility of stroke. Another friend, David Gamble, asked me if I had bought the Aspirin yet, and I laughed and said that I hadn't had time.

The next morning is still a blur to me. Mary says that she came by my house to pick me up to take me to the country. While we were having coffee in my kitchen, she says that a sudden spasm caused me to drop my cup, breaking it and sending a spray of coffee over the wall. I don't remember this.

Mary was dubious about the wisdom of going to the farm. I insisted. We went to Pusateri's, a gourmet food store, to pick up supplies. According to her, I fell down in the aisle, and it wasn't the prices that made me do it, though they might have felled other shoppers over the years. She wanted to take me to the hospital. I said that I would drive myself to the farm if she wouldn't. So we went to the farm.

A few years earlier, the road bridge over the small stream that runs between the road and the house had been swept away. I had replaced it with a footbridge, thinking that it was a good way to keep out intruders too lazy to get out of their trucks to walk the last 150 metres to the farm. On this day, however, I wished I had replaced the road bridge.

Shortly after walking in to the house, I had what I now know was a transient ischemic attack, or TIA. TIAs can be precursors to a stroke. Whatever happened, as a result I was very weak. I was conscious, but I knew that something major had happened. I had trouble walking, though I could do so with assistance. Mary says that I told her that I wanted to stay there. I had had a good run, I apparently said. If I was going to die, I might as well die there, at the farm I loved, surrounded by the gardens I had tended assiduously over the years.

Mary wanted to get me to a hospital, to get me treated. She called all kinds of people, including Dr. Marotta. It is a tribute to her persistence that she got through to him at home on a weekend, after battling her way past the hospital switchboard. When she finally talked to him, his advice was to get me into a hospital as soon as possible. We debated how to get me back to Toronto, having rejected the neurological services available in Guelph or Kitchener.

She wanted to call for an air ambulance. I demurred, both on the grounds that it was unnecessary, and that they would not send one in any event. When she said, "They'll come. I'll tell them who you are," I apparently replied, "You mean, you'll tell them who I *was*."

Supported by Mary, I staggered through the woods and over the footbridge. She drove me to Wellesley Hospital in Toronto and helped me in. I could still walk, though not very well, and talk, though I didn't much feel like it. They brought in a specialist to treat me. He knew I was having a TIA. The question was, where was the blockage?

My drinking and dietary habits were such that it was not unreasonable for him to conclude that there might be occlusions in the carotid arteries, blocking blood flow to the brain. He thought I should have an angiogram, a test in which dye is inserted into the arteries and then an X-ray is taken to see how much of the carotid is blocked by fatty deposits.

There is a small, but still significant, chance that injecting the dye will dislodge some of the fatty deposits in the carotid. This is what happened to me. The angiogram caused a particle to break off. It migrated upward into my brain, where it caused much mischief.

Until the angiogram, I was in rough shape, but more or less intact, both physically and mentally. During the angiogram, I was in big trouble. I had a severe stroke on the left side of the brain, affecting my right-side motor skills and my left-side intellectual capacity.

Mary had alerted my family in Ottawa and they came to Toronto. When I woke up after the procedure, I could speak to them, but the words were hard to find. I was paralyzed on my right side.

Then it got worse. Over the next few days, I lost more of my ability to speak. I could move fewer and fewer body parts. Strokes move through different phases. With me, each phase seemed to take more of my history and consciousness away from me. I remember talking to my sister Martha in the first few days after the procedure, and then the words seemed to fade away. I slipped into a stage between consciousness and coma. People came to see me, and I was only vaguely aware that they were there. I couldn't talk. I couldn't read or write.

My partner at Gowling's, Chris Dassios, was one of those who came to see me. He promptly fainted. His blood pressure was through the roof, and he ended up in a hospital bed for a week. As he is a good twenty-five years younger than I am, it shows that high blood pressure is not to be taken lightly.

The first time Ron Beck came to see me, I couldn't say a word to him, though I knew who he was. This was shocking to me.

Doctors told my family that I would live, but that it was possible that I would not walk or talk again. I took a certain amount of grim pleasure in proving them wrong. I could still communicate, even though the neural connections to my vocabulary were almost completely destroyed. I could wave my good left arm to indicate yes or no. I could communicate through the expression in my eyes. I could even get out the occasional word that was appropriate for the circumstances, though much more often an inappropriate word would come out. If I concentrated as hard as I could, which in my case now included sticking out my tongue, I could print with my left hand some of the letters that made up my name. More often than not, I didn't spell it correctly.

For all intents and purposes, my life as a lawyer was over. The stroke had taken away the law, or at least it had taken away my access to the law. Where once I could retrieve legal principles and apply them instantly to the facts of the case I was arguing, now the principles were buried beneath the rubble of the stroke.

Before the stroke, words were my life. They had come so effortlessly and now they were gone.

I would have to start over. It would be my hardest job.

ELEVEN

Starting
Over

WHEN IT BECAME APPARENT THAT I WOULD LIVE, and that I would regain some of the functions I had lost in the immediate aftermath of the stroke, I was transferred to the rehabilitation unit at Queen Elizabeth Hospital.

At rehab, I was put through my paces. I had to learn to walk all over again. I started off in a contraption with parallel grab bars, like the apparatus that gymnasts use. I didn't feel much like a gymnast, however. I had to learn to use a cane, as my right leg was weak. My right arm was useless, which meant that I had to switch my handedness from right to left, never an easy thing to do. When I was in elementary school, it was still the fashion for teachers to tie up pupils' left hands to make them write the "right" way. Now, the stroke had tied up my right hand and arm, and I had no choice but to learn how to write with the other hand. What made it especially difficult was that I had lost my knowledge of the alphabet. I could not remember which way the curves in certain letters went, and I had no neuromuscular memories in my left arm to guide me.

I had to practice going up and down stairs, a task complicated by the fact that I could not trust my right leg. I used the banister to pull myself up stairs. Going down was harder, as I had to swing out my bad leg and trust that it would eventually connect with something solid. In the beginning, I had very little control over the process. Each step down was an adventure. Try as I might, I could not remember which leg to swing first. I was like a baby learning to walk. When babies fall, however, they usually do not hurt themselves very much. If I was to fall down a flight of stairs, I risked injuring myself severely.

In some ways, a new self was being born. It was strange for me to have to accept advice, however well intended, from occupational therapists. I was used to doing things, in the immortal words of singer Paul Anka, "My Way." Now, I had to listen to people tell me how to walk, how to climb up and down stairs, how to get in and out of chairs. Although I was not quite as unfortunate as Ozymandias, I must confess that sometimes I felt about as useless as Percy Bysshe Shelley's broken statue lying in the desert.

I was not bashful about sharing my feelings on the subject, either. One of the areas of my brain affected by the stroke was the centre that governs restraint, which was now much diminished. As a result, I vented emotions that I might otherwise have kept in check. For the first time in my life, or at least the first time since I was an extremely small child, my rational self was not in control. As a result of the stroke and its depredations in my brain, I was angry. I was frustrated at being so incapacitated, and I had no compunction about letting people know it, within my disgustingly limited ability to say so.

One of the secrets of the success of my previous life was my ability to compartmentalize. In my professional life in law, this ability conferred many benefits. If I was dealing with labour law, for example, I had a finite number of principles to mobilize for arguments. I was good at mobilizing them in a coherent way: that was how I made my living. If I was arguing a constitutional case, on the other hand, I would download the appropriate constitutional principles from my well-stocked legal mind and present them in as persuasive a fashion as I could. At a personal level, I was able to keep my gay social life distinct from my family or professional social lives. It was not a great strain, despite what others may think, to isolate these worlds from one another.

Now the stroke had blasted away the restraints and the compartments, with some memorable results. My brother Brian recalls a moment in my convalescence when, as he was wheeling me in my wheelchair down a hospital corridor to a physiotherapy appointment, we approached a nurse walking in the opposite direction. According to Brian, I waved my good left hand to catch the nurse's attention, and then proclaimed loudly, "Homosexual."

My sixtieth birthday was three months less a day after my stroke. It was arranged that I should go home for a special birthday dinner. My sister Martha had come down from Ottawa to cook it for me. The dinner was the first time I had been home since the stroke. The table was set on the back deck of my home, and my friends and family had done everything possible to make it a very special event for me.

My handyman, Louis Seghers, had been asked to install ramps around the house, so that I would be able to manoeuvre around my house. Whoever made the decision to install ramps, however, had not consulted me, which was the first mistake. The second mistake was to think that I had no opinion on the matter. I did not want ramps cluttering up the place and destroying the appearance of the formal gardens outside or the staircase inside. I was furious.

My friend Ron Beck arrived, several hours before the dinner party was supposed to start, with a huge bouquet of flowers to welcome me home. Then I distinguished myself by falling on the step that leads from the deck to the dining room of my house. I landed flat on my face. Martha was next door at the time. Mary Kiervin had been in the kitchen when I fell and had not seen me stumble. Distraught, she accused Ron of having somehow caused the fall.

Mary's reaction, motivated, I am sure, by her protective instincts, did not improve the ambiance of the occasion. Much shouting followed, accompanied by not a few tears, though none were shed by me. An ambulance was called. Mary jumped in the back with me to ride back to the hospital. I never did get my birthday dinner.

Everyone drew his or her own conclusions from this event. My family was convinced that it meant that I would not be able to cope on my own, that I would need someone with me twenty-four hours a day to deal with any falls. Mary was convinced that she should look after me. And I was convinced that all of these well-meaning people should stop trying to make decisions for me. I wanted to go home, but on my own terms.

One month after my rather unsuccessful birthday party, against the advice of most of the professionals consulted, and in spite of my family's obvious concern that I could no longer look after myself, I came home.

There was no downstairs bathroom in the house. There still is none, despite repeated suggestions from others that adding one would make my life easier. I am stubborn enough to think that climbing the stairs to go to the bathroom is good for me, and that a downstairs bathroom would spoil the aesthetics of my practically perfect house. I did agree, however, to the installation of banister rails on both sides of the staircase, as I needed to hold on to make my way up and down stairs, and could do so only with my left hand.

My family had arranged for a succession of nurses to look after me. I was sure that Mrs. DeSousa, my housekeeper of twenty years, was perfectly capable of providing all the care I required. I didn't want to deal with the professional caregivers, who didn't understand me. Mrs. DeSousa knew me and knew what I needed. I got rid of the nurses and arranged for her to come every day to help me get up, showered, shaved, and dressed, and to prepare my breakfast. I decided to grow a beard. This saved time every morning, as I only needed to have the beard trimmed once a week at my barber's.

Mrs. DeSousa is two years older than I am, but she has the energy of a teenager. She claims to sleep two hours each night. She exists on Coca-Cola; Pepsi is too sweet for her. When she is in prime form, she drinks fourteen Cokes a day. After she leaves my place, she works for her other clients. Although she has worked for me for more than twenty years, I am a junior client for her; she has other clients for whom she has worked for more than thirty years.

Mrs. DeSousa is a wonder, and I am so fortunate to have her helping me. She doesn't need to be told what to do, although that doesn't usually stop me from trying to tell her. Without her, I would have a tough time coping.

Sometimes, especially at the beginning, she had a hard time coping with my impatience at not being able to say what I want to say. Until I went on Prozac after the stroke, I was ill tempered on occasion. She bore it all with fortitude, knowing that when I came to my senses, I would apologize for yelling at her.

One memorable morning, Bob Rae was scheduled to come to my house for breakfast, as part of a group effort to help me regain my speech. Bonnie Bereskin, my speech therapist, and Ian Roland, my partner at Gowlings, organized this program of "breakfast therapy."

Mrs. DeSousa was not unaccustomed to premiers. She knew Bob Rae from his attendance at political events in the Portuguese community. She knew Bill Davis as well, as she had worked for his sister for many years, and had seen him at parties and family events over the years. The day that Bob was to come for breakfast, she showed up in a black dress, and proceeded to put on a frilly white apron, like a maid in a farce by Georges Feydeau.

I thought her costume was unnecessary, and that Bob would think I required her to dress in a formal maid's outfit every day. She thought she was dressing up as a mark of respect for the former premier of Ontario. She was still helping me get dressed when he arrived. He could hear me shouting, "No! No! No! Ridiculous, ridiculous!"

When Mrs. DeSousa, still wearing her frilly apron, and I arrived downstairs to greet Bob, she asked him, after performing a curtsy that would not have looked out of place in Buckingham Palace, "Mr. Rae, do I look ridiculous?" His years of political training paid off in that moment. He replied effortlessly, "Mrs. DeSousa, I think you look wonderful." Then we had breakfast.

The breakfasts were part of a therapy regimen that my speech therapist, Bonnie Bereskin, had encountered while working on her thesis. The actress Patricia Neal had used a group of friends to help her recover from a severe stroke. Bonnie worked out a similar program for me.

People with aphasia are conscious that they do not fit in easily any more. Their problems understanding what other people say are multiplied if several conversations are going on at the same time, as is typical of any cocktail party. Aphasics have problems saying what they'd like to say. Sometimes, the words won't come at all. At other times, the wrong words come, and then much effort must be expended in correcting their unintended remarks. This is embarrassing, and puts a definite crimp in the flow of conversation. The situation can also try the patience of the people who deal with aphasics. Many aphasics sense this, and react by retreating from the world. Retreat is safe, but it means that there is little chance of getting better.

Bonnie wouldn't allow me to retreat into my own, safe world. She called a meeting at Gowling's with a team of my colleagues, assembled by Ian Roland. It was a unique arrangement; in most cases, caregivers tend to come from the aphasic's immediate family circle. The boardroom at Gowling's, usually occupied by dealmakers and corporate strategists, was now full of people intent on learning how to help a colleague and friend learn how to speak again. Most of the lawyers in the room, it's safe to say, were not used to being instructed on how to talk. Talking was what they did for a living. Talking was not a problem for them. Talking to me in terms I could understand was.

At that meeting, Bonnie explained the purpose of my therapy program. People were to help me read and comprehend again. Friends, family, and colleagues were scheduled to have breakfast, lunch, and dinner with me. They were given speech therapy exercises to do with me. The basis of the program might have come from E.M. Forster, when he said that the goal of life was "Only connect." I had to re-establish connections with the outside world, and I was at a loss for words.

Unfortunately, the therapy program did not always run smoothly. I wasn't used to being dependent on people. I had left home when I had just turned seventeen, and I had done quite nicely, thank you. Now, my short-term memory was practically non-existent. The stroke had blasted out my comprehension of numbers, so that if someone gave me a date on the phone, the date meant nothing to me. Consequently, I sometimes left the house when I was supposed to be there to meet someone for a meal. My unexplained absences frustrated people in the support team. Sometimes, the guest didn't show up. As I well understood from my days in practicing law, dates for court appearances would get changed, and the lawyer who was supposed to come to help me learn how to speak again would have to cancel and reschedule.

The breakfasts frustrated me as well. I wanted to talk about politics and law and world events. My support group, meanwhile, wanted me to speak in complete sentences, a task I wasn't up to yet. Some of the sessions worked, and some of them left both guider and guidee in complete frustration. Some people dropped out of the program because they found it too painful to contemplate the damage the stroke had wrought in me.

Bonnie worked with me on a one-to-one basis, using a series of exercises that involved flash cards. It was like doing phonetics all over again. I had a hard time reading. I had dyslexia, and I couldn't spell. She kept trying to convince me that it would take time for me to regain my speech, that babies needed three years before they could speak in sentences, and that *their* brains were hard-wired for the task. My hard wiring had all been scrambled. It was unreasonable to suppose that I would re-learn language skills faster than an infant could. In many ways, it was worse than being an infant again. I knew what I wanted to say, but the words just would not come. I was not the most patient client she had ever had, but I might have been one of the most determined.

Still, learning to navigate in the world was a battle. I was lucky if I could say more than "Ian Scott, Ian Scott," on the telephone to anyone who called me. It was at first very hard for me to dial out, as I literally did not recognize the numbers, and when I found the one I wanted I might have forgotten what number came next. The telephone also made it difficult for me to retract mistakes. When I was speaking to someone face-to-face, if "no" came out where I meant "yes," I could wave my left hand to indicate that in this case "no" did not mean "no." On the telephone, no one could see me wave. I was reduced to saying "Ian Scott, Ian Scott," and hoping that they could figure out what I wanted to say, or that they could contact someone who might know what I wanted to talk about.

In the past, I had worked out at the Y, and jogged for exercise. I always got in shape electioneering, with the daily practical necessity of working the morning bus stops and doing three canvasses a day. Now, it was exhausting to walk to the end of my little cul-de-sac of a street. I could not walk very well, as my right leg dragged. It was hard for me to lift up my right toes, so that when I walked, I tended to pull that foot on the ground. This made it likely to catch on any minor obstruction on the ground. As a result, I got used to falling. It might have been easier to allow myself to be pushed around in a wheelchair, but I did not want to settle for that.

The first big test of my resolve to walk again came at a special ceremony in honour of my appointment as an officer of the Order of Canada. Ray Hnatyshyn, the governor general and a friend of mine from when he had been federal justice minister and I had been attorney general, made arrangements to come to Toronto to present me with the pin that signifies that one is an OC. It was my first public appearance since the stroke. It was a big step for me, and typical of Ray's kindness that he would make a special trip on my behalf. I have been blessed with many wonderful friends.

Mrs. DeSousa and I rode to the ceremony in a limousine. Fifty or sixty of my family and friends had assembled. The usual hum of conversation in the crowd ceased as Ray came into the room. I started to walk down the corridor between the rows of chairs. The sudden silence called for a comment from me. I said, "Ssh, ssh, ssh." The crowd laughed. I might not have been able to speak very well, but I was still capable of making comments that went to the point.

I took another big step toward independence when, at Ron Beck's suggestion, I got a battery-driven sidewalk vehicle. Most of my family was horrified. They didn't think it was safe for me to be out on a scooter when I couldn't even say where I lived. But Ron was right.

The scooter gave me back some independence. If I wanted to go to a movie, or out for a coffee or lunch, I didn't have to rely on friends to take me or worry about calling a cab, which was a hard thing for me to do. What's more, I knew where I wanted to go and how to get there. In cabs, I often couldn't say where I wanted to go, although I could usually direct the cabbie by waving my left arm repeatedly and shouting "No, no, goddammit!" if he went the wrong way.

The scooter gave me word-free mobility, unless, as sometimes happened, the battery went dead, or wasn't charged. In those cases, I got someone to help get me home; then, someone else could deal with the problem of the dead battery.

There was no getting around the fact that I needed a lot of help, a reality that collided squarely with my highly developed habits of independence. I was also getting bored. For my whole life, I had been active, verging probably on hyperactive. Now, for the first time since I was a child, I had no obligations. My universe had shrunk from the arena of Supreme Court appearances to noodling over on my scooter to the Second Cup at Church and Wellesley in the hopes that I might see someone I knew.

Someone suggested that a computer might help me. My brother David bought one for me. I had never used a computer — or a type-writer, for that matter — in my life. As a lawyer, I dictated, and others typed. I had used this system throughout my professional life. When I confronted the computer, I was stymied. I had a sympathetic teacher in Pearl Gryffe, who specialized in teaching disabled people how to use computers. Still, I couldn't remember how to turn the thing on. I couldn't spell. If someone put the word "cat" on the screen, I could hunt and peck and find the letters on the keyboard to spell out "C-A-T." If someone asked me to spell "cat," and the screen was blank, I couldn't do it. Repeated attempts at this training exercise were like rubbing salt in the wounds of my loss. I gave up using the computer.

Other people thought that I might like to take up painting, a diversion that had provided Winston Churchill with many happy hours of recreation in his later years. Roy McMurtry, as Bill Davis once pointed out in a speech I heard him give, specialized in collecting the work of one artist: Roy McMurtry. Despite these examples of successful recreational painters to inspire me, I produced only one canvas, a copy of a Barker Fairley painting I own. The canvas sat on its easel for more than two years before I had it removed.

The breakfast meetings stopped. They were just too complicated to keep going. It was much easier to arrange lunches, where I could meet my friends and have some good food.

I started the lengthy project of working on these memoirs. Neil McCormick's first formal interview with me lasted for about an hour. It was all I could take. Beads of sweat popped out on my forehead before it was over. He sat at the computer, I sat at a chair, and we tried to talk. Neil asked me questions. Often I knew the answers, but the answers would not come. At the end of the session, he had eight lines of notes. It worked better if Neil interviewed someone else about me in my presence. This method jogged my memory, and it allowed me to make corrections in the other person's narrative, something that was much easier for me to do than to construct the whole narrative by myself. But it was a slow process.

One day, Neil took me to Gowling's so that some of my colleagues could reminisce about past cases with me, in the hopes that the visit would trigger my own memories for the memoir. Several people dropped by with war stories of past litigation or political battles. Then Peter Lukasiewicz came to see me. We were laughing about past political campaigns when he said abruptly, "To change the subject, Scott, we need your office." It was the symbolic end of my legal career. My partners had decided that they needed the space. Peter, then the office manager for litigation, was selected to deliver the message. His directness was one of the things I admired about him, but this was a bit of a shock.

Within two days, I had cleared out my office. I brought home the portrait of my great-grandfather, Sir Richard Scott, and the portrait of Oliver Mowat, not only the longest-serving premier of Ontario, but also my model of an Ontario attorney general. He argued the province's cases in person and dramatically reshaped the Canadian

Constitution. He and my great-grandfather had briefly been in the Senate together, with Mowat replacing Sir Richard as Liberal leader in the Senate for a year.

Cleaning out my office was a forceful reminder that I was retired. I knew I would have to find some way to occupy my time. For most of my life, there had never been enough time to do everything I wanted to do. Now, time seemed to stretch endlessly before me. For someone whose hobbies had been gardening, music, and reading, I was running out of things to do.

I decided that I needed to get back to reading. This struck some people as odd, as I could not read very well. I could not understand anything I read to myself unless I read it out loud. I needed to hear it before I could comprehend it. I got Neil to read to me. We tackled the morning paper together. He would read most of a column; I might read a paragraph out loud, which took as long as it did for him to read me the rest of the column. If he read too quickly, which he almost always did, I could not understand what he was saying, and I would have to get him to slow down.

Neil and I spent hundreds of hours plowing through biographies. I liked biographies of musicians, like Glenn Gould, Chopin, and Liszt. Together, we read a massive biography of J. Edgar Hoover. I found it fascinating, not just because it revealed Hoover to have been one of the worst human beings imaginable, but because it triggered memories of political events. We read Kim Campbell's autobiography, and I found it a hoot. We read John Crosbie's entertaining account of his life and times in politics. We started reading Bob Rae's autobiography, but stopped abruptly when we came to the section on the accord, where he did not mention my role in its negotiation. I think he was still mad at me for calling him "the biggest wimp in the Western world" during one particularly heated parliamentary exchange. It sometimes took four months to get through one book. It all helped, but it was slow, slow work.

I started to spend a lot of time with my old partner, Jimmy Smith, who was back in Toronto. He had a new partner in Scott DeWare, and he had throat cancer. He had to have his larynx removed. He learned to speak by holding his finger over the hole in his throat. Then he was fitted with a voice appliance that made him sound a bit like a Swedish computer. As the disease progressed, he would have to have these appliances replaced.

Jimmy started coming around for lunches and dinners. Even though his prospects weren't great, he was determined to extract every ounce of joy possible from his remaining time. At different times in his treatment, he could not speak at all, depending on the state of the prosthetic devices he used to talk. At such times, he carried around a big slate, like a child's Etch-A-Sketch, on which he would write what he wanted to say. Then he would flip a switch, the writing would vanish, and the slate would be ready for his next witticism. He never lost his sense of humour. The problem was that I couldn't read what he wrote on the slate with any facility. Sometimes he would erase his message before I finished reading it. Then I would have to get him to write it all over again.

One nice summer day, Jimmy suggested that we go to my farm for a picnic, for old times' sake. I had just rented the farm to a friend of mine, Philip Edwards. He had installed his new partner there, a South African doctor, who didn't know us from a hole in the wall. It is safe to say that the doctor was somewhat startled by the incursion of Jimmy and me and our language difficulties. Despite the confusion, we had a wonderful day in the fresh air at the farm: it brought back many happy memories for us both.

Jimmy never let his problems stand in the way of a good laugh. Once we were at Prego, a Toronto restaurant. He was carrying his writing device. Michael Carlevale, the owner of Prego and a long-time friend of both of us, was chatting to someone in the doorway, a good twenty feet away. He was consumed with curiosity about what Jimmy was writing on his tablet. Jimmy wiped the slate clean and, with a great flourish, wrote a new message, which he brandished so that Michael could clearly read it. The message was "I have to be careful what I write because Michael is reading my every word."

In the summer of 1997, his doctors told Jimmy that his cancer had come back. It was incurable, they said; he had three or, if he was lucky, six months left to live. He fooled them by surviving for another year and a half, during which time he lived life to the fullest.

Jimmy loved dogs. He came over almost every day to take my dog Billy for a walk. Often he brought along his partner's dog, a self-possessed terrier named Mr. Grimm. Mr. Grimm thought his rightful place was on my bed when I retreated for my afternoon nap. Poor Billy wasn't usually allowed on the bed, but it wasn't fair to him to leave him whinging on the floor while Mr. Grimm stretched out self-importantly above him; eventually, both dogs joined me for my nap.

My trip with Jimmy to the farm was an exercise in nostalgia, but the practical fact was that it was hard for me to get there any more, and almost impossible for me to do the kinds of things that I used to do there. The distance in from the road was now hard for me to cover without exhausting myself. The path was not smooth, which made it doubly dangerous. Worst of all, I could no longer garden, which had been my main source of pleasure at the farm. I only had one good arm. I needed that arm to support my body, which meant that I had no way to weed, prune, or do any of the other gardening tasks that suggested themselves to me daily.

Not being able to garden was intensely frustrating. I could have hired gardeners to do it for me, but it wouldn't have been the same. For one thing, I had enjoyed the intense physical work of gardening. For another, gardeners wouldn't understand how I wanted things done unless I told them, and it was difficult for me to get the words out. Everywhere I turned on the farm, I saw things that needed doing, and I was constantly reminded that I could not do them. Eventually, I stopped going there. I first rented it out to an acquaintance, who, as it turned out, was not very responsible about looking after the place. When his tenancy was up, I decided to sell it. Philip Edwards took it over for a short time. And then I put the farm on the market. My brother Brian, who magnanimously and magnificently had taken on the task of looking after my financial affairs, arranged to have the farm sold.

After I accepted an offer to buy the farm, a gang of siblings and friends gathered at the country place over two weekends to help me clear it out. We caused a great deal of commotion, but we worked out a fairly good system for sorting out over thirty years' worth of accumulations. While I sat in a chair, assorted paintings, pieces of furniture, glass, books, and records were brought to me to categorize. My helpers all had strong opinions about what I should keep, what I should sell, and what I should give to assorted family members. Fortunately, I had the strongest opinions, so these usually prevailed. Once these decisions were made, the items were sorted according to their respective destinations. China was wrapped, books separated into keepers and discards, and furniture sent to my home, or shipped to the auction house.

Most of the house's contents had been sorted by the second weekend. The closing was a few days away, and I had planned to make one more trip to the farm to sort through the remaining bits and pieces. Then the phone rang. It was my country housekeeper, calling to say that the footbridge across the stream in front of the house had been ripped out by a giant steam shovel, and there was no way to get into the house, short of fording the stream.

This incident set off a flurry of calls between lawyers. I alerted Louis Seghers, my maintenance man, who had scheduled a crew to be at the house that day to move out the last of my stuff. He told me, "Don't worry, Ian. We'll build a bridge for you if we have to."

I headed to the country. A light snow had fallen that morning, so when I got to the spot in the road where the path led into the farmthe footing was particularly treacherous. The housekeeper was right. A giant steam shovel was at work, dredging out foundations for a new road bridge into the place. But it was still my property for five more days, and I had certainly not given permission for the new owners to take out the footbridge. It was clearly a case of premature ejection. I started getting out of my car before it came to a full stop, waving my cane and shouting at the work crew. They stopped immediately and came to investigate the cause of all the shouting.

The shovel operator was very apologetic. He had been called by the new owners, and commissioned to put in a new bridge. He knew nothing about the details of the buying and selling of the place.

He made a kind of bosun's chair with Neil, my driver that day, and together they carried me over the stream on a bridge made of some rough planks, and through the woods up to the level ground near the house.

Though I had been shouting, "Trespass!" and "My property!" at the top of my lungs, I didn't really mind the intrusion. It at least indicated that the purchaser was intent on going through with the transaction, something you never know for sure about real estate until the deal actually closes in the registry office.

I sorted the final few things, instructed Louis and his crew about what needed to be carried over the rudimentary plank bridge, had myself carried back out to the car by the linked-hands bosun's chair of the contractor and the biographer, and proceeded to go home. And that was my farewell to the farm that had given me so much pleasure over the years.

I tried to heed the advice of Satchel Paige: "Don't look back. Something might be gaining on you."

T W E L V E

The Long
Road Back

◈

WHILE I WAS RECUPERATING, people like Peter Gzowski were kind enough to want to interview me. Peter was ending his run as the host of CBC Radio's *Morningside*, and he wanted to include me on one of his last shows. I thought hard about the offer, but I did not trust myself to be able to go on the radio without making myself an object of pity.

Somewhat later, however, my friend Steve Paikin asked me if TVO could do a show about my life after the stroke. I had known Steve since my days at Queen's Park, and I had been on the "Fourth Reading" segment of his *Studio 2* show. The advantage of doing a TV show was that they could tape over several days and edit out any glitches. They could also show me using my good hand to indicate that I needed to revise what I had just said. As well, they could interview family, friends, and colleagues, so that the burden of carrying the show would be shared.

The show's producers planned to interview me at home. Later, they would have a cocktail party there with some of my friends, as a way of demonstrating the support group that had helped me so much in regaining my speech. Then they would interview lots of other people and splice all the footage together to give a balanced picture of my life after the stroke.

On the day of the interview, Steve and his crew rearranged the furniture in the house to get the shots they wanted. Then, he started asking me questions. Often I could only come up with one-word responses. Steve had to guess what I meant, and fill in the blanks for me. Sometimes he guessed right; often he completely misunderstood me. It was exhausting, and frustrating. They filmed for hours before they had enough material for the show.

When they filmed the staged cocktail party the next day, they managed to bring together my worlds. Mrs. DeSousa and Mary Kiervin were there. Jimmy Smith was there, as was my good friend John Manuel. Law colleagues like Ian Roland and Doug Hunt attended, as did former political aides like Chuck Birchall and Shelley Spiegel. Neil McCormick and his son Iain also came.

Steve then went to Ottawa to interview my brother David and my sister Martha. My brother Christopher, whose television production company does a lot of work for TVO's Ottawa studio, filmed them.

When the show aired in February 1997, it provoked an enormously sympathetic response. It captured the attention of the Aphasia Centre, an organization founded by Pat Arato in the wake of the devastating stroke suffered by her former husband. He had been sailing on the lake at Milton at the foot of the Niagara Escarpment when the boom came round unexpectedly and hit him on the head. The resultant internal bleeding in his brain caused him to lose his speech in a profound way. He was forty years old, a professional engineer, and he could no longer talk.

Pat was determined to help her husband and others like him. Through much hard work, she created the Aphasia Centre in North York. It served several purposes. First, it simply provided a place where people with aphasia could go, as most people with even moderate aphasia can no longer work. It also provided training for family members and caregivers of people with aphasia. And it served as a scientific research centre. They asked me to become a patron of the centre. I accepted. When the Aphasia Centre held a fundraising dinner in my name, Steve Paikin agreed to be the master of ceremonies, Allan Rock agreed to be the guest speaker, and I agreed to read a short speech.

It would be my first attempt at public speaking since the stroke. Neil wrote a short speech for me, but it was far too long. He wrote a shorter one, and I practiced reading it. During my political career, I rarely stuck to the text of any prepared remarks. Now, faced with the prospect of reading twenty lines or so, I had to go over the material again and again. But I was determined to do it. This is more or less what I said:

Steve, Allan, Ladies and Gentlemen:

It is a pleasure to welcome you this evening.

As I look around the room, I see many friends, family members and colleagues. I thank you all for coming out tonight.

Most of you probably thought that you would never see me with a beard, or stuck for words. Growing the beard was easy. Finding words is the tough part.

Many of you here tonight have helped me to cope with aphasia, and I would like to thank you for your help.

Much remains to be done to understand and help people afflicted with aphasia. The work of the Aphasia Centre is important. I thank you for supporting it.

I am looking forward to hearing Allan's speech, so I will let him get on with it.

Thank you.

It may have been the shortest speech of my adult life. It was hard for me to stand in front of the crowd, clutching the text in my good left hand. I didn't want to make a spectacle of myself, nor did I want people to feel sorry for me. I did, however, want to make people aware of how devastating aphasia can be, and how important it was to work to overcome its effects.

A few weeks after this speech, I went to Florida with Mary Kiervin.

I fell to the floor one morning in the apartment we were renting in Key Biscayne. Mary rushed me to the hospital; my right carotid artery was almost completely clogged. I had an endarterectomy, an operation that involves scraping out the plaque from the carotid. The surgeon later said that one large piece of plaque had been was very loosely attached to the wall of the artery. If it had dislodged, I probably would not have survived the operation.

Later that spring, my alma mater, Osgoode Hall Law School, presented me with an honorary doctor of laws degree. To celebrate, I threw a big party at my house. I perched for most of the evening on a kitchen stool, my back resting against the wall, while a host of my friends and former colleagues streamed by. Mr. Justice Peter Cory of the Supreme Court of Canada, who also received a doctorate that day, had spoken for me at the presentation, as I hadn't felt up to making a speech. At the cocktail party, it was hard for me to follow conversations. I was getting better at one-on-one conversations, but group talk was still hard for me to grasp.

That summer, Jimmy Smith and I went to Chester, Nova Scotia, to a cottage we had rented with my sister Martha and her family. The cottage turned out to be next door to a funeral home, and Jimmy made many mordant jokes about the convenience of it all. Jimmy and I made side trips to nearby Wolfville to take in the summer theatre there and to resume acquaintances with friends who used to run Fenton's restaurant in Toronto, and who now had a charming restaurant in the town. We also visited friends in Prince Edward Island, where my Sullivan ancestors had once lived.

Jimmy was amazing. He was obviously very ill, but he was determined to use his remaining time to maximum benefit. That fall, he tried and mostly failed to get on new experimental drug programs. He was denied entry to one because his tumour was too long and thin; they wanted short and thick. He travelled to Scotland, his birthplace, and to New York. He was set on having some more time in the sun, and so we rented a place in Key Biscayne for February.

I drove to Florida with Christopher Cossonnet, Ian Roland's nephew. Jimmy arrived a week later. It is amazing that he was able to drive down there, but he was determined to do so and he did. He flew back to Toronto for a time, to arrange to get on another experimental drug program, but he returned south shortly thereafter.

The lease on the apartment expired at the end of February, and I planned to leave a few days early, as the Law Society of Upper Canada was conferring an honorary doctorate on me. Jimmy died the day I was to leave. Christopher found his body in the bathroom in the morning. Jimmy had suffered a massive hemorrhage from the tumour in his throat. The police, for reasons perhaps connected with the Versace murder some months earlier, initially treated his death as a murder investigation. Frantic phone calls were made to Toronto to contact Jimmy's doctor. The police would not let me catch the flight I had booked. I stayed in Florida until late that night. By the time my sister Martha flew in from Ottawa to act as an interpreter, the investigation had been completed.

Jimmy had willed himself an extra eighteen months of life, and he had enjoyed almost every moment of it.

The next morning, I went to convocation and received my second honorary doctorate. It sure beat being held as a material witness. Bob Rae also received an honorary doctorate that day. The next week, Jimmy was buried at Mount Pleasant Cemetery, not very far from where Kim is buried. After the interment, we held a wake at my house.

In the spring, the University of Toronto also presented me with an honorary degree. The event was filled with faces from my legal and political past. Rob Prichard, who had been a student of mine, was now the president of the University of Toronto. Roy McMurtry, now the chief justice of Ontario, also received a degree at that convocation. Bill Davis introduced him, and David Peterson introduced me. It was a hot day. The procession wound through the Convocation Hall. I had insisted on walking, rejecting the offer of being pushed in my wheelchair. It was a long way to go in the heat. David Peterson, my partner in the procession, appeared concerned, and tried to help me. I did make it, slowly, up on the stage. I had the chance to rest while the speeches were delivered.

The sense of civility about the whole proceeding reminded me that politics had taken a turn for the worse since my time in government. Davis and Peterson had fun kidding each other and their respective attorneys general. I was proud to have been part of the chain of Ontario AGs stretching back to Oliver Mowat.

This third honorary doctorate marked some kind of turning point in my life after the stroke. Jimmy's death was hard on me, after all the other deaths of friends and lovers. I couldn't do anything about the deaths; I could, however, prevent myself from falling into a morass of depression. I could carry on.

I developed new routines. I rode my exercycle for fifteen minutes most mornings. I worked out twice a week with Henry Carvalho, a personal trainer at the Toronto Lawn Tennis Club. I went to a movie every week. I lunched with interesting people. Some of these lunches were hilarious. John Murray, an old legal friend, reminded me of a case we had had together at the Federal Court of Appeal. The subject matter, now fortunately forgotten, was dry. John was on his feet, making his argument. He saw me start to write a note. Then I rose, bowed to the judges on the bench, walked over to him, and slipped him the note. I went back to my seat. He was afraid that he had made some horrible mistake or that some case he had cited had been overturned on appeal. He looked at the note. On it, I had written, "Can you imagine anything more boring than being a judge on the Federal Court of Appeal?" Elaine Todres, my old deputy minister from the Women's Directorate, came for lunch one day. As usual, she was wearing high heels and a designer suit, with her abundant red hair piled high on her head. Seeing Elaine reminded me of a briefing she had given me once, in the presence of deputy attorney general Dick Challenor and Chuck Birchall. That day, Elaine wore a lavender-coloured leather outfit with a short skirt and a plunging neckline. She delivered her report in her usual crisp, no-nonsense manner. After five minutes, she was done. She asked if there were any questions. There were none. She left. After she was gone, I turned to Dick, a charming but cautious former Crown attorney, and said rather petulantly, "Why can't you be more like that?" He paused, then said, "I don't do leather." Elaine loved the story.

I also decided to take an extension course at the University of Toronto, on the history of opera. I have always loved music. Fortunately, the stroke did not take away my store of music or my ability to appreciate it. As a law student, I had taken a rather cavalier attitude toward attendance. Now that it was a struggle for me to travel to the lecture hall on my electric scooter, I found I really enjoyed going and listening.

I had supportive friends and family. I went on trips to Savannah and Charleston. I went to New Orleans with my sister Martha. I spent more time in Ottawa, visiting my family, than at any time since I left home at seventeen to go to university.

I appeared on *Pamela Wallin Live*, supported by friends and family. Pamela has been kind enough to describe my interview with her as "television that matters." On the surface, however, conducting a talking heads program with someone who is not able to talk very well doesn't seem to me like promising material.

I am still improving, though it seems to me that I am not making very much progress. After many, many hours spent poring over books and magazines, I can now read slowly, without having to say the words out loud. This is a huge step forward for me, though it still takes me a long, long time to work my way through a book.

I count myself fortunate to be able to make this limited progress. Thousands of people each year suffer speech and other disabilities as a result of strokes and other afflictions. Many of them are locked inside their minds, with little ability to communicate with the outside world. I am one of the lucky ones. I have had my share of triumphs and my share of tragedies since that day in the hospital when I lay speechless and semi-paralyzed, my arms tethered to the sides of the bed. The road toward recovery has been a long one, but I am determined to keep trekking on down that road, no matter how hard it might be.

I have never spent much time dwelling on the past, or pondering "what ifs" and "might have beens." When I do look back on my life, I remember best the people I met. I was fortunate to have colleagues in law who were as stimulating as they were competent. I am proud of the work that our little firm did. I was extremely fortunate to get into politics when I did, and to be part of a government that gave me the freedom to run my departments the way I wanted to.

Of all the people I met, I especially admire Tom Berger. The commission he led paved the way toward taking aboriginal rights seriously in Canada. Ironically, many of the young First Nations people who worked for the commission are now in positions of power in the Yukon and Northwest Territories governments, and are competing for the right to build a pipeline. We bought them twenty-five years. If there is a pipeline now, at least it will be at their behest, not the oil companies'.

It has been a long time since Martin O'Malley, covering the Berger Commission for the *Globe and Mail*, described Steve Goudge and me as "looking like two Beach Boys with blonde, close-cropped hair." Goudge is now a judge on the Court of Appeal of Ontario. In September 2000, he invited me to go to the court to witness an appeal argued by my brother David, now one of the top litigation lawyers in Canada. More than three hundred people attended a dinner in Ottawa in 1999 honouring David's contribution to law. I made a brief speech of congratulations.

The case he was arguing, in front of the distinguished bench of Goudge, John Laskin, and Kathy Feldman, was the appeal of the lower court decision upholding the right of Prime Minister Jean Chrétien to invoke prerogative to block the British government from conferring a title on Conrad Black. At the *Black* v. *Chrétien* appeal, Alan Lenczer, Black's lawyer, launched into an articulate and amusing assault on the judicial reasoning employed by Chief Justice Pat Lesage, the judge in the court below. The court recessed for a break when Lenczer had finished his argument.

During the break, three young people who had been assiduously taking notes during the arguments remained in their bench. I assumed they were the clerks to the judges on the Court of Appeal. I couldn't think of the word for "clerks," however, so I asked them, "Are you the blah-blah-blahs?" They all laughed and admitted that they were the blah-blah-blahs, or court clerks. I asked them how many clerks there were. They said twelve. I told them that when I started, only one clerk served the whole Court of Appeal. All things considered, today we have a much better Court of Appeal, and a much better legal system, than when I started out.

When court resumed, I heard David argue for the first time in my life. Like Lenczer, he made his points with eloquence and humour. It was a pleasure to hear them argue, and to be able to follow the arguments. The first time I had visited the court after my stroke, Steve Goudge, not yet a judge, was arguing a case I had started, and I hadn't been able to follow a thing. It was one of the most depressing days of my life. It was a relief to know that now I could follow the arguments with enjoyment.

The next week, I went to Ottawa for my nephew Andrew's wedding. It was a coming together of the family, a celebration of new beginnings, a time for nostalgia and hope.

Then I stayed on for another week to attend the wedding of Chuck Birchall, my old adviser and friend. Chuck had left McCarthy's, the biggest law firm in the country, to establish his own small firm, doing environmental law with his partner Rod Northey. Ian McGilp did some work for them. He told me, "Scott, it reminds me of when I was practicing with you. The cases are fascinating, but quite hopeless."

Chuck was marrying Hillary Geller. As often happens, Chuck and Hillary had lived together for some time before deciding to get married. Their two-year-old daughter, Isobel, accompanied them down the aisle of the church. Upon seeing all the candles set up on the altar, Isobel went running down the aisle, pointing at them and exclaiming with all the wisdom of her two-year-old's knowledge of celebrations, "Birthday candles! Birthday candles!"

And I thought, wouldn't it be wonderful if we could all keep that enthusiasm, running right to the end?

Index

aboriginal rights. *See* native issues
abortion issue, 145, 151–54
Acapulco, Mexico, 41
AIDS, 140, 205, 209, 210, 212
Aird, John Black, 126
Alboim, Naomi, 154–55, 157
alcohol, 3, 16, 22, 44–45, 185, 188, 209, 211, 212, 214
Alexander, Lincoln, 197
Alpha Delta Phi (fraternity), 24
Anand, Raj, 86
Andrew, 243
Andrews, Ted, 177
angiogram, 216
Anka, Paul, 220
aphasia, viii–ix, x, 213, 224, 236–37
Aphasia Centre, 236–37
Arato, Pat, 236
ARCH, 54
Armstrong, Bob, 68–69
Armstrong, George, 78
Arthurs, Harry, 24, 50
The Ashburnian, 11, 12, 14
Ashbury College, 9–15, 16
Ashworth, Gordon, 186, 197
attorney general, viii, 37, 53, 126–71, 174–85
  constraints on, 187–88
  desire to be/love of being, 122–25, 126, 140, 207
  justice system and, 174–83, 204
  sworn in as, 127

auto insurance, 182–83, 189, 198
awards, 12, 226, 238, 239–40
Aylesworth, Justice, 33, 34, 35

Baker, David, 53–54
Barkin, Martin, 173
Barry's Bay, Ontario, 71
Bartenders' Union, 48
bathhouses, 70, 122–23
Beck, Ron, 72, 213, 214, 215
  IS's stroke and, 217, 221, 226
Bedard case, 56
Bereskin, Bonnie, ix, 223, 224, 225
Berger, Justice Thomas, 56–58, 242
Berger, Philip, 147–48
Berger Commission, 12, 56–59, 63, 85, 162, 242
Bhinder v. *CNR*, 84
Bill of Rights, 56, 83
Billy (dog), 211, 231
Birchall, Chuck, 71, 76, 78, 95, 236, 240, 243
  1990 election and, 196–97, 201–2
  at Queen's Park, 127, 131, 157, 167, 168, 175, 179
Black, Conrad, 242
Black v. *Chrétien*, 242
Blainey, Justine, 135, 136
Blair, A.J. (great-grandfather), 2
Blair, George, 7
Blake's, 202
Boo (dog), 43

Bora Laskin Chair, 206
Borden, Ladner, Gervais, 26
Borg, Vince, 197
Boudria, Don, 87
Bourassa, Robert, 164, 166, 167, 191, 192
breakfast meetings, 131–32
Breaugh, Michael, 120, 122
Breithaupt, James, 87
Brewin, Andrew, 7, 26–31, 33, 35, 52, 66,
    77, 150
  NDP and, 29, 47, 75
Brewin, John, 7, 47, 29
Briede, Wayne, 72
British North America Act, 2, 148, 149, 176
Brown, Peter, 39, 40, 71
Brown v. *The Topeka Board of Education*, 56
bureaucracy, 129–30, 135, 143, 158
Bytown, 2

Cabaret, 42
Cabbagetown, 39, 43, 76
Callaghan, Justice Frank, 179
Callaghan, Michael, 105
Callaghan, Morley, 20
Callwood, June, 98
Cameron, Brewin, Weldon, McCallum and
    Skells, 26
Cameron, Brewin & Scott, 36, 47, 174, 207
  merger with Gowling and Henderson,
    85–86, 91
Cameron, Jamie, 166
Cameron, Pat, 47
campaign contributions, 186–87. *See also*
    fundraising
campaign diary, viii, ix, 93–112
campaigning, vii, 75–80, 91–113, 198–203
Campbell, Archie, 129
Campbell, Ken, 152
Campbell, Kim, 229
Campbell, Margaret, 80
camping, 211–12
Campion, John, 51
Canada Temperance Act, 3, 185
Canadian Bar Review, 6
Canadian Commonwealth Federation, 13, 146
Canadian Hearing Society, 105
Canadian Jewish Congress, 101
Canadian Judicial Council, 214
Canadian Officers Training Corps, 21
Canadian Red Cross, 182
Cantinflas, 41
Caplan, Elinor, 80, 115, 143, 168, 173
car driving, 44–45, 131
Carlevale, Michael, 230

Carr, Glenna, 154
Carstairs, Sharon, 191, 192
Carter, Cardinal Emmett, 149
Carvalho, Henry, 240
Cassidy, Michael, 75
Castle Frank High School, 102, 103
Catholic Church, 2, 4, 5, 9, 16, 149
  schools, 2, 88, 108, 122, 128, 138, 145,
    148–51
Catholic Register, 8
Catholic Temperance League, 4
CBC, 100, 101, 102, 103, 235
Centre for Equality in Rental
    Accommodation, ix
CFRB Radio, 44
Challenor, Dick, 209, 240
Charter of Rights and Freedoms, 81, 102,
    130, 158, 160
Cherney, Mike, 118
Chester, Nova Scotia, 238
Chrétien, Jean, 81, 102, 103, 159, 242
Churchill, Winston, 227
cigarettes, 208–9
Civil Rights Movement, 56
CKO, 106
class actions, 182, 204
Claxton, Brooke, 13, 22
Cohen, Paul, 37–39, 43
College of Physicians and Surgeons, 64, 146
Colonial Tavern, 22
Communism, 11
computer, 227
Confederation, 2, 81
conferences
  aboriginal rights, 158, 161–63, 192, 193
  federal-provincial, 155, 163 (*see also*
    constitutional issues; Meech Lake Accord)
Conservative party, Ontario, 31
  dominance, viii, 71, 75, 86, 97, 119, 120,
    122, 129, 204
  elections and (*see* elections, Ontario)
  leadership, 88 (*see also various leaders*;
    Davis; Peterson)
  scandals, 190
Consolidated Constitution Acts, 1867–1982, 151
constituency office, 116–17
Constitution, 81, 134, 159, 161, 163
Constitution Act, 1867, 161, 176
constitutional issues, 127, 128, 134, 158–68.
    See also Meech Lake Accord
contingency fees, 182
Conway, Sean, 72, 120, 122, 124, 143, 144,
    171
  1990 election and, 195, 203, 204

cooking, 210
Cooper (horse), 38
Copps, Sheila, 81, 87
Corner House (restaurant), 196
Cory, Justice Peter, 238
Cossonnet, Christopher, 238, 239
Coté, Joe, 100
courts, structure of. *See* attorney general,
    justice system and
Coveney, David, 82
Cranston, Toller, 199
Creighton, Donald, 20
cricket, 14, 15
Criminal Code of Canada, 42, 151–54, 176,
    187
Crombie, David, 79, 98
Crosbie, John, 229
Curling, Alvin, 115, 144

Darlington power plant, 145–46
Dassios, Chris, 217
Davey, Keith, 78, 91
Davis, Bill, 110, 119, 128, 129, 134, 239
    the Constitution and, 159
    the Pope and, 149
    as premier, 71, 80, 88, 142
Dean, Mugsy, 59–63, 133
death threats, 148
debating, 12, 14, 20, 24, 188, 189
Deer Park, 112
Del Zotto family, 186
Desbarats, Lilian, 3, 5, 7
Desbarats, Mary, 4
DeSousa, Mrs., 212, 222–23, 226, 236
DeWare, Scott, 72, 229
Dickson, Justice Brian, 159
Diefenbaker, John, 56
Dinsmore, Heather, 69
discrimination, 135–36, 199–201. *See also*
    homosexuality; pay equity
"distinct society," 165
doctor of laws degree, honorary, 238
doctors' strike, 146–48
Doer, Gary, 191, 192
Donnelly, Justice Frank, 68–69
Drew, George, 13, 119
Drew, Fiorenza, 13
drugs, 16, 37, 51, 205, 210
Drybones case, 56
Dubin, Charles, 31, 35

Eberle, Ed, 31
education issues, 168. *See also* schools,
    politics and

Edwards, Philip, 230, 231
Eleanor of Aquitaine, 7
elections, federal
    1972, 56
    1978, 36
    1984, 87
elections, Ontario
    1971, 88, 149
    1975, 204
    1977, 204
    1981, vii, 75–80, 91, 204
    1985, vii–viii, 80, 87, 91–113
    1987, 144, 170–71, 198
    1990, viii, 118, 195–203
    1995, 201
elections, student-council, 20, 120
Elgie, Bob, 109
Elmwood private school, 1
Elston, Murray, 125, 143, 144, 147, 171, 175
emotions, 220, 223
employment equity, 157
endarterectomy, 238
Environmental Assessment Board, 101
environmental issues, 59, 63, 104, 145, 168,
    198, 203–4
Erin, Ontario, 38
Essential Services Act, 160
Estey, Justice Willard, 82, 83
Evans, John, 105
Eves, Ernie, 205
Ewart, J.S., 150
extra-billing issue, 122, 124–25, 145, 146–48
Ezrin, Hershell, 120, 147, 197

Fairley, Barker, 228
Family Coalition party, 204
farm, 3, 38, 44, 230–33
Faskens (law firm), 51, 54
Feldman, Kathy, 242
Filmon, Gary, 191, 192
Finkelstein, Neil, 127
Fish, Susan, 79, 99
519 Church Street Community Centre, 199
Florida, 237–38, 239
Fontaine, René, 116
Ford Hotel, 41
Forsey, Eugene, 13
Forster, E.M., 224
"Fourth Reading," 206, 213, 235
Fraser, Blair, 12, 13
Fraser, John, 12, 13
Fraser, Simon, 6
Freedom of Information Act, 128, 130, 146,
    204

free trade, 191
Friedland, Marty, 24
Frost, Leslie, 190, 204
fundraising, 112, 183, 186

Gallup Poll, 110
Gamble, David, 215
Gang of Eight, 159
gardening, 5, 8, 38, 73, 215, 229, 231
Garnsworthy, Archbishop, 110, 149
gay-bashing, 66–67
gay issues. *See* homosexuality
Geller, Hillary, 243
Geller, Isobel, 243
Genesove, B.J., 14
George Bigliardi's (restaurant), 144
Ghiz, Joe, 155
Gilchrist, Peter, 95
Gilmour, Audrey. *See* Scott, Audrey
    (Gilmour)
Gilmour, "Granny," 1, 4, 8
Gilmour, Sutherland (grandfather), 1
Gilson, Etienne, 19
Glasgow, Robin, 40
Glass, Ogden, 10
Globe and Mail, 58, 98, 242
Godfrey, Paul, 98
Goldenberg, Eddie, 106
Goodman, David, 31
Goodman, Eddie, 31, 137
Goodman Lectures, 23, 31
Goods and Sales Tax, 191
Gordon, Walter, 142
Goudge, Steve, ix, 34, 45, 48–49, 51, 54–55,
    57, 133, 207–8
    IS's political career and, 76, 87, 91, 95,
    128, 202
    IS's stroke and, 242, 243
Goudge, Thomas, 48
Gouzenko, Igor, 11
government
    arbitrary actions of, 68–70, 116
    budgets, 134, 175, 176, 201
    defeat of, 126, 202
    media and, 168–69, 189, 191 (*see also* CBC;
    TVO)
    minority, 116, 119, 120, 142, 144, 145,
    169, 204
Gowling and Henderson, 85–86, 207
Gowling's (law firm), 29, 33, 217, 223, 224,
    228
Gowling Strathy & Henderson, ix
Graham, Kay, 72
Grange, Justice Samuel, 84

Grange Commission, 84–85, 133, 175, 187,
    189
Grant, Stephen, 36, 52
Green party, 204
Greenpeace, 197
Gregg, Allan, 110
Grossman, Larry, 88, 169, 171
Gryffe, Pearl, 227
Gzowski, Peter, 213, 235

Haggart, Ron, 104
Haines, Edson, 24
Hall, Barbara, 92, 100, 101, 104, 109
Hall, Glenn, 189
Hamilton Bar Association, 138
handwriting, 219
Hanlan's Point, 72
Harcourts, 24
Hard Choices: A Life of Tom Berger, 57
Harper, Elijah, 192, 193
Harris, Mike, 88, 119, 129, 143
    1990 election and, 201
    as premier, 203, 205
Hatfield, Richard, 155, 159, 190
Hawke, Wayne, 131, 132
Hawkins, Bob, 76, 94, 95, 97, 104, 106, 107
health care, 122, 124–25, 146, 147, 168, 173,
    200
Heeney, Peggy, 18
Henderson, Gordon, 85
Henderson, Paul, 67
Henry, George S., 5
Hepburn, Mitch, 5
Herman, Rob, 53
Heron family, 3
Hinds, Jimmy, 33
Hnatyshyn, Ray, 179, 226
Hogg, Peter, 166
Holland, Justice Richard, 37
homosexuality, 15–17, 39–45, 73
    political life and, 122–23, 199–201
    and social life, 220
honorary degrees, 238, 239–40
Hood, Marilyn, 118
Hoover, J. Edgar, 229
Hosek, Chaviva, 144, 190
Hospital for Sick Children, 84, 85, 103, 133
Houlden, Lloyd, 187
Houlden Commission, 85, 187, 189
housing issues, 144, 168, 187, 189
Houston, Stu, 116, 117, 118
Howland, Justice William, 25, 26, 178, 179
Hoy, Claire, 199
Hunt, Doug, 133, 236

Index

Iaccobucci, Frank, 166
Immigration Act, 83
Immigration Board, 81
Imperial Tobacco, 15
Inch, Jim, 40
Indian Act, 56
Indians, North American, 12. *See also* native issues
insurance. *See* auto insurance
Intergovernmental Affairs, 162, 166
Isherwood, Christopher, 42

Jackman School, 104, 107
Jerome, Jim, 20
J.H. Ryder and Sons, 47
Jim, 186
John Howard Society, 36, 54
Johnson, Dr. Samuel, 7
Jowett, Benjamin, 49
justice system. *See* attorney general, justice system and
Juvenile Delinquents Act, 4

Kaufman Commission, 175
Keely, Helen, 100
Kennedy, John F., 20
Kent, Darrell, 39–40, 43, 92
Keyes, Ken, 188
Kierans, Eric, 142
Kiervin, Mary, 42, 96, 97, 105, 110, 210
   IS's health and, 214–16, 221, 222, 236, 237
Kilgour, David, 23
King, Mackenzie, 13, 160
King Edward Hotel, 39, 131
Kingston Penitentiary, 14, 54–55
Kirby, Michael, 124
Knopf, Paula, 59, 61, 62
Kormos, Peter, 183
Krever, Horace, 23, 31
Kwinter, Monte, 115, 118
Kwinter, Wilma, 118

LaMarsh, Judy, 142
Landreville, Leo, 85–86
Laskin, Bora, 23
Laskin, John, 213, 242
Lastman, Mel, 92
Laurence, Margaret, 98, 100, 104
Laurier, Sir Wilfrid, 2
Lavelle case, 56
law
   administrative, 36, 64
   boards and commissions and, 64 (*see also* various commissions)

career, ix, 14, 19, 23, 26, 36, 207, 217, 228
   (*see also* Cameron, Brewin & Scott; Gowling's)
   civil procedure, 36
   constitutional, 206 (*see also* Meech Lake Accord)
   criminal, 132, 133
   family, 52
   labour, 48, 214
   litigation, 24, 132, 133
law school. *See* Osgoode Hall Law School; University of Toronto, Law School; York University law school
Law Society of Upper Canada, 37, 55, 136, 211, 239
LEAF. *See* Women's Legal and Educational Fund
Leal, Alan, 24
LeDain Commission on Drug Use, 51
legal clinics, 54, 55, 174–75
legal secretary, 52–53
legal system. *See* attorney general, justice system and
Lenczer, Alan, 242, 243
Leon, Barry, 109
Lesage, Justice Pat, 242
Letros (bar), 39
Lewis, Stephen, 88, 119
Liberal party, federal, 13
Liberal party, Ontario, vii, viii, 5, 13, 86, 88
   cabinet, 131, 141, 143–44, 168, 197
   caucus, 80, 81, 87, 131, 144, 196
   elections and (*see* elections, Ontario)
   NDP accord with, viii, 118–22, 128, 145, 168–70, 204
   political reform and, 169, 173–74
Lord's Day Act, 184
Louise (cat), 38, 43
Lukasiewicz, Peter, 71, 76, 94, 113, 212, 228
   as executive assistant, 118, 127, 131

Macaulay, Bob, 73
MacAuley, Ned, 105
MacDonald, Annie, 109
MacDonald, John A., 13
MacDonald, Ramsay, 100
Macdonald, Sir John A., 20, 139, 150
Macdonnell clan, 5, 6
MacKay, Justice, 33
MacKay, Moses, 30
Mackay case, 77
Mackenzie, Hugh, 120
Mackenzie, William Lyon, 13

Index

Mackenzie Valley, 56
MacNeil, Robert, 10–11
MacNeil-Lehrer NewsHour, 11
MacPherson, James, 206
Magder, Paul, 184
Mahoney, Steve, 195
Malloch v. Aberdeen Corporation, 65
Maloney, Arthur, 68
Management Board, 135, 168, 175, 179
Manuel, John, 40, 236
Maritain, Jacques, 19
Marks, Jack, 152, 153
Marotta, Dr., 214, 215
Martin, Arthur, 26, 35
Martin, Paul, 20
Matlow, Ted, 53
McCallum, Jim, 47
McCarthy's (law firm), 243
McCarthy Tétrault (law firm), 196
McClellan, Ross, 120
McClelland, Jack, viii, 93
McCormick, Iain, 236
McCormick, Neil, viii, 69, 233, 236, 237
  IS's memoirs and, ix, x, 18, 228, 229
McDougall, Barbara, 155
McGillivray and Hamilton, Re, 32
McGilp, Ian, 28, 49, 82–83, 243
  at Queen's Park, 127, 128, 131, 150, 166
McGrath, Ted, 118
McGregor Lake, Quebec, 7, 15, 18
McIntyre, Dan, 188
McKenna, Frank, 155, 190
McLeod, Lyn, 201, 205
McLuhan, Marshall, 19
McMillan Binch (law firm), 25
McMurtry, Roy, 68, 80, 81, 126, 137–38,
  175, 239
  the Constitution and, 159
  painting and, 227–28
  student years of, 22–23
McNaughton, David, 201
McPherson, James, 151, 192
McRuer, J.C., 26
media and government, 168–69, 189, 191.
  See also CBC; TVO
medicare. *See* health care
Meech Lake Accord, 81, 145, 155, 158,
  163–68, 190–93, 197
Mencken, H.L., 205
Merritt v. City of Toronto, 32
Metro Morning, 100
Metropolitan Toronto Park Commission, 30
Mexico, 41, 214
Miller, Frank, 88–89, 98, 99, 104, 110, 115

  as premier, 118, 119, 120, 129
  resignation of, 126, 169
Milner, J.B., 24
Milner, Marilyn "Pete," 42, 52–53, 118
mineral rights, 161
Minnie (housekeeper), 8
Moffat, John, 53
Monahan, Pat, 128, 151, 166, 196
Moore Park, 78, 80, 106, 107, 108, 110, 117
Morales, Hiram, 9, 10
Morgentaler, Henry, 151–53
Morin, Guy-Paul, 175
Morningside, 213, 235
Mowat, Oliver, 150, 228, 240
Mr. Grimm (dog), 231
Muirhead's Restaurant, 31
Mulroney, Brian, 87, 110, 164, 165, 166,
  191, 193
Murphy, Tim, 206
Murray, Bill, 170
Murray, John, 240
Murray's Restaurant, 39
music, 4, 11, 229, 241
"My Way," 220

Nader, Ralph, 53
National Action Committee on the Status of
  Women, 155
National Council of Jewish Women, 185–86
National Energy Policy, 161
native issues, 12, 56, 58, 63, 117, 126, 127,
  136, 145, 158, 242
  conferences and, 160–63, 192, 193
Neal, Patricia, 223
Nelles, Susan, 84, 175
New Democratic Party, viii, 30
  auto insurance and, 182–83, 189
  Bob Rae and, 36, 75, 118, 119, 143
  Brewins and, 29, 47, 75
  elections and (*see* elections, Ontario)
  government, 141
  Liberal accord with, viii, 118–22, 128, 145,
    168–70, 204
  Sunday shopping and, 185
Nicholson, Harold, 100
Nicholson, police constable, 64–66
Nicholson case, 66
Nineteen Eighty-Four, 86
Nisga'a, 56
Nixon, Bob, 88, 120, 122, 123, 124, 143,
  144, 147, 171
  1990 election and, 195, 201, 202
  as Liberal leader, 204
  Patti Starr affair and, 186, 187

Index

Northern Ontario Gas Pipeline, 86
Northey, Rod, 243
North West Company, 5, 6
Northwest Territories, 56–57
Norton, Keith, 199
notwithstanding clause, 160, 191
numbers, comprehension of, 225–26
Nunn, Robin, 94, 95

Oag, Donald, 55
O'Driscoll, Justice, 61
Ogonquit, Maine, 37
O'Malley, Martin, 58, 242
Omnibus Equality Bill, 158
O'Neill, Tip, 80
Ontario Court of Justice, 181
Ontario Hospitals Association, 103
Ontario Human Rights Code, 26, 135, 136,
    158, 200
Ontario Human Rights Commission, ix, 126,
    213
Ontario Hydro, 145–46
Ontario Medical Association, 120, 146, 147
Ontario Place, 186
Ontario Public Employees Union, 66
Orange Order, 2, 5, 149
Order of Canada, 226
Orwell, George, 86
Osborne, Coulter, 25
Osgoode Hall Law School, 23–25, 151, 206,
    238
Osler, Justice John, 55, 174
Ottawa, 2, 3, 8, 9, 38
Ottawa Civic Hospital, 1
Ottawa Journal, 5
Ottawa Symphony, 4
Ottawa Valley Hunt, 9
"outing," 199

Paikin, Steve, 206, 213, 235, 236, 237
painting, 227
Paliare, Chris, 50, 57, 59–62
Pamela Wallin Live, 241
Pape, Paul, 109
Pare, Paul, 15
Parkdale Legal Clinic, 55
parliamentary system, 141–46
patronage, 138–39
Patti Starr affair, 85, 174, 185–87, 189, 190
pay equity, 145, 154–58, 204
Pay Equity Act, 158, 160
Pearson, Mike, 141, 142
Peckford, Brian, 191
Perks, Gordon, 197

Peterson, David, 81, 86–101, 104, 115, 134,
    239
    the Constitution and, 166, 167, 193
    1987 election and, 170–71
    1990 election and, viii, 195, 197, 198, 201,
        203
    as opposition leader, 118–23
    Patti Starr affair and, 186
    as premier, 126–29, 140–44, 147, 153, 169
Peterson, Heather, 186
Peterson, Shelley, 87, 99
Phillips, Gerry, 115
Pickering airport, proposed, 68–70, 116
pipeline. *See* Berger Commission
political career. *See also* attorney general
    early, 13, 71, 73
    elections and (*see* elections, Ontario)
    love for, 174, 203, 204, 242
    resignation as MPP, 205
Porter, Anna, 92
Porter, Dana, 92
Porter, Julian, 92, 93, 95–110
Porter, Katherine, 108
Port Hope, Ontario, 39
Potts, Dawn, 113
Pouper, Bob, 41
Prego (restaurant), 230
Price, Mary, 18
Prichard, Rob, 36, 166, 239
Prime Minister's Office, 142
prisons. *See* Kingston Penitentiary
Privy Council Office, 142
Progressive Conservative party. *See*
    Conservative party, Ontario
Prozac, 223
punishment, 10, 54–55
Pusateri's, 215

Queen Elizabeth Hospital, 219
Queen's Counsel, 137–38
"The Queen's Mafia," 71, 76, 202
Queen's University, 71
Queen v. Yule, 32
question period, 188–89

race relations, 188, 204
Rachlis, Michael, 147
Rae, Bob, 36, 75, 143, 223, 229, 239
    1990 election and, 198
    as MPP, 118, 119, 170, 171
    as opposition leader, 188–89
    as premier, 185, 205
Ramsay, David, 170
reading, 229, 241

REAL Women, 155
recession, 195–96
recording, campaign, 106, 112
Reference Case on the Constitution, 1981, 159
Reference on the Anti-Inflation Board case, 66
refugee claims, 82–84
Regent Park, 79, 80, 112, 113, 202
Rémillard, Guy, 164
Retail Holidays Act, 184
Rideau Club, 9
Ritchie, Charles, 17
Ritchie, Roland, 17
Robarts, John, 71, 115, 119, 146, 204
Roberts, Frank, 105
Robinette, John, 26, 35, 138, 150, 159
Robinson, Kathy, 197, 201
Rochdale College, 37
Rock, Allan, 237
Rockwell, Norman, 147
Roe v. *Wade*, 152
Roland, Ian, 49, 50–51, 57, 94, 223, 224, 236
Roman Catholic Church. *See* Catholic Church
Romanow, Roy, 81, 159
Ronson, John, 71, 76, 95, 202
Rosar, Frederick, 20
Rosedale, 39, 72, 76, 78, 80, 105, 106, 110, 113, 117
Rosenberg, Ken, 112, 113, 118
Rothstein, Linda, 29, 101
Rubin, David, 76, 112, 183, 186
Ruby, Malcolm, 33
Russell, Peter, 21, 22, 139
Russell, Robin, 91
Ryder, Alick, 47–48, 57, 95, 105
Ryder, Tom, 67, 71

Sackville-West, Vita, 213
sales tax, 201–2
Salvation Army Retirement Shelter, 96
same-sex benefits, 200–201
Saturday Evening Post, 147
Saunderson, Bill "Max," 21–22
Saunderson, John, 50
schools, politics and, 2, 88, 108, 122, 128, 138, 145, 148–51
Schroeder, Justice, 8, 33
scooter, 226–27
Scott, Audrey (Gilmour) (mother), 1, 7–9, 16, 17, 18, 38
Scott, Brian (brother), 9, 16, 17, 18, 38, 221, 231
Scott, Christopher (brother), 9, 16, 18, 236

Scott, Cuthbert (father), 1, 7, 8–9, 16, 17, 18
  IS's law career and, 26
Scott, David (brother), 211–12, 236, 242, 243
  early years of, 7, 9, 10, 16, 17, 18, 21
  IS's law career and, 26
Scott, Ian
  birth of, 1
  legal career (*see* law, career)
  political career (*see* political career)
Scott, Martha (sister), 9, 16, 18, 216, 221, 236, 238
Scott, Mary (Heron) (great-grandmother), 3
Scott, May (Sullivan) (grandmother), 4, 8
Scott, Nancy (sister), 7, 9, 16, 17
Scott, Sir Richard (great-grandfather), 2–4, 13, 148, 150, 185, 228, 229
Scott, W. L. (grandfather), 4–5, 6–7, 8, 21, 148, 150
Scott, William (great-great-grandfather), 5–6, 21
"Scott Act," 3, 4
Scott and Aylen (law firm), 26
Scrivener, Margaret, 76, 79, 80, 92, 112, 116
Scrivener, Paul, 92
Seghers, Louis, 221, 232, 233
Senate reform, 192
separate schools. *See* Catholic Church, schools
separatism, 161
sexual orientation. *See* homosexuality
sign law, Quebec, 191
Sikhs, 84
Singh case, 82, 84, 131, 180
Sissinghurst, 213
SkyDome, 145
Smith, Hillsden, 60, 61, 62
Smith, Jimmy, 17, 21, 43–44, 70, 72
  IS's recovery and, 229–31, 236, 238–39
Smith, Joan, 189
Smith, Stuart, 75, 76, 80, 81, 87
smoking, 208–9
Sopinka, John, 30, 31, 44–45, 68–69, 84, 175
Sorbara, Greg, 115, 158, 197
Sousa, Juan de, 9
speech competitions, 12–13
speech therapy, ix, 223–26, 236
speech writing, 13, 94
speeding, 67
Spence, Wishart, 29
Spiegel, Shelley, 127, 236
sports, 14–15, 16, 72, 135, 205
St. Andrews, New Brunswick, 8
St. David riding, vii, 76, 79–81, 92–93, 101, 110, 115–17

St. George–St. David riding, 117, 170, 193, 198, 202, 206
St. Jamestown, 112, 170
St. Laurent, Louis, 13
St. Michael's College, 9, 13, 16, 19–23, 213
Stanley Cup, 1
Starr, Patti, 185–87
Steele, Justice
Steelworkers union, 48, 50
Stewart, Ed, 119, 129, 142
The Story of English, 11
Strathy Archibald, 207
stroke, viii, 215–17
    recovery from, 219–33, 240
Studio 2, 206, 235
stuttering, 12, 20
Sullivan, Justice, 4
Sullivan, May. *See* Scott, May (Sullivan)
Sunday shopping, 184–85
Swackhamer, Bill, 14, 41, 54
Swayze, Carolyn, 57
Sweeney, John, 153, 173
Symes, Beth, 53

taxes, 191, 201–2
teachers
    at Ashbury College, 11–12, 13
    at St. Michael's College, 19, 20
teaching
    career choice and, 19, 23
    at Osgoode Hall, 206, 207
    at Queen's University, 71
    at U of T Law School, 36, 37, 50
television. *See* media and government; TVO
tennis, 72
therapy. *See* stroke, recovery from
Thomson, Ken, 117
Timbrell, Dennis, 88, 120
Tiny Township case, 149
Todres, Elaine, 154, 155, 157, 240
Tonks, Alan, 171
Toronto Islands, 30, 72
Toronto Star, 97
Toronto Sun, 106, 113, 199
Toronto Symphony Orchestra, 214
Trainor, Dick, 33, 53
transient ischemic attack, 215–16
Transitions, 173, 198
Trudeau, Pierre, 45, 86, 141, 142, 159, 161, 165, 166
Turner, Brenda, 11
Turner, John, 11, 86, 142
TVO, 206, 213, 235, 236

Underhill, Frank, 20
unions, 48, 50, 66, 77, 118
United Farmers of Ontario, 141
United Way, 105
University Naval Training Division, 21
University of Toronto, 239, 241 (*see also* St. Michael's College)
    Law School, 23, 25, 36, 50
University of Western Ontario, 9

Varsity, 213
Vaughan, Colin, 103

Waddell, Ian, 57
wage and price freeze, 66
Waitzer, Ed, 53
walking, 219–20, 222
Ward, Chris, 202, 214
Watkin, Bob, 72
Webster, Beth, 197
Wellesley Hospital, 216
Wells, Clyde, 191, 192, 193
Wells, Ross, 86, 107
Williston, Walter, 29, 44–45
Wilson, Cairine, 8, 18
Wilson, Senator Cairine, 8, 15
Winters, Robert, 142
Women's Directorate, 154–56, 240
women's issues, 126, 134–35, 152, 153, 154–56, 160
Women's Legal and Educational Fund, 134–35, 204
Woodburn, Irene, 11
Woods, Dale, 170
Woolf, Leonard, 213
Woolf, Virginia, 213
Wordstruck, 10
World War II, 7, 8
Wright, Carolann, 202
Wright, Dean, 24
Wright, Dick, 13, 15

Yaeger, Lesley, 116, 117, 118
Yakabuski, Doreen, 72
Yakabuski, James, 210
Yakabuski, Kim, viii, 71–73, 140, 205, 209–13, 239
Yakabuski, Paul, 71, 72, 211
Yellowknife, NWT, 59, 63
Yorke, Liz, 95
York University law school, viii, 206

Zuber, Justice Thomas, 178